CALLED BY THE WILD

The Dogs Trained to Protect Wildlife

Conraad de Rosner

with Graham Spence and Elaine Bell

AD LIB

First published in the UK in 2023 by Ad Lib Publishers Ltd
15 Church Road
London SW13 9HE
www.adlibpublishers.com

Text © 2023 Conraad de Rosner

Paperback ISBN 9781802471380
eBook ISBN 9781802471984

A CIP catalogue record for this book is
available from the British Library.

Printed in the UK
10 9 8 7 6 5 4 3 2 1

CONRAAD DE ROSNER was born and schooled in Gqeberha, then Port Elizabeth, in South Africa's Eastern Cape province. He studied nature conservation in Pretoria before starting work, in 1993, at Windy Ridge Game Park in KwaZulu-Natal, South Africa. In 2009, he was appointed assistant anti-poaching manager at Sabi Sands Game Reserve. Then, in 2011, he formed his company, K9 Conservation, at Thanda Game Reserve. In 2015, he moved to his base training farm in Hoedspruit, where for the past six years and more, he has developed and expanded his training of rangers and dogs. Conraad is also involved in training and transporting dogs to India, to guard wildlife and track rogue tigers who have attacked villagers. In 2022, Conraad married his wife, Anke, under the ancient branches of a baobab tree growing at the highest altitude ever recorded for a baobab.

ELAINE BELL has had a love for the bushveld of Africa all her life, a passion engendered by her father from early childhood. Retired, she now lives in the beautiful Midlands of KwaZulu-Natal, South Africa. Her daughter and family live in New Zealand; her youngest son, Jayson, is in the international film industry; and Conraad will always have his roots in Africa.

Born in Africa, GRAHAM SPENCE was a journalist for twenty-five years during South Africa's turbulent apartheid era. He has written several books on Africa, including the global bestseller *The Elephant Whisperer*, which he co-authored with the 'Indiana Jones of conservation', Lawrence Anthony, as well as *Saving the Last Rhinos* and *Rewilding Africa* with environmentalist Grant Fowlds. He currently lives with his family in England.

In memory of Zingela

Contents

CONTENTS

Prologue

By Elaine Bell

My eldest son was born on a cold and windy day in Port Elizabeth (now Gqeberha) on South Africa's south-east coast on 15 May 1973, three weeks premature and given no more than a twenty-four-hour chance of survival. Lying froglike in the incubator, tubes and needles hiding his face, his little chest laboured for every breath. I looked at him struggling for life and I heard myself whispering fiercely, 'Fight, my son.'

Fight he did and he still does – fifty years later.

He and his teams of rangers and dogs are in a life-and-death struggle against illegal poaching in a fight for the survival of all wildlife. They guard rhino, elephant, lion and all manner of other creatures from the unrelenting, unceasing, increasing war taking place in the bush, on the plains, along streams and rivers, and in the mountains and hills of Africa. Many dedicated rangers, men and women, battle this scourge, with frankly no end in sight.

The illegal killing of and trade in Africa's wildlife is all to appease the markets of the Far East, with their erroneous belief in the curative powers of animal parts and organs. The greed to possess ivory, rhino horn, lion's teeth, bones, claws and all manner of other gruesome body parts serves to line the pockets of the masterminds behind the smuggling cartels, as well as those of the highly placed people who turn a blind eye in return for thirty pieces of silver. What price betrayal?

This is the story of my son's personal odyssey. His rite of passage to reach the present day, where his contribution to conservation has made a small difference.

His journals, notes and reports over the past years piece together the story of his struggle to pay his dues to Africa, his land of birth. To protect Africa from itself and from each and every person who feels by right they should have a slice of the cake merely by virtue of the fact that they were born on the soil of this continent, without adding virtue or value to their claims.

The reports documenting all the poaching incidents, plus all the animals that have been slaughtered and died, make one wonder how there is any wildlife left in Africa at all.

I am grateful and give thanks that Conraad has survived all the danger he has encountered from both man and beast over the past years. These years demonstrate not only his dedication to nature and the wild, but also his years of discovery and study of San rock art he documented for the public domain for the first time.

These years also include the time spent pioneering the use of dogs for anti-poaching in the bush and the story of Zingela, who was born to be my son's wonderful and faithful friend, guardian and protector during his years in the bush.

If Conraad's story can serve as an inspiration to just one person who is passionate about stopping the slaughter and decimation of fauna and flora, then this book has served its purpose, the message it contains understood.

About six months before my ninety-seven-year-old mother passed away on 23 July 2017, I had a vivid dream in which a disembodied voice urged me to write a book on Conraad. Of course, not being a writer, I was totally at sea about how and where to begin. I awoke the following morning and told my mother about the dream.

'Well, what are you waiting for? Get on with it,' she said. 'My vibes tell me this is what has to be done.'

Her vibes were a matter for gentle teasing from the family. They were either 'Yes' or 'No' or 'Do' or 'Don't' and she was seldom wrong in her summation of either people or events.

With the Abba song 'I have a dream' swishing around in my head all day and my mother's urging, I began to give credence to her vibes.

First and foremost, this is Conraad's book that he has related for posterity. May I therefore say in all humbleness: I have a son of Africa. He lives on a small farm nestled below the castellated top of Mariepskop Mountain and Moholoholo peak in Limpopo Province. The farm lies in the valley formed by the Blyde and Olifants rivers, where the Drakensberg Mountains begin their journey down to KwaZulu-Natal, and there form a great backdrop fortress with the mighty Maloti Mountains of Lesotho.

This is the story of the small footprint he has left on the soil of Africa. One day the winds of time may wipe this footprint away, but I dare say his spirit will hover over the bushveld forever.

His mother,
Elaine Bell

1

The Assassination Attempt

A fundamental lesson of tracking in thick bush is that *dongas*, dry riverbeds, are potential death traps.

To emerge headlong from a steep ravine onto higher ground is the ultimate 'sitting duck' situation. Any predator such as a hunting lioness, an irate buffalo – or more likely these days, an AK-47-toting poacher – will have an immediate jump on you.

This was drummed into me from a young age by my grandfather, Coenraad Havemann, whom I called *Oupa*, as well as my uncle and mentor, Louis John Havemann. They both continually stressed that I must always first scan the bush from below the river bank to check every angle before exposing myself. They were both wise outdoorsmen and I listened to whatever they said.

That's why I am alive today.

I was patrolling a river in South Africa's Mpumalanga province on the northern side of Mthethomusha Game Reserve that borders the Kruger National Park with my dog Zingela when *Oupa*'s advice was put to the ultimate test. Zingela was a Weimaraner – in my opinion the most loyal, intelligent and beautiful gun dog in the world. I used him extensively in the bush to track poachers or injured animals. He was my first line of defence, and I could tell just by a brief growl or whine exactly what species of animal was nearby. Humans are infinitely more deadly, and his body language was enough to alert me if there were any around.

Zingela was also my best friend.

This was a routine patrol. I had no reason to be on full alert, although that state is second nature after decades in the bush. I parked the Land Cruiser above the river bank, and Zingela and I clambered down the steep slope to the rock pools below. The water was crystal clear and bubbled with life. Zingela jumped in to cool off, and with ears flopped forward and nose to the water, he started looking for fish. This was one of his favourite pastimes and I let him swim in the stream, as there were no crocodiles that high up in the mountain valley. As Zingela fished, I started making my way downstream, marvelling at the swarms of iridescent dragonflies hovering and darting this way and that as I carefully scrutinised the game trails leading down to the pools for any signs of poachers' snares. There were none. It was just another day in paradise.

Or so I thought.

Suddenly Zingela leapt out of the pool and ran up the bank, barking with an alarmed aggression I had not heard before. He had obviously scented something, as the hair on his neck and back was raised. I knew that whatever – or whoever – was above us was dangerous. My survival instinct kicked in, adrenalin flooding my system. I needed to think fast, and act immediately. There was no time to make a mistake.

Remembering *Oupa*'s words, I did not follow Zingela up the slope but sprinted behind a large granite boulder, about forty yards long and twenty high. Drawing my firearm, a .45 ACP pistol, I silently crept around the side of the massive rock. Zingela instinctively sensed what I was doing and did not follow.

Instead, he held his position facing up the bank, his agitated rapid-fire barking acting as a decoy.

I peered cautiously around the boulder and gasped silently at what I saw. Two men armed with R1s, automatic rifles previously used by the South African military, were pointing their weapons down the bank.

I recognised them instantly. To my utter astonishment, they were game rangers who worked for the provincial parks board. Not only that, but both had also been named in a damning report I had earlier submitted to the authorities concerning the poaching epidemic raging across the Mthethomusha reserve. They were key suspects with alleged links to gangs targeting highly endangered animals, while brazenly using their parks-issued rifles to gun down buffalo for the greedy bushmeat industry. The same rifles pointed at where they thought I would emerge.

At first it struck me as strange that they had not fired at Zingela, who was still barking frantically. Then I understood.

'My God!' I whispered. 'They're after me.'

There was no question about it. They were waiting for me to emerge from behind my dog. If I had charged headlong up the slope – which most people without the benefit of *Oupa*'s sage advice would've done – I would have been shot stone dead.

Silently, I approached from behind the boulder, placing one foot carefully in front of the other. A snapping twig or crunch of sand would give me away faster than a striking mamba. When I was about twenty yards from the men, I ducked behind a large tree for cover.

'*Wenzani?*' I shouted in Zulu. What are you doing?

They spun around. The first thing they noticed was my hands locked around the large-calibre .45 swivelling from one man's torso to the next – the most effective area to shoot in the event of an attack. Like most people who have spent their lives deep in the bush, I am a skilled shot. I could take them both out before they could swing their rifles my way. And they knew it.

'Drop your weapons. Now!'

They did so with alacrity.

'Move back!'

By now, both men had turned fifty shades of pale and hastily backed away from their dropped R1s.

'Why are your rifles cocked and aimed at my dog?' I shouted. 'Was it because you knew I would come up the bank after him? And then you would *dubula* (shoot) me?'

They denied this vehemently, but I could clearly see by their body language they had been caught out. Not knowing how to react, they stuttered and stammered that they thought Zingela was a hunting dog with a poacher coming up behind him.

'Oh really? You thought it was a poacher's dog? But you see me with this dog every day.'

I then pointed to the rusty, banged-up Land Cruiser behind us. 'There is my *mova*. You see me driving it every day. You knew it was me down by the river. How stupid do you think I am?'

I walked towards the dropped weapons, quickly stripped the rifles and threw the action pieces as far as I could into the bush.

Still pointing my pistol, I slowly walked up to the rangers, who were beside themselves with fright. Zingela ran up the bank, his distinctive stiff-legged gait indicating he was aware of extreme danger. He crouched at my side, baring his fangs, growling viciously. One word from me and he would have attacked.

'You bastards meant to kill me,' I said, my voice shaking with shock and anger. 'You were going to shoot me.'

They shook their heads vigorously. They repeated that they thought they were up against a poaching gang with dogs. That was rich; every ranger in the reserve knew Zingela belonged to me. A muscular Weimaraner with distinctive blue-grey fur, he looked nothing like the slim, lurcher-type mutt that poachers use.

This was far from just being an honest mistake. These two guys planned to pump me full of lead and later claim that poachers were responsible, or else leave my body rotting somewhere deep in the bush for hyenas and vultures. Any doubts were dispelled by the fact that they were pointing their weapons at the exact spot where I would have emerged from the river bank. Not to mention that I had recently exposed their alleged poaching activities just a few weeks before.

It was a blatant assassination attempt. I continued swinging the pistol from one man to the other. 'The next time you try me, I *will* act in self-defence and kill you both.'

I then backed towards the vehicle, started the motor and drove off, leaving them to find the bits and pieces of their rifles' firing mechanisms scattered in the veld.

Two things were now certain. One was that Zingela's incredible alertness and my mentors' wise words of advice had saved my life. The other was that the enemy was now truly entrenched within. Some of my fellow conservationists and game rangers wanted me out of their way. Permanently.

I took a few minutes to absorb this. There was no pill more bitter to swallow. I have put everything on the line to protect Africa's unique heritage – its magnificent wildlife, unsurpassed anywhere else on this planet. It's been my lifelong quest.

But how could I continue to do so against such overwhelming odds, when even some of the people I worked with were out to get me? Who could I now trust?

I silently thanked Zingela, lying on the passenger seat with his head on my lap, for saving me. For him, it was no big deal. It was what he did. I knew with granite certainty that I could rely on him in any situation. His loyalty was set in stone. He would lay down his life for me in the blink of an eye. He was incorruptible. A true force of nature.

The battle for Africa's last wild places will only be won by those with total, unwavering commitment to the natural order of the planet. That we all knew. But where were they? I mean … a few moments ago I had almost been taken out by two supposed 'good guys'.

In the darkness of despair, I suddenly realised that right next to me was an answer. Zingela. At that moment I grasped that perhaps the ultimate combatants in this conflict for the soul of the wilderness were dogs; creatures that have no conception whatsoever of human vices such as corruption, insatiable greed or utter betrayal. Their loyalty was absolute, their courage immeasurable. Their allegiance to us was not negotiable.

I stroked Zingela's head. It was a small spark of hope. For me, that day was an epiphany. I knew what I had to do.

How I got there was a long journey …

2

Where it all Began

My mother, Elaine, says I was an adventurous child. In fact, she claims I drove her to exhaustion, never still for a moment, incessantly questioning everything.

She says she sometimes wished I was more like my older sister, Kendyl, wise beyond her years, or my younger brother, Jayson, quiet and introspective.

Be that as it may. What I do know is that one of my earliest recollections of school was terrifying classmates by bringing various bugs, beetles, spiders, frogs and even snakes into the classroom, usually resulting in a mass scattering of kids and teachers alike.

As I say, I knew from the very beginning that my life was destined to be lived in the wilderness. So much so that when I was six, my mother says I told her I no longer needed to go to school and should instead be left to wander in the hills. She had no idea how prophetic those words would be.

But perhaps I had no option. I come from an unusual gene pool, from both branches of the family tree.

Let's start with the paternal bloodline. The name De Rosner sounds aristocratic, and to my surprise, it is. My grandfather

Geza de Rosner (hence my second name) was a Hungarian Baron, a hereditary title that dates to the Crusader Wars of Richard the Lionheart. The baronetcy was awarded to the family for bravery on the battlefield.

Baron Geza de Rosner was, by all accounts, a man of many talents – a writer, adventurer, amateur archaeologist, Egyptologist and film maker – who travelled the world lecturing on ancient civilisations such as the Incas and Aztecs. He married Mignon Beaumont, scion of a prominent British family who were among the earliest of the colonialist pioneers to settle in present-day KwaZulu-Natal. Mignon's grandfather, William Henry Beaumont, was born in India, arriving in Durban in 1873 and appointed Judge of the Supreme Court of Port Natal in 1902. William's son, Baron William Richard Beaumont, married into the Platt family, also early settlers from Britain, who were on the founding board of the multinational sugar corporation, Tongaat Hulett.

Geza and Mignon had two children, Marcia and my father, Zoltan, who married my mother, Elaine Havemann. My parents divorced when I was five and we lived mainly with my mother, although my dad has been a guiding influence in my life and was a wonderful father. He was calm and wise, with a dry wit that made his remarks and numerous wry puns even funnier. To my sorrow, he passed away in early January 2022.

On my mother's equally adventurous side of the family, Heinrich Havemann left Germany as a young man, arriving in Port Natal, where Durban stands today, in 1839. He married Hester Maré, who is the ancestral mother of our branch of Havemanns. Hester's parents joined the Great Trek, the exodus of Dutch-speaking settlers into the African hinterland to escape British rule in the Cape Colony, when she was thirteen years old, taking two years to reach Natal. Family lore has it that it was the teenage Hester who led the trek oxen of the first wagon down the precipitous cliffs of the Drakensberg Mountains at Oliviershoek Pass into their new homeland.

Once over the mountains, they outspanned near the Bloukrans and Bushman's rivers. The *voortrekker* laagers, fortified camps encircled by wagons, were spaced far apart to ensure enough grazing for their cattle herds, so the Maré family was about four miles from the Bloukrans settlement.

On 16 February 1838, Hester's mother was urgently called to assist in delivering the baby of a trekker woman at the Bloukrans camp. The Marés packed their wagon, but one of the team of twelve cattle they used to pull it, a white ox, was missing. They searched for it in vain and the eleven oxen were tied to their yokes for the night to enable the family to leave at sunrise.

The next morning, they woke to terrible news. Zulu warriors had raided the Bloukrans settlement and massacred everyone, including women, children and servants. The delay in searching for the white ox had saved the lives of Hester and her family. Also, to their astonishment, the white ox that went missing was now calmly lying next to the rest of the yoked animals.

The Maré family finally settled in a laager in an area that became the site of the present-day city of Pietermaritzburg. Heinrich and Hester were married along with two other couples in the first church erected in the settlement on 15 February 1841.

Then we have my grandfather Coenraad *Oupa* Havemann, who was a huge influence on my life. *Oupa* was a practical man of the soil, a Zululand pioneer in the 1940s, overcoming scorching summers, droughts, floods, tsetse fly, rampant malaria and repeated crop failures to carve a living from the land on his farm, Windy Ridge. He was also an old-school hunter, and Windy Ridge in the Ntambanana district was one of the first privately owned farms to be rewilded – a novel concept in those days. *Oupa* ploughed up his cotton and pineapple fields and let nature take its course as the land reverted to wild acacia grassland and thornveld.

When the bushveld came alive again, *Oupa* stocked Windy Ridge with zebra, wildebeest, impala, rhino and giraffe, and actively encouraged the return of nyala, kudu and bushbuck. He was a founder member of the Natal Game Ranchers Association and was widely recognised for his ground-breaking conservation efforts. The 1950s was a pivotal era in Zululand conservation as frontline game rangers such as Dr Ian Player, Ken and John Tinley, Nick Steele, Jim Feely, Graham Root and Mark Astrup were valiantly trying to save the area's wildlife, particularly its white and black rhino, from extinction.

Oupa married into the Rudd clan, a family synonymous with the early days of the Kimberley diamond fields, and my grandmother had English, Scottish, Irish, French Huguenot and *Boer* blood.

So, there we have it. My DNA is a chaotic mishmash, ranging from Hungarian aristocracy to hardscrabble *Boer* rebels. Indeed, the family joke is that the De Rosner bluebloods arrived in style, sailing into Port Natal on a handsome ship, while my mother's paternal forbears couldn't afford the boat fare, so had to trek over the rugged Drakensberg Mountains in rickety ox wagons.

My mother remarried in the 1980s, and a few years later we moved to a game farm called Mauricedale outside the town of Malelane, the southern gateway to the world-renowned Kruger National Park, an iconic wildlife reserve roughly the size of Wales. During school holidays I, along with my brother, sister and stepsisters Teresa and Belinda Bell, would disappear into the bush, walking dogs, riding horses and exploring the untamed countryside. I learnt how to hunt responsibly, but mainly I honed my tracking skills and spent hundreds of hours just watching wild creatures in their natural habitat.

All five of us kids had a privileged childhood and went to private boarding schools. I first was sent to Somerset House near Cape Town and then to Woodridge College outside what was then Port Elizabeth (now Gqeberha) in the Eastern Cape province. My last three years of schooling were spent at Weston Agricultural College in Mooi River, KwaZulu-Natal. I loved it there and my nickname was Bush Cat, as I was always running around, either illicitly fly-fishing for trout on a neighbouring farm, raiding beehives, or white-water rafting down the beautiful Mooi River.

I couldn't wait to start a career as a game ranger. I not only cherished being in the bush more than anything else, for me it was a holy place.

The planet's cathedral.

3

Windy Ridge Game Reserve

With my formal schooling at last done and dusted, I was ready at last for my real education – going into the wild.

It happened when my uncle Louis John Havemann offered me a game ranger apprenticeship on Windy Ridge, the Zululand reserve my grandfather rewilded. Even though I would be paid a meagre salary, it was exactly what I wanted. *Oupa* had now retired, handing over Windy Ridge to his only son, and to be offered a job there was a dream come true. As a boy, visiting *Oupa*'s game farm was the biggest treat imaginable and where my all-consuming love of nature and choice of career took root. As far as I was concerned, Windy Ridge was without question the greatest place on the planet.

I had recently turned nineteen and despite Louis John being my mother's brother, I was not given any special treatment. On the contrary, he was a hard, demanding taskmaster and not the easiest person to work for. But I had huge respect for my uncle and his knowledge of the bush, and I possibly deserved the frequent bollockings that came my way.

The experience was invaluable. In fact, I don't think I could have had a better bush internship under a greater tutor even if I felt like clocking him at times, even though I knew he would probably hammer me in a physical confrontation. Thanks to him, I learnt how to become a skilled ranger, taking part in game captures, anti-poaching patrols, snare sweeps and fence inspections, and working with many different types of animals. I also had to become a Jack of all trades, as on Windy Ridge we did everything ourselves. Consequently, through sheer necessity I became a hands-on bricklayer, plumber, electrician and, most importantly, a bush mechanic to keep the fleet of often dilapidated vehicles and tractors chugging through some of the roughest terrain imaginable. On top of that, I had to polish up on my people skills, taking tourists and guests on game drives and handling school groups who came to the reserve for wilderness experiences.

In many instances, I was thrown in at the deep end, being pretty naïve after a privileged childhood. But that was good. With Louis John as a boss, people either sank or swam ... there was no in-between. Wake-up calls were at 4 a.m. sharp in summer and 5 a.m. in winter and there were times when I was late and got fired minutes after getting out of bed, only to be rehired after breakfast. I constantly had to walk on eggshells, never knowing if I would incur Louis John's wrath for some minor infraction, or whether I would still have a job when he calmed down. But his wildlife knowledge, learnt through tough experience, is right up there with the best. He's a genuine bush maestro – and I am greatly honoured to have had one of the best teachers in the business. The hard lessons he taught have stood me in good stead throughout my life.

I got to know the rugged thornveld and the magnificent acacia grasslands of Windy Ridge like the back of my hand and became very fit from constantly being on the move in the heat and humidity of the unforgiving Zululand bush. I loved the sheer adventure of it all, as well having the complete freedom to roam and explore the outdoors. To keep me company, I got a puppy; no special breed but definitely with a sprinkling of genes from the indigenous, semi-domesticated but largely free-ranging *Canis Africanis* lurking in the background. I named him Bamba, which in Zulu means 'to catch' or 'grab hold of', and today I cannot imagine a life without a trusting dog as my companion.

My accommodation was in one of the *rondavels*, a round room attached to the main house, which I shared with Louis John's son Brandon whenever he came home from boarding school. However, it soon became apparent that another 'resident' shared the premises with us, something far more sinister. I regularly heard ghostly footsteps at night and there was a creepy feeling of being watched by invisible eyes in the lounge.

I was not alone in sensing this spooky spectre. Hopeful rangers looking for work would arrive for a job interview, and as we were far out in the sticks, they usually stayed overnight in an empty room near the disused cattle dip behind the house. Almost without fail, they would emerge wide-eyed the next morning saying a 'demon' had grabbed them by the throat and attempted to throttle them.

It transpired that some years before, a ranger who worked at Windy Ridge had disappeared after payday one month and was never seen again. Human bones were later found by Brandon under a tarpaulin in a drainage line at the old dip, and it is believed the ranger had been killed and his body dumped there. I became convinced that the strange noises and bumps in the night were caused by the restless spirit of the murdered man.

Despite the hazards, supernatural or otherwise, my most dangerous job had nothing to do with wild animals. The old borehole at the Inthibane camp, which we used to accommodate our wilderness education groups, was out of action so I regularly had to ferry in water. This entailed driving an ancient Bedford lorry down to the Enseleni River with two massive water tanks mounted on the back. Once the tanks were pumped full, I had to coax the groaning vintage rattletrap up the bank and often imagined myself being crushed if it toppled backwards into the river. The sloshing water tanks also made the archaic lorry top heavy and I was certain that the stressed brakes would one day spectacularly fail as it careered downhill, with potentially fatal results for the unfortunate driver. Me, in other words. That was the worst and most onerous task on my long list of duties – far more precarious than any charging rhino!

The field rangers at the time were Ovambo trackers from Namibia. Most had served with Koevoet – a crack paramilitary unit during the South African border war that ended in 1990 – and were seasoned bush fighters. I had a good relationship with these hard men, regularly going out on patrol with them and learning the art of tracking both humans and animals.

Louis John also had a lot of friends in the military special forces, and they often came to Windy Ridge to do clandestine training. I latched onto these men as well, joining in the undercover operations and running around in the bush wearing a sweaty camouflage ghillie suit during 'pursue and catch' practices. As they were a sniper unit, they also taught me elite marksmanship skills. I didn't know it then, but both the Koevoet and special forces guys taught me a lot of crucial skills that would become extremely useful when the rhino horn poaching conflicts erupted with a vengeance at the turn of the twenty-first century.

Many hunters also visited Windy Ridge, and I would go on hunts with Louis John before getting my professional licence through the well-respected Ian Goss Hunting Academy and leading safaris myself. These were particularly popular with hunters of Indian descent, who mainly came from the Durban area, and the buck curry they cooked was the best I have ever tasted.

While my bush education was on-going, I also became attuned to the mysteries and mythologies of this intensely spiritual continent – something I have always been interested in. For example, I noticed that the rangers meticulously avoided a sharp bend in the Enseleni River, which winds its way through Windy Ridge, taking the longer route on their patrols. It seemed illogical, so I asked them why.

The answer was unanimous. '*Eish*. A *tokoloshe* lives there,' one replied. 'It will attack anyone who goes there. Stay away.'

A *tokoloshe* is a small, hairy demon and has a terrifying influence in African folklore. Many people – even in the cities – sleep with their beds raised on bricks to ward off its evil power.

I asked more questions and reluctantly they took me to where the mythical creature lived. On the bend of the river, high up an undercut rock crag, is a gaping hole that disappears into the eroded cliff face. That, they said, was the evil creature's lair. Although they called it a *tokoloshe*, they said that it was more like an *mkovu* – a wild humanlike dwarf creature. Something like the Yeti of the Himalayas or Big Foot of the Rockies, but smaller.

Whatever it was, it was as spooky as all hell and I involuntarily shivered as the hairs on my arms stiffened. I agreed that this was a spine-chilling place and understood why the rangers zealously avoided it.

Indeed, there was never a dull moment. I remember one morning driving to fetch the reserve's secretary, Maureen Tracy, when a man came running down the road with a large pack of *Canis Africanis*. These extremely hardy, lightly built animals resemble a cross between a greyhound, a terrier and an Australian dingo, and are widely used by the locals to hunt bushmeat.

I slammed on brakes and shouted at him. 'What the hell are you doing? Where are you going with those hunting dogs?'

Instead of stopping, the man charged towards me, brandishing a large panga (a type of machete). Alarmed and thinking the dogs were a poaching pack that would run amok on the reserve, I started to shoot at them. Highly agitated, the man screamed that they were not his dogs, but belonged to the people in the nearby village. Some of the dogs were now also getting aggressive, and with snarling animals and a panga-wielding man coming at me, it took some deft footwork to force him into the back of the car. I was lucky not to be slashed or bitten.

I drove to the office and Louis John started questioning him. It was soon evident that the guy was mentally unstable so we called in the local headmen who confirmed it. Nonetheless, he would have to face retribution from residents for rounding up their dogs, taking them onto a game reserve and endangering their lives.

Not long afterwards, I had another hair-raising experience while building wooden chalets at the Inthibane educational camp – literally, in this case.

Our farm workers had been tasked with the manual work and I noticed we were often a staff member short. I suspected that this was because one of the workers was sneaking off to the river to do some illicit fishing, so I sent two rangers out to investigate. I told them not to detain the man, but to report who it was directly to me as he was a staff member, not some grubby poacher.

The next morning, while having breakfast, a sweating and alarmed ranger burst into the room.

'Big trouble,' he wheezed. 'Makhathini has been shot.'

It transpired that the rangers had caught the worker, whose name was Makhathini, fishing and tried to arrest him – contrary to my instructions. Makhathini resisted and, in the ensuing melee, he was mortally wounded.

I raced down to the camp to find the now dead Makhathini, with his incensed colleagues accusing the rangers of being murderers and threatening to lynch them.

Shouting above the noise, I tried to restore calm. Eventually, when everything quietened down, I examined the body and started piecing together the full story.

What finally emerged was that Makhathini had allegedly tried to smack a .30-30 lever-action rifle out of one of the rangers' hands with a spade, striking the barrel and accidentally triggering the firing mechanism. The bullet hit him under the left armpit, killing him instantly.

However, the sorry saga didn't end there. Soon afterwards, a distressed ox stumbled into the yard at the main house with an axe wound cleaved down its back. Again, the local headmen were summoned, as it was believed that a disgruntled villager had inflicted the gaping injury.

We all agreed that the most humane thing to do was to put the critically injured animal out of its misery. I took my .30-06 Winchester and, aiming for the centre point of a cross between the horns and eyes, shot it in the brain.

I slotted another round into the chamber in case the animal was not dead, clicked on the safety catch, and placed the rifle next to a tree. I then cut through the animal's throat with a razor-sharp knife to bleed it out.

While bending down to do this, the ranger whose rifle had killed Makhathini picked up my Winchester, slipped off the safety and with the barrel pointing at me, pulled the trigger. Whether this was by accident or design, I do not know. What I do know is that the bullet lifted the hairs on the nape of my neck, missing my head by a fraction of an inch. I paled and spun around, asking what the hell he was doing.

'Sorry, *Nkosana* (little master),' the man pleaded. 'I was just trying to make your gun safe.'

'Safe?' I snarled. 'Safe by taking off the safety catch?'

I was so angry that I nearly beat the crap out of him – and so did the headmen. It was a very, very close call indeed.

But one of the strangest experiences at Windy Ridge concerned a man the other workers all called 'Mfaan'. It still haunts me.

By now, I had been at Windy Ridge for about two and a half years, and although Louis John said I was still wet behind the ears, I had certainly come a long way in getting to grips with the realities of working as a wildlife game ranger. It was a tough gig, but one that I relished with a passion.

One morning I was taking roll call and noticed a newcomer standing at the end of the line. He was a short, stocky man dressed in tattered rags and there was a stench about him that would repel a hyena. His teeth were rotten black stumps and his gnarled hands were rough and calloused, the nails broken and dirty.

Louis John was also there and asked the regular staff where this guy came from and why was he at roll call. They told us that he lived close to the reserve and his name was Mfaan. Although he didn't talk much, they said he could outwork any man when it came to hard physical labour.

I looked at him closely. His expression was unfathomable, his eyes radiating both fear and bewilderment, and there seemed to be something a little out of kilter about him. However, Louis John agreed to take him on the payroll for a trial period.

As the staff said, he was an unbelievably hard worker. He could dig like an excavator and had the strength of five men. Whatever we showed him to do, he did exceptionally well, as long as it was simple, such as digging ditches or other manual labour. He never initiated conversation and, if spoken to, would react with a rotten-toothed smile, nod his head and simply say, 'Eehh.' That seemed to be the extent of his verbal communication.

Mfaan was delighted when we gave him his first staff uniform, a pair of overalls and gum boots. He beamed with pride, strutting and prancing around like a king. I have never seen anyone so ecstatic. I looked on in amazement, particularly as otherwise Mfaan seemed to have no material desires whatsoever. In fact, on pay days he would hand over his money to his workmates, who would laugh while pocketing his hard-earned cash.

However, it was a completely different story with his weekly food ration. This he jealously guarded, snarling and mock charging if anyone came close, and the rest of the staff soon learnt to keep a respectful distance during meal times.

I watched this unusual behaviour with interest. Why did he have no use for money but love his uniform? Why did he guard his food exactly as a wild animal would? Something was amiss and I became increasingly convinced that Mfaan's story was much more complex than simply one of mental disability. I was determined to find out more.

For me, most puzzling of all his behaviour was that he never cooked food, eating his maize meal, salt, sugar and dried bean rations raw – again, just like a wild animal. I questioned the staff about this but they just pointed to their heads making circular motions indicating that they thought he was *wathlanya* (crazy).

A few months after Mfaan joined the squad, I took out two international clients who wanted to shoot baboons for their trophy collection. We tracked down a troop close to Inthibane camp and the first client had a clean kill, bringing an animal down with a single bullet. But the second client botched his shot, wounding the baboon, and it ran off clutching its stomach. We then spent the next two days searching for it in thick bush, eventually finding the unfortunate creature lying crumpled in shallow water up against the Enseleni river bank. It had been shot in its gut and must have suffered an agonising death. I shook my head in sadness. Taking out trophy hunters and having to track wounded animals was beginning to take its toll on me. I couldn't see the point of having a once-beautiful creature stuffed and decorating a wall with accusatory glass eyes.

I retrieved the baboon and took it back to Inthibane camp, which was closer than the main skinning shed, as we needed to prepare the decomposing animal quickly before its hair started slipping. Mfaan was hard at work in the camp excavating foundations for a new building and I asked him to help with the skinning.

When Mfaan saw the dead baboon with a bullet hole in its gut, he went ballistic, jumping up and down and shrieking in distress. Baring the black stumps of his teeth and with his eyes rolling with fear, he ran off and shinned up the nearest tree, howling uncontrollably.

At roll call the next morning, I asked why Mfaan was not present. The staff made the usual 'he's crazy' gestures, but this time I demanded a reply. Why did the dead baboon have such an effect on him? We would not leave until I got an answer.

Eventually the *induna* (headman) stepped forward, and for the first time I was told the truth. As a young child, Mfaan had attended the small rural school at Ntambanana village and was extremely bright. However, others in his class were jealous so arranged for some older boys to beat him up. This they did repeatedly, so much so that Mfaan suffered brain damage.

'Then both his parents died,' the *induna* continued. 'With no one to care for him, he wandered off into the bush and was taken in by a family of baboons that lived in the hills of KwaBiyela, further up the Enseleni River.'

With a start, I realised that was roughly the same area where I had taken the trophy hunters. It all made sense. I had inadvertently asked Mfaan to skin the corpse of one of his family members. The dead baboon had most likely been a friend. As a bullied orphan and outcast, these animals were the only kinsmen he had left.

I cried a silent tear for being so naïve.

Mfaan never did return to Windy Ridge. I was later told that he re-joined his adopted family and was once more living in the KwaBiyela hills along the winding river valley. Sometimes cattle herders would see him with the troop, but he avoided them at all costs.

His trust in humans had been shattered forever.

4

Death in the Guarri Bushes

It's a Thursday morning I will never forget. I even remember the exact time: seven-thirty. The workers had gathered in front of me as I gave instructions for tasks scheduled that day.

Then the quiet buzz of daybreak shattered with the sharp crack of a gunshot echoing in the hills from the valley below. Then another.

I saw birds flapping skywards, squawking wildly. I knew exactly where the shots had come from: a lush, terraced hillside that had been planted with cotton many years ago but was now rewilded. It was a favourite grazing ground for wildebeest.

At first, I thought it might be rangers shooting at poachers' hunting dogs that had somehow got in through the game fence. But whatever it was, I needed to check it out.

Although not envisaging a major problem, I grabbed the R1 automatic rifle I had been issued after enrolling as a police reservist and ran down the valley. Finding nothing unusual, I then ran along the reserve's boundary fence to the top corner on the hill, which was a good lookout position. I sat in the long grass, watching and listening, my weapon at the ready. I had two twenty-round magazines taped together for instant use but did not think that I would need them.

Then, down in the steep valley, a herd of *blesbok* appeared, running panic-stricken along a contour of the hill in the distance. Their snow-white faces glinted in the blazing early morning sun and, looking through binoculars, I noticed one of the animals at the back floundering. It was obviously wounded.

Then, amazed, I saw two men following the animal. One appeared to be armed with a rifle, although at that distance I couldn't be sure. Could they be poachers? This early in the morning?

I kept low, watching from my vantage point on the high ground. This was highly unusual, as poachers usually only operated under cover of darkness. They were never so bold as to shoot animals on a game reserve in broad daylight – especially with the main house no more than a mile away.

What the hell was going on? If they were poachers, why were they so brazen?

Suddenly the two men broke off the chase and left the *blesbok* herd. They then came up the hill directly towards my position. I tightened my sweaty grip on the R1. Those two magazines I had hurriedly grabbed as I sped off now seemed very useful. This situation could go south at any moment.

Taking cover behind a guarri bush, I waited for them to come closer. In front was a young man holding a spear, while behind was a large, heavily built older man carrying a .303 rifle. It was obvious that he had shot and wounded the *blesbok*. Having been in the odd fray and arrested poachers a few times, I instinctively knew that this was going to be serious. I was on my own with no backup.

My heart was beating like a locomotive, my entire body wildly pumping adrenalin. Louis John, who had been in many shoot-outs with poachers, told me that at times like this, I needed to be totally focused and controlled – and always have good cover. He also stressed that I would instinctively know when to act with deadly force. It was something I had to decide for myself; no one could teach me how to do it.

I steadied myself, remembering Louis John's words, breathing evenly and steadying my emotions. I waited until they were about fifteen yards away, then stood and, pointing my automatic rifle at the armed men, shouted in Zulu.

'Stop right there!'

The older man panicked and swung the rifle off his shoulder. He had a strange expression on his face, and I watched as he brought the weapon up, almost in surreal slow motion, and levelled the barrel at my chest. There was no doubt he was going to shoot me. Without having time to aim, I fired, shooting from the hip.

He winced as the bullets struck but didn't fall. I continued pulling the trigger until the magazine emptied. I then hurriedly changed over to the next one.

The younger man sprinted off while the gunman ducked into the guarri bush thicket. The bushes heaved as he barged through, then stopped. I knew he would be lying in ambush, expecting me to follow.

With my heart now pumping even more ferociously, I stood dead still, barely moving, waiting to see what would happen next. To follow the gunman into the thicket would be suicide, as he would shoot the instant I entered. After about ten minutes, I decided there was nothing I could do except go and get help.

As I did not have a mobile phone or handheld radio, I ran as fast as I could down the hill to the main office, shouting to Maureen, the reserve secretary, to call the police.

'I've hit a contact,' I wheezed as I charged into the office, my tortured lungs gasping for air. 'He tried to shoot me and I don't think I missed him.'

Maureen dialled the police dog unit in Richards Bay, who said they were on their way. However, we were about forty miles inland on mainly dirt roads and it took them close on an hour to reach Windy Ridge. I waited anxiously with dire images flashing through my mind. Was the man dead? I knew even shooting from the hip that I could not have missed at that range and with the amount of ammo I had fired off. He also had run into the bush as if he was wounded.

However, my biggest concern was that the younger poacher might return to the crime scene and take the rifle from the shot man. If that had happened, there would be no way that I could prove self-defence. I would, in all likelihood, be charged with attempted murder – or murder if the man died.

Eventually the police arrived and I took the captain and his men to the shoot-out scene. As the poacher was armed, the police were ultra-cautious, advancing at little more than a couple of steps a minute. Once we got to the guarri, the police sent a tracker dog into the thicket. It started barking as soon as it entered.

'He's definitely still in there,' said the captain, referring to the poacher. 'But we don't know what the situation is. Whether he's dead or alive.'

We waited for a while, but nothing moved in the bushes. Eventually, one of the policemen warily parted the dense foliage.

'*Hy's dood*,' he said. He's dead.

I looked inside and the first thing I saw was the poacher propped up against a tree, eyes staring vacantly ahead. In his hands was the .303, pointing directly at where I would have entered. It was cocked with the safety catch off and his finger still in the trigger guard. If I had followed him into the thicket, there would have been two dead men.

The police captain made the poacher's rifle safe. We then noticed that the bullet heads were all coated with toilet paper and animal fat. This was clear witchcraft medicine – or *muti* as it is commonly called – and the dead man was also wearing other occult paraphernalia around his waist and neck. Even his knife in its sheath had protective charms. One of the Zulu police officers said that with all this *muti*, the poacher believed bullets fired at him would turn to water. A big mistake on his part.

We returned to where the gunfight started, and the captain asked where I had been standing. This was obvious by the many spent R1 bullet cases on the ground. He then asked how many rounds I had fired.

'I don't know,' I replied. 'I didn't stop shooting, as the guy didn't fall. He kept on aiming in my direction, trying to shoot me.'

The captain wrote down every detail in his report book.

He then asked where the poacher had stood. I pointed to the pool of blood.

'Why did you wait until he was so close?' he asked. 'He was almost on top of you.'

'Because I would have preferred to arrest rather than shoot him,' I replied. 'I thought he would drop the rifle when I challenged him.'

'That was very foolish,' said the captain, shaking his head. 'In future, keep a good distance before you take any action – especially if the other person is armed.'

The police pathologist vehicle arrived to collect the body, but as the poacher was so hefty, there were not enough hands to lift the body up and carry it to the closest road about a hundred yards away. I offered to help, but the captain refused, saying it was better I did nothing as I might later have what he called 'psychological repercussions'.

I insisted, saying that even though it was self-defence, I was still responsible for taking this man's life. The captain was not happy but relented, allowing me to help carry the body to the police van.

Louis John returned later in the afternoon and we went into the lounge bar, or den, as we called it. He cracked open a beer and handed it to me, staring straight into my eyes.

'You have taken a life and now you are a man. You did your duty. You have crossed a line and you can never step back over it. You will see the next time will be easier. Never hesitate when it comes to self-defence, in saving yours or another person's life.'

It didn't go down well. I was trying to process the incident, and after my third beer I started to feel angry as well as upset. Why did this man even attempt to draw on me when I so obviously had the upper hand? I had the high ground, a firearm at the ready and the first draw. There was no way he could have won the gunfight. If he had simply surrendered, he would still be alive.

There was little doubt that the *muti* had played a pivotal part in his demise. He had thought himself to be invincible. By acting as he did, he had forced me to take his life.

I was later told that the dead poacher had been an *induna* from one of the surrounding villages. The younger man armed with a spear was one of his three sons. They were a well-respected family in the area. There would be repercussions.

A few days later, the *induna*'s family came to the reserve to collect his spirit from the death scene, a sacred funeral rite in Zulu culture. A branch of a buffalo thorn tree (*umlathla nkosi*) is used to sweep the area where the person died, and the spirit is summoned to jump onto the branch so that it might be taken back to its final resting place in the village homestead. In this case, the person sweeping the death zone was the dead *induna*'s mother.

For reasons I did not understand, I was instructed by Louis John to accompany the mother to collect the spirit of her son. I was extremely uncomfortable about this and thought it insensitive in the extreme. However, I suppose Louis John did it because he thought it would 'toughen me up' and send an uncompromising message to the poacher's family. Throughout the ceremony, the mother stared at me with absolute hatred. The venom in her eyes literally blazed. I couldn't blame her. Just as it was not over for me, it certainly was not over for the family.

The inquest later that week ruled that I had acted justifiably in self-defence and no charges were laid. But even though I was completely absolved, the ruling did not bring closure. Far from it. I still felt extremely upset that he had acted in a manner that made me end his life.

However, just because the courts cleared me, it didn't mean I was home-free by any stretch of the imagination. I still had the law of the jungle to contend with, something far more vicious and lethal, and it wasn't long before I heard what I already suspected. The family had vowed vengeance. There was only one acceptable outcome for them: I had to die. An eye for an eye.

The first warning came from one of our staff. I was just about to drive to Heatonville, a nearby farming village, and our garden caretaker rushed up to me looking extremely agitated.

'Don't go, *Nkosana*,' he said. 'The *induna*'s sons and family are waiting for you on the Ntambanana road. They have AK-47s.'

I hurriedly got out of my truck. The hit was now official. There was no escape from this.

Even more unsettling for me was the precarious location of Windy Ridge. The Ntambanana road is the key route in and out of the reserve and I travelled along it often. In fact, I had little choice when getting supplies or going to town. Being unable to use it basically meant I was a prisoner in my own home. And with assassins waiting for me day and night, there was no doubt they would get me in the end. All they needed was for me to make a single mistake. I would then drive into a hail of lead and that would be the end.

Only one option remained. I would have to leave Windy Ridge, the place I loved more than anywhere else on earth at the time. With a heavy heart, I started to make plans to go.

That was my first deadly contact, and unfortunately, not the last. Over the years I have been involved in many others, as the poaching conflict in South Africa today is as pitiless and nasty as any war zone. Most shoot-outs are short, sharp and brutal, often in bush so thick you are only yards apart. It is terror personified: the frenzied heartbeats, the dry-mouthed choke of fear, adrenalin surging like wildfire, and one overriding mission – kill or be killed.

But Louis John was wrong, at least in my case. It never gets easier. Killing someone, even someone trying to kill you, does not make you a 'man'. It is something you live with forever. I still sometimes wake up sweating with a pounding heart as violent dreams merge with reality in a terrifying collage of violence.

However, when fighting side by side with dedicated fellow rangers, there is some small comfort in that usually no one knows who fired which fatal shot. But in the case of the dead *induna*, my first ever gunfight, there was no doubt. Not only had I killed a man, I had looked straight into his eyes as the bullets struck. I will not forget the shock of seeing that expression on his face for the rest of my days.

I know I will be in more firefights; I have chosen the path of a warrior. That's just the way it is with the insatiable demand for the body parts, horns and organs of Africa's wild animals in the Far East. But for many of us, the wounds are increasingly psychological as well as physical, and I have frequently sent fellow field rangers for post-traumatic stress disorder counselling or a cleansing by the local *sangoma* (tribal healers). We know it, accept it and, as far as possible among the often-taciturn men and women of the bush, we sometimes talk about it – but only among fellow combatants. Those who understand the pain; those who relive lucid flashbacks of shoot-outs, machete or knife attacks, and bareknuckle brawls in the dark recesses of their minds. The bond that bush warriors have for each other is forged in blood, just as it is with any frontline combat soldier.

I was then offered the chance to do field-guide training at Phinda, a famous Big Five game reserve in northern Zululand. It was a great opportunity. But before starting the course, to clear my head I went off on holiday as I had some days leave due to me.

While relaxing, I got a call from Louis John. He got straight to the point. 'I'm phoning to tell you that I have shot your dog.'

After a shocked silence I asked, 'Why?'

Louis John said that Bamba had brought a duiker onto the front lawn of the main house and killed it. He said the dog had turned rogue and was 'duly dispatched'.

I was shaken to the core. Bamba was more than just a dog; he was my closest friend. I could not for the life of me understand why, at the very least, Louis John hadn't just told me to come and take the animal off the reserve. He knew how much I loved Bamba. I was now starting to understand that this world can be brutal and ruthless. To survive in the bush, where there is often little time for emotion, it's best to toughen up and get on with it.

POSTSCRIPT: In 1998, more than two years after I left Windy Ridge, the reserve was sold to Lawrence Anthony and the name was changed to Thula Thula. Lawrence's book about rehabilitating a herd of elephants at the reserve, The Elephant Whisperer, *became a global best seller and the reserve is now internationally famous, with the elephants as a star attraction.*

But fate plays weird and wonderful tricks. Lawrence's son, Dylan, married my cousin, Tanith, and they have two sons. The Havemann gene pool is still rooted in what was once my ancestral home – something that would make my grandfather beam with pride. Oupa's love for the patch of wilderness he called Windy Ridge was infinite.

5

Shamans of the Past

Phinda Private Game Reserve is considered one of the top ecotourism destinations in Africa.

Close to the Maputaland coastline in South Africa's northeast with the best coral reefs in the country, it has seven distinct habitats: woodland, grassland, wetland, mountains, rivers, marshes and pans, as well as a spectacular one thousand hectares of Africa's rare dry sand forests. Apart from that, it's home to the iconic Big Five – lion, leopard, elephant, buffalo and rhino – as well as an incredible 436 bird species. Close-up sightings of the lightning-swift but shy cheetah are not uncommon.

So, when I was offered the opportunity to do ranger training there, I grabbed it with both hands.

My tuition at Phinda had been organised by Mark Taylor, the newly appointed manager of the Bongani Mountain Lodge in Mpumalanga. The idea was that once qualified, I would be employed at Bongani as a field guide. Mark was previously a highly rated trail ranger on the Bushmans Wilderness Trail in the southernmost area of Kruger Park, and I had previously been on one of these informative three-day hikes with him. For the first time on this hike, I was introduced to San rock art and was immediately bowled over by the beauty and spirituality of these eons-old paintings. In fact, I was bouncing like a madman up and down the cliff from one image to the next, and no doubt Mark took note of my keen interest.

In November 1996, I started my new job at Bongani, which lies in the heart of the Mthethomusha Game Reserve nestling in the Krokodilpoort Mountains. Although the land is owned by the Mpakeni tribe, a private company called Inzalo Holdings had a ninety-nine-year lease to provide local employment and train the local community in conservation and ecotourism, the lifeblood of the reserve. CC Africa – the company I worked for – sublet from Inzalo.

As I drove up Zulweni Mountain to the lodge with fellow trainee Ashwell Glasson on our first day, I stopped to admire the wild paradise unfolding below us. The rugged bushveld is strewn with majestic granite boulders, while streams snake through woodlands studded with marula trees before plunging down glittering gorges into the Crocodile River flowing to the south-western corner of the Kruger National Park.

The beauty was unbelievable. But it was more than just that. The land itself was spiritually primal. I could feel the raw energy of the earth, throbbing like a magnet, coursing through my body. To say I was enthusiastic about my new job is understating the case.

Once at the lodge, two guys came out to greet us, both called Mark. I already knew the general manager, Mark Taylor, who introduced me to the head ranger, Mark Griffiths. We instantly hit it off and remain good friends to this day. He took me on a tour to get to know the area, and one of the first things I noticed was an overhang between two giant granite boulders at the entrance to the lodge. Pointing at them, I remarked, 'I bet there are San paintings up there.'

Mark Griffiths nodded and said rangers frequently took visitors to see the paintings. My excitement mounted. 'Are there any others?'

'There are five sites that we know of. But there could be many more.'

It then struck me that this panoramic, undiluted, hard-wired wilderness surrounding Bongani Mountain Lodge was exactly what the San encountered when they followed the ancient game trails in search of food and water. They had even painted those epic migrations on the rocks. We were truly stepping in the footprints of the world's first conservationists.

The San hunter-gatherers are one of the world's oldest cultures, living in total harmony with the planet, and the legacy they bequeathed through hundreds of beautiful rock paintings and other artefacts is beyond priceless. Most San rock art is found in the Maloti–Drakensberg mountains in KwaZulu-Natal and the Cederberg mountains in the Western Cape. And here, on my doorstep deep in the wilderness of Mpumalanga, there could be more. From that moment, I was hooked. Searching for San rock art became an obsession, taking up every minute of my free time.

Then I got my first breakthrough. One blazing morning, crawling through an almost impenetrable tangle of *Dalbergia armata*, a woody liana vine with four-inch thorns, I momentarily paused to wipe the sweat streaming down my face. The climb had been taxing, and sucking in deep lungsful of crisp mountain air, I suddenly noticed how the leaves in a nearby tree canopy were throwing a kaleidoscope of shadows over a gigantic boulder. Like a lodestone, it was drawing me in.

Suddenly the shadows dancing on the rock seemed to merge for an instant. Then I saw it. A painted animal. It was barely visible, as if in fear of being discovered. My heart skipped a beat. It was a magnificent eland, sketched in the unmistakably ethereal style of the San people.

My eyes focused like a laser, and a granite canvas of ancient art emerged. Many more images adorned the walls. I had found my first San shelter – a wonderfully painted sanctuary. I barely breathed, so great was my awe and astonishment. To me, this was the bush equivalent of Michelangelo's paintings on the roof of the Sistine Chapel. The colours were red, orange, beige, cream and charcoal. Some of the paintings were faded, some clear and some seemed to glow. There were mountain reedbuck looking over their shoulders, giraffe and, of course, eland, the holiest and mightiest of animals to the San. Most poignant of all was a procession of human figures engaged in a trance-like dance, all painted in red ochre. It was the same colour as their blood that flowed after the onslaught of settlers and pastoralists that consumed the land and chased them from it.

I felt an overwhelming sense of melancholy. Sorrow for ancient times gone forever and sadness that San would never again visit this Eden that they were the first to inhabit.

And then, as if by magic, the gloom vanished, replaced by exhilaration that the connection I was feeling and the energy swirling around the shelter meant that I could work at making some sort of communication with these long-lost people. Through their art, I could record their irreplaceable passing heritage.

That thrill never left me. I felt it whenever I unearthed a new site and I knew why it meant so much. The superlative San hunters and gatherers were probably the last people able to coexist and commune at the purest level with the natural environment. For them, the environment held absolute power over life and death, and so spiritual communication with nature was essential to their survival. Few cultures, past or present, come anywhere near as close to instinctively knowing the elemental balance of the earth as they did.

At first, San rock art was interpreted by archaeologists in a basic narrative fashion with little understanding about the beliefs and culture of this all-but-lost race. Even now, we will never know many of the deeper meanings of these paintings, but by simply acknowledging the universal spirituality that exists within ourselves, we can gain some insight and understand San art with a clearer vision. These ancient images convey a simple yet profoundly fundamental message: the earth is our mother and should be treated with respect. Keeping that natural balance is integral to our future survival.

There had to be more shelters like this, and most of my days off involved boulder hopping along *koppies* (hilltops) and valleys, river courses and plains, discovering more and more wonderful painted home shelters along the way. Unwittingly, I had uncovered a treasure trove that few knew about, and by the end of 1997 I had logged more than a hundred new sites. I meticulously photographed each one, little understanding their importance and significance. It was mainly for my own interest, although I felt a strong spiritual connection that touched me to the core.

That changed dramatically when Tanya Vost, who worked at CC Africa's head office, visited Bongani. She had completed an archaeology course at the University of the Witwatersrand's Rock Art Research Institute, and when I showed her these new sites, she was mesmerised. Tanya instantly grasped that these discoveries were extraordinary – particularly because so few people apart from me knew they existed. Also, some of the subject matter and motifs painted were unique to this area, not found on rock art sites anywhere else in Africa. She notified Wits University, and the research institute's deputy director Geoffrey Blundell came out to see what all the buzz was about. He was blown away. This was to become one of the most important collections of rock art in the world, surpassed only in the Drakensberg and the Cederberg. Most paintings were estimated to be around one thousand five hundred years old, although some were considerably older, and Dr Blundell emphasised the importance of scientifically recording every painting we found. Each site was given GPS co-ordinates, marked on a 1:50,000 area map, photographed from all angles and the images traced with painstaking accuracy.

This task largely fell to me, mentored by Dr Blundell. I loved every minute of it.

Tracing San art is an art in itself and, at the time, was the most exact means of reproducing images for posterity. It takes a steady hand with a 0.35-millimetre lead pencil to do this, as the tracing has to be accurate to within a millimetre. It also takes infinite patience. In fact, my mother often shook her head wondering how I, a hyperactive child, could now happily hang from a harness in a cave for many hours tracing ancient art in minuscule detail. During the years I spent wandering in the hills of Bongani, I discovered about two hundred and fifty different rock art sites that possibly would otherwise have fallen unknown into the shadows of antiquity.

I regarded the opportunity to do this work as a great privilege as I was creating a gateway into the spiritual world of the mystical San, unravelling secrets and stories that perhaps would never have been told. But for me, it was also a journey of inner discovery, tapping deep into the soul of Mother Africa. This feeling is difficult to describe, so my chance meeting with a nyala in a rock art cave will have to suffice as a metaphor for this intensity.

It was a warm summer's day and I was making my way through the bush to a site listed simply as Thlati Pools 3 as it's on the Thlati River that winds eastwards towards Kruger.

It's breathtakingly beautiful with large granite boulders, rock pools, crystal clear water, and is safe to swim as it's above a waterfall so there are no crocodiles. There are plenty of leguaans, or monitor lizards, though – so many that I named one of my favourite spots Dragon's Pool. It's a special place, and the San artists must have thought so too as this area contains one of the highest concentrations of rock art paintings – fifteen sites within a third of a square mile. There also is a huge mound of giant land-snail shells, leading me to believe that the San enjoyed eating these molluscs, as well as an old iron spearhead and a large ash heap, testament to frequent habitation over time.

For me, the most intriguing painting in Thlati Pools 3 is of a human figure with spines projecting from its shoulders. The same figure also appeared in other nearby sites, and to this day no one is sure what the spines mean. As far as we know, the figure is unique to the Bongani reserve and is what archaeologists call 'a regional diagnostic reoccurring motif'. When I traced the painting, I called it the 'Human Shoulder Spines Man'.

I approached the overhang cautiously, as one never knows what beast lurks in a wild cave. Edging through the thorn scrub entrance, I suddenly noticed a flash in the shadows behind the thicket. Peering through the undergrowth, I saw an old nyala bull standing motionless in the overhang. I could see it was old and emaciated and had obviously come here to die. In the African bush, it is extremely rare for an antelope to die of old age. Only the fit can outrun predators.

Slowly, I stepped inside. The nyala remained motionless. It showed no fear; the calmness of death reflected in its dull eyes. It watched me enter. I crouched in a non-threatening manner, turning my face and body sideways so I would not look directly at it.

For a minute or two I sat quietly, then spoke.

'Hi, my name is Conraad and I mean you no harm. Would it be okay with you if I sit here for a while?'

My voice was the only sound in the cave.

'I see you are at the end of your life, but I must tell you that you must have been a very handsome nyala, and I am sure your progeny is now inhabiting the hills and valleys of Bongani. So, die in peace; you have left a proud heritage.'

The animal barely moved; the only flicker was the widening of its nostrils. It seemed to sense I was no threat. A soft breeze moved the thorn bush.

'You are so lucky that you will have a peaceful and honourable death and that you have lived a life with your dignity intact. No predator has torn you to pieces and devoured your flesh and left your bones to the vultures and hyenas, so I wish you a peaceful journey into the next world.'

The nyala continued looking at me.

'I will not talk and disturb you anymore but would like to sit with you for a while longer,' I said.

I sat quietly for almost an hour. Then the nyala swayed slightly. It was weakening. A soft spiritual calmness circulated in the cave. The tranquillity was tangible.

It was time to go. Very slowly, I stood and backed away towards the entrance.

'Goodbye,' I said, raising my hand in a farewell salute. Whatever had to be said, had been said. I knew deep down that this was something raw and profound and touched the depths of my soul, something organic about the cycle of life and spirit energy, our souls and our role on the planet.

I returned the next day. The grand old nyala lay dead, gone like the San of long, long ago. Above it, like a headstone, was the painting of the shoulder spines man.

6

Stories of the Weird and Wonderful

Few dispute that Bongani is a spiritual place. But perhaps there's also a geological explanation for this, as the dramatic granite caves and boulders that so inspired the venerated San artists have a remarkably high quotient of quartz crystal.

These electron-rich crystals store electromagnetic energy, and I believe that the mystical hunter-gatherer artists tapped into that cosmic voltage. Standing on these monoliths more than fifteen centuries later, I, too, could sense the pulsing primal heartbeat of the continent.

But it's not just idealists like me who say this. Many archaeologists researching these San sites have also spoken of strange vibrations and peculiar extrasensory perceptions that are inexplicable to science. If hard-data boffins say there are strange forces at play, who am I to argue otherwise?

Not only that, Bongani lies squarely on the Golden or Nilotic Meridian, the geographic centre of the Earth's landmass. This is a mythical axis around which ancient civilisations believed the universe rotated. Consecrated in deep-rooted folklore, the Golden Meridian runs horizontally along the 31° 14′ east longitudinal line from the Egyptian pyramids and Great Sphinx through the Great Rift Valley, ending at the Indian Ocean just below Durban. Among African shamans, this meridian is the arterial blood of Mother Earth, a subterranean river of energy mirrored in the cosmos by the Milky Way, hence its alternative name River of Stars. Mythical or not, there are more sacrosanct sites dotted along this revered meridian – including the Giza Plateau, the Temple of Philae, the ruins of Great Zimbabwe and Timbavati, birthplace of the white lions – than anywhere else in the world. It also crosses the source of the Nile, Africa's mightiest river.

Unfortunately, not all of this is good energy. In fact, some of it is downright scary – such as what happened to me at the site of what I now call the 'screaming banshee'.

I had spent a whole day on a ladder in a cave tracing a panel of a herd of elephants and supernatural potency dots – a common feature of rock art associated with shamanistic activities – when I suddenly became acutely aware that I was not alone. There was a presence watching behind me, invisible but palpable. The hair on the back of my neck was fairly bristling. I tried to ignore the negativity and uneasy feeling and concentrated on completing the job.

The atmosphere in the cave then turned cold, as if a freezer switch had been flicked. I looked behind to see what was causing it. Nothing – just a chilled draught swirling around me.

It was getting late and I started finishing up, relieved that I could get out of this spooky place. I packed my equipment and hurriedly walked out of the cave down to where my vehicle was parked.

Suddenly, I heard a high-pitched scream just behind me. It was a woman's voice – a terrifying shriek that nearly burst my eardrums. Spinning around, I could see nothing, but there was no doubt that this invisible entity was now directly facing me. I could feel the air churning.

Gooseflesh tingling down my spine, I spoke as calmly as I could in a loud voice. 'I am here out of respect and not to cause harm to this place, so leave me alone.'

I turned, scuttling down the path on my now-rubbery legs, jumped into my truck and sped off, shaken to the core.

I never heard the screaming banshee again, but the next supernatural encounter was just as bizarre. It was literally a bolt from the blue.

I had discovered an eerie, dark hole beneath two granite monoliths that turned out to be the entrance to an ancient mine. What was particularly interesting about the mine – apart from its ghostly access – was that the shaft had been dug using fire force tunnelling, a time-consuming and extremely dangerous excavation method where a fire is lit next to the rock surface and heated to blistering temperatures. When the rock starts cracking, cold water is poured onto it, causing a steam explosion that scatters razor-sharp stone shrapnel like a grenade blast. The process, preferably done when standing some distance away, is repeated hundreds of times, probably until one or more of the miners is either injured or dies from sheer exhaustion. I don't know if gold or any other precious metal came out of this spooky, hundred-foot-deep pit but judging by the amount of work needed to dig it, the incentive was definitely there.

Mark Griffiths wanted to see the mine, so we set off on a clear, big-sky day. Bad weather was the last thing on our minds as there was only one small puffy-white cloud directly above as the sun scorched the veld. A troop of baboons sat on the rocks lining the pathway, staring at us in utter silence. I looked at them, puzzled. This was extremely unusual behaviour for baboons, who normally shriek and bark at any sign of humans.

We then passed a mountain spring and I warned Mark to be on the lookout for an enormous black mamba that I often saw on the path. It was the biggest I've ever encountered and I have bumped into more than a few. Fortunately, it slithered off at the vibrations of our footsteps.

Then, as we approached the mine, a bolt of jagged lightning blitzed down directly in front of us. It was storm lightning, sparking fiercely off the rocks and sending up spurts of dust and pebbles. The air turned cobalt blue, acrid with the reek of burnt electricity.

Mark and I stared at each other in shocked disbelief. There were no rain clouds around, and certainly no thunder rolls. What was going on? Where had this blistering fireball come from?

Up on the rocks, the baboons maintained their silent vigil, as still as statues. We continued walking, now considerably rattled.

As we reached the entrance, we heard what sounded like the sharp crackling of cellophane wrapping but magnified a thousand-fold. We looked up. On the roof, a vast colony of paper wasps were flapping their wings – an unmistakable warning that they were getting ready to swarm and sting.

For us, that was more than enough for one day. From strangely behaved baboons to a monster mamba, a lightning bolt hurled by some strange force, and now squadrons of stinging wasps – well, we got the message. As we fled towards the safety of the lodge, the impassive baboons continued staring at us. I also noticed that the single puff of cloud had disappeared.

Unsurprisingly, the secrets of the mysterious mine shaft remain just that – a mystery.

Another mystery that defies logical explanation is the night we saw two 'full moons' rising over Bongani.

It happened during a late afternoon/early evening game drive where we take visitors out for close-up animal viewing. For most, it's the highlight of their stay at the reserve, and on this particular drive our passengers were mainly foreign tourists loaded onto three Land Rovers. The vehicle drivers were in close radio contact, so if one group came across a lion kill, for example, they would alert each other and all guests would get to view what for most would be a once-in-a-lifetime sighting. No two game drives are the same, which is one of the most magical things about the bush.

As the sun set, we stopped for the traditional sundowners to savour the wilderness with a glass of chilled wine, gin and tonic, or whatever tipple the guests wanted. It was a beautiful evening, and up in the mountains the night skies always seem clearer and the stars closer. If the guests are interested, I usually point out the Southern Cross – which most tourists from the northern hemisphere have never seen – as well as *Alpha Centauri* straddling the Milky Way, Scorpio, the bright evening star of Venus and other dazzling constellations.

Suddenly the radio crackled into life. Meshach Nyawu, a hefty Shangaan field guide, was calling me.

'Hey, Con, can you see that orange ball in the southern sky?'

At first, I thought he was referring to a full moon, which in the bush is sometimes coloured orange due to dust particles in the air. I looked up, surprised, as this was not a full moon phase – something all rangers are acutely aware of as it's often called a poacher's moon.

Then I saw it: a large round orange object hanging motionless in the upper atmosphere. It definitely looked like a full moon. As I pointed it out to the tourists, the radios from the other vehicles started crackling. Everyone was gaping at this strange phenomenon. What the hell was it?

Then another guide came on the radio, voice bursting with excitement. 'Look north. There's another orange ball.'

Indeed, there was. But this one was smaller and moving directly towards the first ball. As the two spheres collided, a huge white flash lit up the sky for a nano-second. The larger one seemed to expand and then contract. It had, it seems, 'swallowed' the second ball.

It then slowly headed off in a westerly direction, disappearing into the cosmos.

When we arrived back at the lodge, the guests were on a total high, gushing enthusiastically about the sighting, and throughout dinner it was the sole high-charged topic of conversation. As all of us had seen the orange balls as well as the spectacular flash as they merged, there was little doubt that this extra-terrestrial happening was not a figment of anyone's over-fertile imagination.

The next morning at breakfast, I expected the animated discussion to continue. But strangely, there was not a single mention. It was as if nothing had happened – the entire episode scrubbed clean from everyone's memory. Maybe some thought it had been a dream and were fearful to say so. Or perhaps it was too bizarre, too galactically incomprehensible to digest.

Not for me. The sight of those two orange moons is as vivid in my memory today as it ever was.

No discussion of supernatural Africa is complete without mentioning *sangomas*. They are an integral – in fact, fundamental – feature of this magnificent continent and, because of my interest in San rock art, I sometimes visited these shamans while delving deep into African folklore. Most of the time I would join them in drum beating and dances, but I stayed away from some of the more esoteric rituals. I also went out into the bush with tribal healers, collecting different herbal medicines and learning the curing properties of wild plants.

One of the first times I consulted a *sangoma* was when my .458 rifle was stolen from the safe at Bongani Lodge. This was a serious matter as these heavy calibres are designed for thick-skinned animals such as elephant and rhino, and are consequently much prized among poachers. I had to get it back and quickly. We questioned our staff and the surrounding villagers, but all my investigations and those of the police drew a blank.

Eventually, my colleagues suggested I confer with a *sangoma*, so a group of us went to a respected shaman who lived in

Impakeni village, high in the mountains bordering Bongani. *Impaka* means stray or feral cat, and villagers claim that on dark nights some of the *sangomas* transform into felines and become hybrids or therianthropes (shape shifters). So, the entire area is steeped in superstition.

I was not sure if our *sangoma* was considered a shape shifter by other villagers, but there certainly was no doubt he was an established medicine man. He watched intently as we entered his hut, and the first thing I noticed was the large array of dried skulls, animal skins, various bones and other arcane paraphernalia that African shamans use in divination.

Once seated, I told him we were concerned about an item stolen from Bongani Lodge, without specifying what it was. He nodded, then went into a hypnotic trance, throwing a handful of magic bones called *matambo* and watching how they fell.

'This thing that is missing makes a very loud noise,' he said.

'That is so,' I replied. 'What else can you tell us?'

'The bones tell me again that it makes a very loud noise. Tell me what this thing is.'

'It is a firearm,' I said.

He nodded. 'I told you it made a loud noise.'

He continued staring at the bones, then said, 'You will never find this item. It has been taken and hidden somewhere in the mountains. You can look anywhere you want but you will never see it again.'

I was disappointed, but a little sceptical. Stolen firearms are usually traced if they are in use and, in the case of a .458 hunting rifle, the most likely suspect would be an active poacher. A careless shot at an animal, or, say, a love rival in the village, could be easily linked to a stolen weapon. As any cop will confirm, often it is just a waiting game.

But not in the case of my rifle. The *sangoma* was correct. It never was found.

The overwhelming majority of Africans believe in the supernatural powers of a *sangoma*, but a surprising number of Europeans are equally fascinated by the continent's most ancient occult. I cannot remember how often tourists to Bongani have asked to meet 'a fortune teller', or 'medicine man'. I was always happy to oblige, as this also was a source of income for the *sangomas*.

But it backfired spectacularly when an Argentinian couple asked me to arrange a visit. And not only because the husband – who was about thirty years older than his wife – only spoke Spanish, meaning everything had to be triple-translated from siSwati to English to Spanish.

We sat down in the *sangoma*'s thatched hut as he threw the bones, humming and muttering to himself. He then looked at me and said, '*O'n'tonda ga le belungu angi sebenza gathle.*'

I wasn't sure I had heard him correctly, so said, '*U thini Baba?*' (Please repeat that, Father).

The *sangoma* repeated his words – but, to my surprise, in English. 'The penis of this white man is not working properly.'

The wife blushed to the roots of her hair, while I tried without much success to keep a straight face as William, my tracker at the time, started giggling uncontrollably.

Now that the cat was truly out of the bag, there was no stopping the *sangoma*. Ignoring the wife's discomfort, he said he had very good *muti* that would clear out the 'old man's pipes' and get things going again. Rummaging around his herbal accoutrements, he ground up various roots and barks and presented the mixture to the Argentinian woman with perhaps more explicit user instructions than necessary.

The husband was blissfully unaware of what was going on, although his wife's scarlet-faced embarrassment might have been a giveaway. Even so, it was a very subdued group that drove down the mountain back to the lodge.

I never did hear if the *muti* worked.

7

Fun and Games with Big Cats

A huge granitic rock protruding like a throne from the flank of Zulweni Mountain overlooking Bongani and the Insikazi River provides one of the most spectacular panoramas anywhere in the world.

Perched on its edge, you're on the precipice of eternity as the glorious expanse of wild paradise sweeping below seems to stretch to the curvature of the planet.

For me, this is a spiritually charged, sacred place – somewhere to meditate and fine-tune my senses to the natural world. When doing so, I sit on the rock cross-legged, breathing in the mountain air through my diaphragm, concentrating on the body's seven *chakra* – core energy – points and focusing with peripheral vision on a specific spot across the valley. The mystic and author Carlos Castaneda referred to it as 'gazing', as after several minutes, everything in one's line of sight merges into a single central focal point. In this state of awareness, one can envisage the earth in its energy form, breathing, pulsating and moving.

During one 'gazing' session, I became aware of another presence on the mountain boulder. Without reacting, I continued deep in meditation.

As I slowly drifted back to reality, I readjusted to the here and now. Right beside me, about ten yards' away, sat the scariest and most beautiful leopard I have ever seen. It was his presence I had sensed while in this meditative state. Curiously, the leopard was looking in the same direction I was and not at me. Both of us were 'gazing' – our peripheral vision fixated across the wide valley. I could feel a strange bond throbbing electrically between us, fellow travellers on this deeply mysterious planet. I knew, somehow, I was not in danger even though I had not brought a rifle with me. In fact, I didn't even have a knife or a Leatherman.

I also knew that to do anything could cause a negative vibe, so I didn't react. Being close to a leopard is not like stroking a house cat; it's a profound, even insane experience, so I sat still. I have no idea how long the two of us remained like that. Time was irrelevant.

The leopard eventually rose slowly and silently, stretching his body and paws to full length, and flicked the snow-white tip of his tail nonchalantly over his back. He then walked imperiously off the rock without a backward glance.

Spellbound by the mystical encounter, I remained rooted to the rock. I wondered in awe whether this had happened to anyone in the wild before. There we were, two apex predators, sitting close together in total harmony. I have no explanation for it, other than that the big cat must have sensed my harmony and energy.

There was one vast difference, though. One that shames me to my core. Wildlife predators kill to eat and stay alive. Conversely, most humans kill wildlife for sport or financial gain. In fact, leopards, who have been exterminated in many of their eons-old habitats, must surely regard us as their greatest enemy. Their fear and suspicion of us should be entrenched and infinite. Yet here we were, sharing a magnificent moment of spiritual accord.

In the stillness that followed, I sent a silent but abject apology to the leopard on behalf of mankind – as well as my gratitude for the magnanimity shown by him for not eating me. Many believe that when it comes to speed and sheer ferocity, a leopard is the most cunning and formidable of the Big Five. If he had decided to attack me, I would not have stood a chance. I would not even have sensed him as he approached from behind. Instead, this noble creature chose to share some kind of joint experience. The privilege of a brief but magical moment of space and time with this master of the bush is incomprehensible. It was one of my greatest experiences. I had no hesitation or fear. In fact, I was on an exhilarating high as I climbed down the mountain, even though I knew that the leopard was almost certainly watching me from some other vantage point.

Not all my contacts with big cats have been mystical or harmonious, however. On the contrary, nature red in tooth and claw is the more common occurrence, as I found out when I stumbled upon a lion kill not long after my leopard encounter.

It was a beautiful sunrise, warm with a slight breeze, and the mocking chats and red-winged starlings were in full-throated morning song. Feeling on top of the world, I wrapped a bright Swazi sarong around my waist and decided to take a short walk in the veld before getting dressed for work.

Strolling happily, I headed off in a northerly direction towards a large granite outcrop called Mpukweni Rocks. Years in the bush have taught me to be constantly aware of my surroundings as problems can come from anywhere. But on this occasion, there was no warning whatsoever as I walked straight into a lion kill. Two lionesses had brought down a zebra the previous night, and barely twenty yards away they were feasting on the carcass with four cubs and two sub-adults.

I froze in my tracks. The nearest lioness, blood dripping from her mouth, looked up, no doubt unsure what this apparition in a garishly coloured loincloth was. Then, enraged at having her meal disturbed, she crouched down in a menacing pre-charge posture, her tail swishing like an angry cobra.

I raised my hands in a universal gesture of submission and looked directly at her. 'Sorry, sorry, sorry,' I kept repeating in various languages as I slowly started backing away. Every instinct screamed at me to turn and run, but that would have been suicide. Lions, like most felines, will give chase if you flee. Instead, I continued looking directly into her blazing tawny-yellow eyes, trying not to show fear as I moved backwards, one agonising step at a time. This was the complete antithesis of a beautiful spiritual moment. Unlike the curiously complacent leopard, this big mother cat had one thought on her mind: to kill me.

She growled, a low, guttural, rattling snarl, and the cubs scuttled over the carcass in their haste to get behind their mother. I was now facing the entire pride of eight lions.

I continued retreating ever more rapidly, and the crouching lioness seemed to relax slightly, but never taking her eyes off me. Nor did I take my eyes off her. Then, as if given some silent signal, the pride started feeding again. Fortunately, on the zebra and not me.

But by far my closest shave with lions came from a coordinated ambush I had with three large male lions that we called the Mapogo males.

In 2006 I had moved from the staff village at Bongani to a safari-style campsite built specifically for me and the game ranch manager, one of my best friends, whom I'll just call Pete. Not being in formal staff quarters and halfway up Zulweni Mountain allowed me the liberty of coming and going as my duties dictated, while living permanently out in the wild was a dream come true. In short, I was in my element.

To give us even more freedom of movement, Pete and I often used motorbikes for bush work. The bikes, mine being a Honda XR500 thumper, saved petrol and time, but the downside was mambas gliding across dirt tracks, recalcitrant elephants and giraffes causing traffic jams, or charging rhinos to spice up a journey.

Returning to camp late one afternoon, I had just reduced speed on a tight, winding road leading up to the lodge when out of the corner of my eye I noticed a yellow blur heading towards me. This got my attention fast – especially when the blur happened to be a large black-maned lion. Within seconds he was on me and the only thing I could do was to boot him hard in the face with my left foot. He gave a guttural grunt, briefly backing off, and as I twisted the accelerator throttle to full speed, I saw another lion crouching fifteen yards directly ahead. I was being ambushed!

I had no choice but to slam on brakes, kick out the side-stand and jump off the bike. I now had one lion in front of me and another on my left with only the Honda as a flimsy buffer. Drawing my .45 ACP pistol, I aimed at the closest lion and yelled loudly in a forlorn attempt to scare him off. Then, to my horror, I saw a third lion stalking me on the right. It was the Mapogo brothers and they had me well and truly boxed in. I could not risk firing warning shots as with only seven rounds in the magazine, I couldn't spare bullets. A charging lion can cover a hundred yards in four seconds, so to take out three with a pistol is a big ask.

At that instant, I heard a Land Rover engine start up. It was a tourist game drive vehicle a couple of hundred yards away and perhaps the last hope I had of getting out of this scrape alive. They had been following the Mapogo brothers, believing they were about to witness a lion kill, unaware that I was the dish of the day.

The Land Rover came around the corner in the nick of time, and as luck would have it, the driver was William, who had once been my tracker. When he saw me surrounded by three hungry lions, his mouth dropped in astonishment.

The tourists, presented with a rather macabre photo opportunity, started snapping away as I frantically signalled to William to come and fetch me. But worried about his guests' and his own safety, he instead slammed the Land Rover into reverse and hastily started to back off. I had my radio in one hand – the other was pointing the .45 at the closest lion's face two yards away – and so I quickly called out to him.

'If you don't come now, I am going to have to start shooting these lions!'

William shifted into first and cautiously drove forward. The lions, like most reserve animals, were thoroughly habituated to Land Rovers and ignored the vehicle, concentrating solely on me. As soon as William got to the bike, I made a flying leap into the vehicle. The excited guests must have thought I was on a candid camera show.

We remained still for several minutes, watching to see what the lions would do next. It was extremely unlikely they would attack the Land Rover, and sensing the hunt was over, they moved a short distance away.

'Okay,' I said. 'I'm going to jump back on the bike and hightail it out of here.'

William protested strongly, fear in his eyes. 'It's too dangerous. Leave the bike here.'

That might have been the more sensible option, but I was concerned that the lions would damage the machine if it was left unguarded. I jumped back onto the saddle, gave a quick kick-start and twisted the accelerator throttle.

As the engine roared into life, the lions came storming out of the grass and started chasing me again. I took off down the track with them hot on my heels – and William hot on theirs. On the right was another loop back to the lodge and I decided to take that detour.

Eish – big mistake! As I turned, I looked to see where the giant cats were and, to my dismay, they had taken a short cut and were about to cut me off. I could hear William and the tourists screaming at the top of their voices, 'Faster! Go faster!'

It was touch and go as the lions started gaining on me. But big cats are sprinters rather than marathon runners, and despite a few extremely anxious moments, the powerful thumper clawed back some distance, eventually leaving the disappointed lions in the dust. The tourists definitely had a story to tell around the fire that night.

Not long afterwards, Pete and I were having a morning cup of coffee when we noticed bits and pieces of chewed metal scattered around our camp. It was Pete's motorbike, and judging by the teeth and claw marks, the culprits were obviously lions, if not the actual Mapogo brothers. From then on, we always carried pepper spray and did not ride at night. Except once. Several years later, I was on a Yamaha 660 Tenere pursuing poachers in Sabi Sand Wildtuin (also known as Sabi Sands Game Reserve) and rode like a bat out of hell into a pride of lions lying in the road. There was no time to stop, so I did the only thing I could: I went even faster, hooting and shouting as loudly as I could. Fortunately, the lions got a bigger fright than I did and leapt out of the way.

Another time when I was up a little too close and personal with a lion was while walking along the Mbiyamithi River, one of the most beautiful drainage courses in Kruger Park with an impressive number of leopards living along the banks. The handheld radio shattered my reverie, with a game drive group reporting that they had spotted a nearby lion that appeared to be seriously ill.

The park's veterinarian, Okkie Kruger, answered the call and said he was fetching a dart gun to sedate and treat the animal.

I had my .375 HH rifle with me so decided to wait for Okkie to arrive. A few moments later, my nose started twitching. It was a smell I knew well. Too well – the sickly stink of a rotting carcass.

Looking sideways, I saw the source of the stench. Then I got a huge shock as the 'carcass' gave a low, guttural rasp. It was the sick lion spotted by the game drive vehicle – and just a yard or two away. Fortunately for me, the poor animal was so weak it could barely move its back legs and was unable to pounce, or else I would not be writing this story. Instead, it painfully dragged itself forward, stretching out a paw to try and hook me.

I jumped backwards. Still snarling – albeit somewhat weakly – the ailing animal inched towards me.

At that moment the vet arrived and I shouted, 'Okkie, dart it quickly or I will have to shoot it!' That was the last thing I wanted to do as I believed we could treat the chronically ill cat.

I heard a thump and the animal became even more enraged. But the dart had found its mark and the drugs soon took effect.

We managed to get the maggot-riddled lion to Skukuza, the park's headquarters. Sadly, it was too far gone and had to be euthanised.

It was not only sick lions that were put down. Unfortunately, sometimes entire prides were destroyed if they roamed out of protected reserves. This was a problem for us at the Mthethomusha Game Reserve, which surrounded Bongani Lodge, as we shared a long border marked by a railway line with Kruger Park. As a result, roaming lions would, on occasion, move from one park to the next in search of food and water, only to be shot for their efforts.

As a result, scores of lions were killed for the crime of 'transgressing the borders of the protected areas' during the twelve years I was at Bongani. If I ever got word that lions were out, I would go and chase them back into their designated areas – kind of like a cat and mouse game, only I was the mouse.

The authorities would later arrive, brandishing their rifles and asking where the lions were, only to discover they were already back inside the reserve.

However, we couldn't save them all, and whenever the authorities destroyed roaming lions, a fresh pride would be introduced. We placed the new animals in a lion boma on Bongani to give them time to settle and habituate before being released, and one of my jobs was to feed them. This entailed going out into the bush after game drives and shooting a couple of impala every few days.

On one occasion, field guides spotted a zebra with a broken leg limping on the eastern side of the reserve, which would soon be killed by lions in any event. However, I had a permit only to cull impala so asked the provincial park manager if I could instead shoot the injured zebra to feed the new pride. This was far preferable to killing a healthy buck.

The manager said yes, go ahead, but told me to call him after I had shot the zebra and we would take it to the lion boma together.

It was a Saturday and I was taking several of Bongani's private shareholders out on a game drive when we came across the injured zebra. It was hobbling about seventy yards ahead and I explained to the shareholders that it was to be culled to feed the new lions. They asked if they could watch the proceedings, something I would not normally do with guests. But as they were executives in the company that held the ninety-nine-year lease on Bongani, it was a different story.

I aimed the .375 rifle over the steering wheel and with a single clean shot, put the animal out of its misery. I then, as instructed, called the reserve manager, who told me to wait for him.

So, we waited. Then an hour later a truck came speeding around the corner, slamming on brakes and smothering us in a cloud of dust. About five or six armed provincial rangers jumped out of the vehicle and aggressively approached me, clutching their weapons. I looked around for the reserve manager I had just phoned, but he was nowhere to be seen. At that moment everything clicked into place with sickening reality. I had walked straight into a trap.

The real reason he was not there was because he knew I was part of a team investigating him for allegedly shooting game and illegally selling the meat to his cronies in Daantjie village on the western side of the reserve. We became suspicious of this when Bongani field guides came across the unmistakable tyre tracks of one of the reserve's vehicles as well as swept-over blood trails of shot animals next to the roads. We had also found the carcasses of a couple of kudu and a giraffe that had been shot and run off to die in the bush.

The manager was obviously aware that I was conducting an internal investigation and now had the chance to strike first. He knew all I had was his verbal permission to shoot the zebra, which he would deny and have me arrested. For this, he sent his henchmen.

In front of the shareholders – extremely embarrassing for me – one of the rangers, a corporal, belligerently asked, 'Did you shoot this zebra?'

'Yes.'

'Where is your permit?'

'Your superior gave me permission. Call him.'

The corporal shook his head. Along with the reserve manager, he was being investigated for alleged poaching as well, so was also an enemy of mine. He said he was not aware of any such permission being given and proceeded to charge me for shooting a zebra unlawfully within a provincial park.

The rangers confiscated my rifle and wanted to arrest me right away. If that happened, I would spend the weekend in the dreaded Kabokweni Prison and, as anyone who knows anything about South Africa's awful jails knows, that was not an option. I was in serious trouble and had to think fast.

'If you try and arrest me, I will run into the mountains and you will never find me,' I said. 'Instead, I give you my word that I will present myself to the court on Monday morning at Kabokweni.'

I could see that they were itching to throw me into a cesspit of a cell, but luckily one of the senior shareholders intervened on my side. The rangers knew that he had some clout with the authorities, so were wary of him. They also knew I was far more at home in the mountains than them and if I did run off, they would never catch me.

They grudgingly relented, warning me to be at the courthouse on Monday, and we took the zebra to the lion boma.

I arrived at the Kabokweni court early on Monday and, tightly handcuffed, was whisked down some mouldy stairs and locked in one of the overcrowded, filthy cells. About forty rough-looking characters glared at me in the gloom.

However, knowing how the jail system worked, I arrived well prepared with a few packs of cigarettes and a mobile phone hidden in my clothes. I backed myself against the vomit green wall and waited for the cell boss – usually the most hardened criminal in the packed cage – to approach. As I was the only white person, it didn't take long. Perched on top of the highest bunk, one of the meanest looking guys I have ever seen barked down at me.

'What are you doing here, white boy?'

I politely greeted the man in siSwati, the dialect of the area.

He looked surprised. 'Oh … you speak our language. Why were you arrested?'

'For poaching a zebra.'

With that, the whole cell erupted in cackling laughter and tuberculosis-hacking coughs. I laughed as well, producing a pack of cigarettes and handing them to the cell boss. He exploded in another fit of laughter.

'Hey, white boy, I did not even get a chance to search you and you're already giving your stuff away.'

'I brought cigarettes because I knew I was coming here.'

I then handed my mobile phone to the boss and said he could make as many calls as he and his friends wanted. I only required my phone back before leaving.

Needless to say, from that moment on I was taken into the protection of the cell boss and was not messed up or assaulted. I later discovered that he was in jail for what are called 'farm murders'. Thousands of mainly white South African farmers are murdered each year with extreme brutality, so to call the cell boss hardcore is understating the case.

However, he was friendly and we chatted away amiably. Most of the inmates were also smoking *dagga* (marijuana) and clouds of the narcotic weed billowed pungently in the stuffy cell. Three hours later and as high as a kite from second-hand *dagga* smoke, I was led up the stairs into the dock of the court room.

I paid a R1,500 (about £60) admission of guilt fine as I did not want any more time in jail, and not long afterwards I was out, breathing fresh air again.

In an ironic twist of fate, the park manager who had set me up was nailed a few months later in a joint investigation led by the provincial authorities, Pete and me.

But we didn't get him on poaching charges. Instead, he was dismissed for theft of a Lister borehole pump engine.

8

The Gathering Storm

The dawn of the millennium was a watershed in the struggle for the essence of South Africa's wildernesses. Although none of us knew it, the new century would herald a new era in the fight for the wild lands. There was no sudden event. Instead, a gradual dividing line formed between what can loosely be termed the old world of conservation and the new.

I'm generalising, of course, but before the turn of the century, poachers were mainly corrupt officials who thought themselves above the law, or rural people shooting and snaring for the pot. It was prevalent, but manageable.

No longer. Today, some South African reserves are bloody bush battlefields where rangers and poachers clash, often with deadly results. Poaching gangs are no longer mere subsistence hunters – they are run by highly organised multimillion-dollar cartels smuggling rhino horn for spurious health reasons, elephant ivory for mantelpiece ornaments, or big cat bones boiled for traditional medicine. Game rangers, whose key function is supposed to be stewardship of the planet's remaining wildernesses, now find themselves fighting for their lives, and are often outnumbered and out-gunned.

As I write this, clashes between rangers and poachers are raging uncontrolled, and in the process, many who had started out as idealists, deeply immersed in the spirituality of the land as well as the magnificent wildlife, have morphed into hardened bush warriors. But as I say, it happened gradually, and I was extremely fortunate to have had a foot in the old world, largely through my interest in San rock art.

In 2003 I left Bongani after being offered the position of head ranger at the eight-thousand-hectare Jock of the Bushveld Concession in Kruger Park. This was close to where I had seen my first San painting before starting at Bongani, so I eagerly seized the opportunity.

Soon after arriving at the 'Jock' concession, one of the rangers showed me a San rock art site on the opposite bank of the Mbiyamithi River, and from there I started exploring the overhangs and shelters in the *koppies* along the waterway, as I had done at Bongani. It paid dividends and I discovered twenty-seven new sites within my first few months.

That was the tranquil side of the job. But there was plenty of action – not least because the concession had the largest population of white and black rhino in Kruger at the time. On one occasion, I was guiding eight international guests on a walking trail through thickets of tamboti trees when we came across seventeen white rhinos at a series of waterholes. Rhinos loved wallowing in the muddy pools on hot days, and as we were downwind, they were unaware of our presence.

Suddenly the wind shifted. I saw one rhino lift its head and glance in our direction. Then another ... then the earth shook as the entire crash of rhinos came charging towards us.

Lazarus Mkhonto, my back-up trail guide, shouted at everyone to climb the nearest tree, which all the guests did with alacrity. Well ... almost all. One woman was unable to move as her panic-stricken husband was clambering over her to get up a tree first. Without hesitation, Lazarus yanked her husband's flailing foot off her head and squashed her flat against the tree at the exact moment three rhinos thundered past.

Everything happened so fast that there was no chance to even load my rifle. Instead, I waved my hands in the air, shouting '*voetsek*' (go away), trying to divert the beasts.

When the clouds of dust and debris cleared, the guests cautiously climbed down the trees and we moved out of the area on very shaky legs. I noticed the husband studiously avoiding his wife's furious gaze.

Another close call was when Lazarus and I were walking along a hippo trail on the Mitomeni River. We had four guests with us, and as we rounded a large leadwood tree, I walked right into a black rhino calf. The animal raised its head and, seeing me, started to whinny. Suddenly its mother appeared. I shouted at Lazarus to get our group under a buffalo-thorn bush behind me. The panicking guests started to scramble in all directions, but Lazarus skilfully managed to shepherd them to safety.

Fortunately, the mother rhino got such a fright that she took off in the opposite direction with her calf. It took some time to extract the guests from the spikey thicket, but better a few scratches than the business end of a rhino horn. We had been very lucky.

Lazarus is now head ranger of the 'Jock' concession and does a great job. He's a close friend and – speaking from experience – one of the toughest and bravest men I know.

It wasn't only in the bush that I was getting adrenalin rushes. It was also at the lodge, as I discovered after being woken one night with someone frantically banging on my door.

'Conraad, there is a big black snake in my cupboard. Come quickly!' As the accent was French, I knew it was Saskia, a staff member who came from Reunion Island, south of Mauritius.

Whenever someone says a snake is 'black', the immediate reaction is that it's a mamba, although that is usually not the case. Taking no chances, I grabbed a shotgun loaded with birdshot, an air rifle, a *sjambok* and a long stick and ran to her room. Indeed, there was a black snake. And yes, it was a massive black mamba hissing and slithering behind a wooden board inside the cupboard.

Not wanting to use the shotgun at close quarters and not being an expert snake catcher, I opted for the air rifle and proceeded to shoot the mamba with copious amounts of lead pellets. It was a shame to destroy the snake – a magnificent specimen measuring more than two yards – but mambas and ladies' lingerie are not a compatible combination. It was also midnight and pitch-black outside, so the decision was made for Saskia's safety.

Despite these adventures and the concession's spectacular range of wildlife, I started getting restless. Most of the time I was taking guests out on walking trails, which, compared to the rugged bush and granite rocks of Bongani, were mere strolls. Unless, of course, one was interrupted by charging rhinos. But more than anything, I missed the challenges and physical hardships of Bongani.

Also, although the Jock of the Bushveld was a private concession, we were under the jurisdiction of the state-owned South African National Parks (SANParks), with a far more rigid bureaucracy than the freewheeling life I enjoyed at Bongani. The one rule that really got to me was the dress code, as the camp is named after South Africa's most famous dog and has huge historical significance. The original Jock was a Staffordshire bullterrier and his owner, Sir James Percy FitzPatrick, had been a transport rider bringing supplies to the Lowveld gold miners in the 1890s. In keeping with the ambience of that era, all rangers had to wear long khaki trousers.

I am no fan of fancy dress and prefer to walk and explore in shorts, especially in summer. As ridiculous as it sounds, I was contemplating resigning simply because I was forced to wear long pants. But just as I was about to do so, a new management company took over the concession, so I handed in my resignation without having to stipulate my aversion for historical attire.

I was not unemployed for long. A few weeks later, Purple Plum Properties, which had taken over the lease at Bongani Mountain Lodge from Inzalo Holdings, offered me a job as habitat manager and game warden at the nearby Ingwe Lodge. My good friend Pete was now the game reserve manager at Bongani, so I happily returned to my old stamping grounds of mountains and rough terrain.

However, my six-month stint at the Jock was time well spent, as the work I had done discovering new San rock art sites there as well as at Bongani resulted in me teaming up with Mike English, the renowned former section ranger who pioneered rock art research in the Stolzneck area of Kruger. SANParks had recently received a grant from mining company Anglo American's Chairman's Fund to revisit the sites originally documented by Mike in the mountainous southern section of Kruger, and I was contracted to go with him.

We located the paintings, recorded GPS co-ordinates, filled in site record forms and traced selected panels. All relevant information was documented for the one hundred and twenty sites previously discovered by Mike, as well as a further sixty new sites that we found this time around. Fortunately, none of the rock art had been defaced or vandalised, which made our discoveries all the more awesome.

It was an effective and diverse working team, with me, champing at the bit as always, Mike, a genuine wildlife guru patiently guiding me, and Sergeant Aaron Nkuna, a huge, powerfully built Shangaan with an encyclopaedic knowledge of the bush protecting us. Aaron was our guard and we certainly needed him, as much of Stolzneck was untouched wilderness and Mike and I were unarmed, concentrating solely on mapping and tracing selected panels of art. On one occasion, we were walking along an old elephant path and spotted a buffalo cow with a calf about one hundred and thirty yards away that had separated from the main herd. We stopped and watched quietly as the cow stared back. Then without warning, she charged. We all knew that a charging buffalo is one of the most dangerous of the Big Five, and as Aaron stepped in front, raising his rifle, Mike bolted to the right. I decided the best bet was to stand next to Aaron, who was a crack shot.

But for some reason, Aaron didn't fire, despite the fact that a juggernaut with wickedly curved horns was coming at us fast. Alarmed, I shouted *'Dubula! Dubula!'* (Shoot).

Still Aaron didn't fire. Then, a split second before impact, we both jumped sideways and yelled at the top of our voices, clapping our hands.

Miraculously, the cow veered and ran off.

'Aaron,' I wheezed, getting my breath back, 'why didn't you shoot?'

'It was not necessary,' he replied, as cool as anything.

It was only years later that Aaron admitted to me that he had forgotten to click off the rifle's safety catch. That's how close it had been! And he never made the same mistake again. Several years later at the Mdluli Concession reserve, Aaron saved a group of international students from certain injury, if not death, after they stumbled directly into the path of an old buffalo bull. The bull instantly charged, but Aaron – a true hero – stood his ground, calmly making a kill shot under extremely harrowing circumstances.

These were master veterans of the veld and I was privileged to work with them. Mike and Aaron had been through a lot together and their stories of Kruger back in the day were absolutely riveting. Often Rob Thompson, the hugely respected section ranger of Stolzneck, also joined us, and sitting around the campfire, I would listen spellbound to their yarns of wild men and wild animals in simpler times.

It was sad to admit those days were gone. The poaching conflicts were now gathering momentum and my new job at Bongani catapulted me directly into the fray. Apart from my normal duties, I was also contracted to monitor illegal hunting on behalf of the leaseholders and report my findings to the Mpumalanga Tourism and Parks Agency, who were responsible for the protection of the animals on the Mthethomusha Game Reserve that incorporated Bongani.

I was shocked rigid at what I found. The demand for rhino horns, big cat bones and ivory for the lucrative Far East markets was still growing, so most of the poaching at that time was for bushmeat. Animals were massacred wholesale, either shot or snared, for their flesh. Kudu and giraffe meat was openly sold at informal wet markets. It was so rampant that we even caught field guides quartering carcasses snatched from lion and wild dog kills.

We found snares virtually everywhere we went, indiscriminately strangling animals in their hundreds. It wasn't just small game and antelope caught in these gruesome wire loops that slowly garrotte an animal to death; lion, giraffe and buffalo were also either killed or lost limbs in this most barbaric method of slaughter. As a result, Pete and I spent many days with Dr Cobus Raath, an exceptional wildlife veterinarian, removing snares from every species of animal found on the reserve. One of the most traumatic incidents was finding skeletal lion cubs starving to death after their mother had been strangled by a snare. But the worst of all was coming across twenty-three animals trapped by nooses attached to a single long line. The howling, crying and bleating was heartbreaking.

It was mayhem. But no matter how hard we tried, no matter how many culprits were identified, nothing was done to staunch the bloodbath. In fact, from 2005 onwards, it got worse.

To my dismay, some of the chief suspects were field rangers. And the more they featured in my poaching reports, the more unpopular I became. I wasn't alone. Other honest rangers and field guides who lived within communities surrounding the reserve were also threatened, often with their lives.

It wasn't only poaching. General lawlessness was escalating on a scale I never imagined. Fuel and spare parts were regularly stolen from game drive vehicles, protected trees in the parks were chain-sawed for firewood, while packs of semi-feral village dogs chased animals on reserves almost at will and gun-shots fired near game lodges sent top-dollar guests scampering for cover. On top of that, at least three hijacking attempts on park visitors were thwarted at the last minute. I personally stopped one when I noticed a blockade of rocks strewn across the road and two armed men hiding in the bush. I got out of my truck to apprehend them and they ran off. Fortunately, this happened before the visitors arrived.

At the height of this chaos, something good arrived in my life. On 13 February 2006, a Weimaraner puppy was born. Out of a litter of eleven, he was one of only two left when I bought him.

I named him Zingela. It means 'to hunt' in Zulu.

9

Zingela

Zingela didn't come into my life by chance. He was no impulse buy.

On the contrary, I had researched every variety of sporting/hunting dog I could find before making my choice. I had to know exactly what I was looking for, as any dog working with me would be doing so in a particularly unforgiving environment. I needed a highly intelligent, hardy animal with plenty of stamina, great tracking skills, huge courage and fierce loyalty to its owner.

Weimaraners fitted the bill in every way, as well as being conveniently short-haired and ideal for the hot climate I operated in. The pedigree, a blend of bloodhound and greyhound genes, goes back about three hundred years and was first bred by German aristocrats to hunt bear, boar and deer. With their bloodlines, Weimaraners have an acute sense of smell, as well as exceptional sight and speed. Due to their high energy levels, they are not ideal pets and far better suited as purpose-bred working dogs. Their loyalty is legendary, so much so that they often suffer from separation anxiety when their owners are away.

One needs permission to keep a dog on a game reserve and, after the debacle of my first dog, Bamba, being shot at Windy Ridge, I wanted to be sure everything was above board before Zingela arrived at Bongani. A ranger's life is solitary and most of the time not easily shared, so Zingela would be a companion as well as my eyes and ears in the bush. The fact that I named him Zingela meant that his destiny was forged the moment I took him home after getting clearance from the authorities. He would be a hunter. But not of animals. He would target a 'species' far more deadly. Poachers.

Right from the beginning, Zingela never left my side. We were inseparable from the word go, and on my days off I only visited places that allowed dogs. We shared a bed and I never booted him off. Not for anyone.

Wherever I went, he followed, whether checking out San rock art sites, searching for snares, chasing poachers or tracking animals. His eager little legs always trotted behind me, and when he was tired I carried him. But he never gave up.

He took to the wilderness immediately. By the time his eyes turned from blue to yellow at about seven months, he was well on his way to becoming a seasoned bush dog, absorbing new survival lessons every day. He learnt to recognise different animals, not only by sight, but also scent. A zebra was not a kudu and a giraffe was a creature that towered to the heavens. He knew them all. Imagine how fast his puppy heart started beating when he first saw an elephant.

He learnt the sounds of the veld: the various birdcalls, the roars, grunts, growls, yips, trumpets, snorts of different animals. He also learnt that unnaturally silent landscapes hid a hushed anticipation of something about to happen.

He mastered the myriad smells in the wild, which was critical as a Weimaraner can sniff blood, death and decay as well as vehicle fumes, fires and human settlements from up to two miles away.

He also grasped the dangers. I taught him, through cautionary commands, that big-fanged, sharp-clawed predators such as lions and leopards were deadly. Baboons and razor-tusked warthogs could kill as well. Crucially, he learnt to warn me of humans hiding in the bush.

Zingela soon mastered this almost clairvoyant intelligence gathering while perched on the bouncing front seat of my truck with his nose twitching in the air. When he picked up a certain scent, he would nod his head and start whining softly. As soon as I stopped the vehicle, he would jump out and lead me either to a dead carcass or a wounded animal. He adopted distinctive stances and whines for various animals, making different sounds for buck or zebra, lion or elephant. Importantly, he made a different noise altogether when he perceived human threats.

He was completely in tune with life in the wild and became an indispensable, infallible early warning system for me. In turn, I learnt how to interpret his various sounds and movements. Through this almost telepathic synergy, we learnt how to read each other.

However, this only came about through a school of hard knocks and some very near misses. In fact, I nearly lost him when he was only eight months old while taking visitors to a rock art site behind Bongani's lion boma. We were returning to the vehicle and it was getting dark when we noticed a leopard crouching ahead of us. It was just off the path, but in a stooped stalking stance with its eyes fixed on the dog, considered by leopards to be the tastiest of meals. Just as ominous was that it was also the exact place where the lightning bolt out of the blue nearly struck Mark Griffiths and me years before.

'Careful, careful,' I whispered softly. Zingela immediately came to heel.

My first responsibility was towards the tourists, so I had my rifle ready, but I could only legally shoot if the animal charged at humans – and at that moment, the leopard was fixated solely on Zingela. The visitors, incidentally, were enthralled at seeing a leopard in stalking mode and all had their cameras clicking.

We continued walking in single file towards the Land Rover parked up on the ridge. The leopard followed. I was now extremely worried. The big cat seemed oblivious to the humans, only eyeing Zingela, who was glued to my legs and did not utter a sound. Even at such a young age, he was aware of the potential danger.

With a huge sigh of relief, we reached the vehicle and I hurriedly tossed Zingela onto the front seat as the tourists clambered in. The leopard lay in the grass and watched, knowing the stalk was over.

Incredibly, when I later looked at photos I had taken of the leopard, I noticed there were actually two of them. We had been so focused on the closest one that we hadn't noticed there was another big cat behind in the bush. I was very lucky not to lose Zingela that day.

Another even closer shave was when Zingela was about eighteen months old and we were out looking for snares in the Mpunzi valley on the railway line bordering Mthethomusha and Kruger. Zingela was running in front of my truck when he suddenly disappeared into a deep drainage line near the train tracks.

As he vanished, to my absolute horror I heard the chittering and yipping barks of African wild dogs. Zingela had plunged into a pack resting in the gully and I knew they would tear him to pieces in an instant.

The next thing I saw was a grey blur shooting out of the far side of the trench. It was Zingela at full sprint with thirteen African wild dogs hot on his tail. I shouted to him, and with the pack snapping at his heels, he veered and sprinted towards me, leaping into my arms.

A split second later, I was surrounded by the snarling pack. Holding Zingela above my head, I yelled as loudly as I could and kicked out at the animals.

The pack backed off and started circling me, now a little hesitant. African wild dogs hunt on the run, ripping chunks of flesh off their prey until the animal drops dead from blood loss. Being kicked and shouted at by an irate human was something new to them.

But what really saved the day was that I somehow managed to barge my way through to the truck and, as with the leopard, desperately threw Zingela inside. Seeing their meal disappear, the disappointed wild dogs chittered and ran off with noses and tails in the air to find easier and more obliging prey.

In those early days, it was almost routine for me to save Zingela while out on the trail. It was a debt he would soon repay with interest – the most dramatic being when two field rangers attempted to assassinate me, as recounted in the first chapter of this book. Zingela's warning barks when we were at the river and then holding the rogue rangers' attention while I crept up the side behind a boulder to disarm them is the sole reason I am here today. To give an indication of how anarchic the situation had become in the bush, I didn't even bother to report that blatant attempt on my life to the authorities. It would have been my word against the field rangers, but even if I had had witnesses, I doubt any action would have been taken.

However, it was now obvious that my dog was as high a priority on the hit list compiled by corrupt rangers as I was. Despite that, we somehow continued to thwart them. One such time, we approached a vehicle one morning after a game drive and Zingela suddenly started sniffing at a cool box used to store drinks for guests. He made a sort of whinnying sound and kept looking at me, determined to catch my attention. I lifted the lid to find the meat and innards of a wild animal inside.

When I pointed this out to the tracker in charge of the tourist vehicle, he tried his best to act surprised. In fact, he was so 'astonished' that he was at a complete loss to explain how all this meat had 'miraculously' found its way into the cool box on his watch. I reported the incident, but as usual, nothing happened except that the hatred directed at me and Zingela ratcheted up to an even higher level.

To protect Zingela, I taught him never to accept food, no matter how delicious, from anyone but me. He learnt quickly; he had to or else he would soon be poisoned. Every day we were on full alert. Our lives depended on it.

And so it went on. The more efficient Zingela and I became in exposing the crimes perpetrated by the people who should have been guardians of the wild, the more we were threatened.

I was determined to continue taking the fight to them, however, regardless of constant intimidation. One of my more creative – some might say harebrained – schemes was to do anti-poaching patrols by air. But as planes and helicopters were absurdly expensive, we used motorised paragliders instead. We would catch thermals with the vultures while also catching poachers.

The benefits were irrefutable: we would be flying low so poachers couldn't see us far in advance and hide; we could land close by to make arrests; and we would have a bird's-eye view of the entire reserve. No one could escape us.

It was brilliant. Except it wasn't. For a start, I hadn't considered the inconvenient fact that hanging from a harness in the sky provided a wonderful target for a poacher to put a bullet up our backsides – or '*poephols*', as my mother quaintly put it. Another not so minor flaw was that we couldn't do this after nine o'clock in the morning as that was when the winds picked up and started gusting through the gnarly scrub. As we were flying low and slow, this was hazardous, graphically illustrated by some of my friends making extremely undignified landings in thorn bushes and having to get their girlfriends to remove deeply embedded spikes from their butts. They were the lucky ones; a couple ended up with broken arms and ribs as well.

This provided us with a few laughs … well, not for the thorn victims … but to cut a long story short, I decided that I had enough problems with rogue rangers trying to assassinate me without adding falling out of the sky to my list of headaches.

Meanwhile, the fact remained that it was becoming increasingly obvious that my enemies were determined to get me off the reserve or eliminate me, whatever came first. I was under no illusions about that.

Matters came to a head late one afternoon at the northern entrance of the reserve when I was with Pete and some Bongani staff members. As we were chatting, one of the Mpumalanga Tourism and Parks Agency field rangers arrived at the gate from outside the park.

That was strange. I walked over and asked him, 'Why are you coming from outside the reserve? Aren't you supposed to be patrolling inside?'

He glared back sullenly. Then without a word, he lunged, grabbing my shirt and trying to wrestle me to the ground. I resisted and a fight erupted.

We were eventually separated, with Pete and the Bongani staff holding me back and other provincial rangers restraining the attacker. We both had handguns, but fortunately these remained holstered. Even so, it was a nasty incident. I had to attend a disciplinary hearing and almost got fired. There were no repercussions for the other man, even though he had first attacked me.

That night back at our tented camp on top of the mountain, Pete spoke some harsh home truths.

'Con, you'd better get the hell out of here. They WILL kill you. You have pointed the finger of guilt at so many of them and have proved such a problem with all the crimes you have exposed. All for nothing.

'It is a losing battle, my man. You have been here too long; you are getting too close to the top echelon of crooks. Better resign and leave now before you're taken out in a body bag.'

He was right. My time at Bongani had included some of the most enriching years of my life, but it was time to go.

At least Zingela and I might then live to fight another day.

10

Untamed Mdluli Concession

It was with a heavy heart that I packed up what had been eleven years of my life and handed in my resignation to the board of directors of Bongani Mountain Lodge.

The directors from both Inzalo Holdings and Purple Plum Properties were amazing people and had always supported both Pete and me, but as Bongani is only a leasehold, they could not help me. The undeniable fact was that I had made too many enemies inside the provincially managed Mthethomusha Game Reserve that ran Bongani's anti-poaching patrols.

Thankfully, I soon landed on my feet and was offered a job with the wildlife eco-company Untamed, which managed a large chunk of bushveld known as the Mdluli Concession. Although inside the Kruger Park, the land had been returned to the original inhabitants, the Mdluli tribe, with Untamed running the business for the community. The concession headquarters was a bustling base between Kruger's Numbi Gate entrance and Pretoriuskop camp and, apart from catering for tourists, Untamed also ran very popular student wildlife research programmes.

My position was concession ranger, and I accepted on condition that Zingela came with me as a working canine. This involved getting a special permit from SANParks, which administers Kruger, and after much begging, cajoling and pleading, the paperwork came through. Zingela was 'official'.

Still smarting from the Mthethomusha experience, I arrived at my new job hoping it would be different as far as crime was concerned. Sadly, it wasn't. Poaching with guns, dogs and wire snares continued just as it had at Mthethomusha, and game fences were regularly cut by illegal bushmeat hunters entering Kruger. Theft was also rife, with everything from ammunition, solar panels, air-conditioners and freezers to crockery, food and even bed lamps simply 'disappearing'. Much of this happened, allegedly, with either help or direct involvement from so-called security guards.

Untamed is also where I met a lifelong friend, Ruud Alders, whom I nicknamed *Bajüwe* (stuck in the mud) as he had the habit of getting the camp vehicle stranded in the most ridiculous places. Ruud, originally from Holland but now living in Switzerland, appointed himself as my personal manager and mentor, as he saw right away that I was a wild bush boy with zero camp organisational skills. We made a good team as Ruud was a diplomat who knew how to control guests, many of whom were foreign students, while I knew the ways of the bush. Apart from getting a stronger tow rope to keep bailing his vehicle out of various quagmires, Ruud's other claim to fame is that he's so tall he has to sleep with his feet zipped up outside the tent. He kept Untamed's camp impeccable, which gave me free time to set about carving my reputation as an enemy to the poachers in the area.

Life in the bush is never dull – especially with Ruud around – and working for Untamed certainly proved that. In fact, it provided more than its fair share of 'interesting' moments. As any ranger will attest, one snake you really have to watch out for is the puff adder. While not as venomous as the black mamba, the puff adder is responsible for more bites than any other snake in Africa for the simple reason that it will not get out of the way for anything or anyone. It also strikes with unbelievable speed, and unless treated rapidly, the extremely painful bite of cytotoxic venom can be fatal.

On one occasion, my cousin Brandon Havemann and I were leading a walking trail with a group of students and we stopped to watch a herd of elephants relaxing in a marshy area. Brandon and I were distracted while looking through binoculars, when suddenly Zingela rushed forward and grabbed a thick, writhing, chevron-striped cord of muscle exactly where Brandon was about to step. It was a puff adder, poised to strike the moment his foot landed. As Zingela shook the thrashing reptile to snap its spine, the dying snake managed to hook a fang into Zingela's right cheek, delivering a full dose of venom.

The deadly countdown had begun. 'Okay guys,' I said to the students. 'We are returning to camp. As fast as you can run.'

Within five minutes, Zingela was unable to walk and I had to carry him as we half-sprinted, half-jogged for the next thirty minutes. Once at camp, I grabbed five ampoules of anti-venom then drove like a maniac to the closest veterinarian in Nelspruit, more than fifty miles away.

By the time we arrived at the surgery, Zingela's face was the size of a football and the vet hurriedly injected four of the five ampoules I had brought along. After three anxious days, the swelling subsided. It was only then that we knew for certain Zingela would live.

Another major headache for us at Untamed was the prolific number of *Canis Africanis*, the semi-feral indigenous dog often used for illegal hunting, that came onto the reserve's land. As there was no fence between us and Kruger, the concession area was a major poaching corridor, and as a result, rabies was rampant. Any stray dog had to be shot on sight, its head cut off and a brain sample sent to the Onderstepoort Veterinary Hospital at the University of Pretoria.

This was done not only to protect wildlife, but humans as well. And being charged by a dog frothing wildly at the mouth is pretty damn scary, as another group of students I was taking on a wilderness trail discovered.

It happened as we were walking along the Mbabala (bushbuck) drainage line near the Numbi Gate with Zingela trotting ahead when a poacher's dog came hurtling out of the bush. I could tell straight away by the foam lathering its mouth and flopping tongue that it was rabid. Shouting at the students to get behind me, I unslung my .458 Win Mag rifle, usually only used for protection against big game such as elephant or buffalo.

As I was about to shoot, Zingela suddenly ran directly into my line of fire. He was going to protect us from the rabid animal, but in so doing, my clear shot was now reduced to a tiny gap. If I missed that, I would almost certainly kill my own dog. There was no time to do anything else so I swiftly adjusted my aim and fired. To my infinite relief, the snarling, frothing animal dropped instantly. I'm certain Zingela must have felt the whiplash of the bullet that zinged past his head with less than an inch to spare.

There was silence as we tossed the dead animal, its mouth still slick with bubbling saliva, into the back of the truck. Most of the students were a little traumatised, but they were there to learn bush survival and unfortunately not all lessons are pleasant.

Even though Zingela had no visible injuries, to be on the safe side, I took him to the vet for anti-rabies injections. That was one of his first of many jabs, and I'm pretty sure no other dog in the Lowveld could claim to have had as many anti-rabies shots as him.

With so many rabid animals around, the law of averages was that I would one day be bitten. And sure enough, a couple of months after Zingela's narrow escape, I got a call from the Pretoriuskop section ranger asking for help in shooting a suspected rabid dog on the tar road outside the camp.

I hadn't been driving for long when I spotted the animal, but this being the world-famous Kruger National Park, there were several tourist vehicles already parked around the dog. I had to first clear them out of the way in case a bullet ricocheted off the tarmac and into a visitor's car.

As politely as I could, I explained the situation and asked the tourists to kindly vacate the area. To my surprise, they took the side of the diseased dog. As is frequently the case with well-meaning do-gooders, their misplaced sympathies often do more harm.

'*Ag* shame, poor dog,' shouted one tourist.

This caused a chain reaction, with me being the bad guy. 'Can't you take it to the vet instead of just killing it?' shouted another.

'What about getting it to the SPCA [Society for the Prevention of Cruelty to Animals]? Don't just shoot it.'

Seriously, had these people never heard of rabies?

By now, totally frustrated and with the panting dog at the side of the road becoming increasingly frenzied, I grabbed it by the scruff of the neck and tail, lifting it onto the back of my Land Rover.

As they say, no good deed goes unpunished. I was savagely bitten on my hand.

I drove to the boundary of the park, and as I opened the vehicle's tailgate, the dog jumped out and hightailed it down the old railway track. By the time I had got my rifle up, it was running at full speed about sixty yards away and I managed to shoot it in the rear. I then cut off its head and sent it to Onderstepoort for testing.

Four days later I was in a helicopter assisting section rangers in an elephant management exercise when an urgent message cackled over the radio from Kruger's head office in Skukuza.

'Conraad, the rabies test from Onderstepoort is positive. Tell the pilot to get you to the doctor's office ASAP!'

After the elephant job was sorted, the pilot flew back to the Skukuza doctor's office, torquing up the turboshaft to maximum speed. As I arrived, the nurse pointed to the bed.

'Just lie down,' she said. 'I have never had to inject someone with so much stuff before!'

The 'stuff' was eight ampoules of immunoglobulin to be jabbed into my butt. It was more of a jelly than a liquid, so had to be injected with a heavy-gauge needle. I felt as though I'd had an overdose of Botox. Thankfully, the high-dosage shots worked and I dodged the rabies bullet, albeit with a very black and blue backside.

Not long after that, we received a call for help from a village about three miles outside the Numbi Gate where a leopard was said to be eating the residents' livestock and they were now worried about their children. It appeared to be wounded and the villagers asked us to track it down.

I phoned April Lukhele of the Mpumalanga Tourism and Parks Agency at the Nelspruit head office, requesting assistance to dart the leopard so we could move it back to Kruger. I told April we also believed it was injured and I would contact him once we located it.

Any animal when wounded and on the run is extremely dangerous, but few are more cunning and lethal than a leopard. Thinking about this, I remembered what my grandfather *Oupa* Havemann had repeatedly told me when I was a youngster at Windy Ridge: 'If ever you go after a wounded leopard, my boy, make sure you take a shotgun. Load one barrel with shotgun pellets, and the other with a solid slug.'

Oupa's wise words had saved me during the assassination attempt at Mthethomusha and I certainly heeded anything else he told me. But this time I not only took his advice, I decided also to take along his shotgun, a side-by-side double-barrelled Geco that I inherited from him. It was a magnificent weapon, a prized collector's item designed for German game keepers, but I rarely used it as I am not a hunter or bird shooter. I silently repeated his words as I thumbed a solid slug into the right barrel and multi-pellet SG shot into the other.

With a handful of cartridges in my pocket, I set off with Zingela and Sergeant Aaron Nkuna, who had been with me and Mike English on the San rock art project at Stolzneck several years previously. Aaron had since retired from SANParks and become a close friend and trusted colleague, so I employed him at Untamed where we took guests on many walking trails together.

Heading for the village through the agricultural fields bordering Kruger, we bumped into a group of meat poachers with a pack of scrawny dogs. They nervously approached when we called them over, thinking we were going to arrest them. Instead, after explaining the situation, we asked them to help track the leopard with their dogs. For once, they were on the right side of the law and happy to oblige.

Zingela, with orders from me only to track and not attack, led the pack up the hill. They soon locked onto the scent of the big cat and we could hear them barking excitedly about three-quarters of a mile away.

When we arrived, it appeared that the dogs had chased the leopard into a hole next to a tumble of granite boulders, as the animals were howling hysterically at the entrance. At first, I couldn't believe that the leopard had squeezed into such a small gap, but a few seconds later it barrelled out of an even smaller hole, and once again the chase was on.

Leaping downhill, the dogs sped off with Zingela in the lead. My progress was seriously hampered as the hillside was covered in *Dalbergia armata* – or thorny rope creeper – sprouting multiple clusters of four-inch thorns that can pierce to the bone. I tried, not always successfully, to dodge the wickedly sharp spikes while running and, coming around some bushes, I saw the leopard just ahead of me. She was a young female, about three or four years old, but not in good condition. The poachers' dogs were baying around her and she was totally exhausted. Even so, she clawed two or three of her yelping tormentors, flinging them around like wet rags.

Aaron came up behind as I frantically called Zingela to heel. I then pressed the speed dial on my mobile phone, telling April Lukhele that we had cornered the leopard and giving him the GPS co-ordinates to come and dart it. April replied that he was about fifteen minutes away.

As we were talking, the leopard turned towards me and glared, her blazing almond-shaped eyes boring into me with terrifying ferocity. That was the only warning I got as, despite her fatigue, she leapt clean over the entire pack of dogs as effortlessly as a ballerina. It was surreal and I almost didn't react, instead admiring her incredible grace and beauty.

Then with a second leap she flew at me. I was still on the phone to April, so hadn't raised the shotgun to my shoulder. Everything seemed to happen in silent slow motion. I fired from the hip when she was about five feet away.

The SG shot hit dead centre in the chest as she was in the air, but that was not enough to stop her acrobatic momentum. Her head then smashed into the right barrel of the shotgun, causing the second trigger to jerk and fire the solid slug. It smashed into her skull just above the right eye, and she landed on one of my feet.

I can't swear to it, but I don't think many people have shot a leopard while talking on a mobile phone. It was actually the second shot, accidentally triggered by the leopard striking the barrel, that killed the animal, as it was too close for the initial body shot I fired to slow her down. If the solid slug had not struck its mark, I would either have needed numerous stitches and surgery, or not been around to tell the story. I'm pretty sure *Oupa* was beside me in those few crucial moments. Knowing him, he would have just grinned and said, 'What did I tell you, my boy!'

When April arrived shortly afterwards, his mouth dropped in disbelief. 'How could you have shot the leopard while talking to me?'

'It was so fast I didn't have time to drop the phone,' I said.

That counted in my favour, as I heard later that certain senior officials who were not very fond of me had attempted to charge me with illegally shooting a leopard within a Mpumalanga Tourism and Parks Agency area of jurisdiction. They were surely disappointed to discover I had been talking to a senior-ranking agency official when I fired and there was absolutely no question that my actions were justified. The fact that the big cat landed on my foot was pretty much a giveaway that any trumped-up charge would not stand up in a court of law.

Aaron summed it up perfectly when, laughing and shaking his head, he said, '*Eish*, Con! You nearly met *Nkosi gaKulu* (God) today.'

Sadly, Aaron died in 2020 after dedicating his entire life to conservation. I will always remember him for his pride, bravery and loyalty, and he will always share a special place in my soul. He was as pure as a man can be.

But the most significant event at Untamed was yet to come; the arrival at the camp of a beautiful Englishwoman.

Her name was Catherine.

11

Anti-poaching Patrols at Sabi Sands

Catherine Corrett was unlike any other woman I had previously met. And not just because she came from a country six thousand miles away that some of my ancestors had once waged war against in an epic David versus Goliath clash.

Dark-haired with honey-brown eyes, she is beautiful and has blue blood coursing through her veins as she is related to the Earl of Cavan peerage. There is little doubt that she moved in more rarefied social circles than I did.

But despite being an English rose, she is as tough as a *sjambok* and blended well into the wilds of Africa. She was as at home in the bush as she was in jet-set London.

She arrived at the Untamed concession in late 2008 as a student doing a wildlife film academy course on elephant birth control, and soon we were dating. On the face of it, it was an unlikely combination: me, a son of wild Africa, and Cat, as we called her, a born and bred metropolitan Brit. But we also had a lot in common as we both loved the wilderness, wildlife and dogs. Perhaps a guy living in the outback and whose sartorial choices are limited to khaki shorts and *veldskoene* (simple, sturdy shoes made from animal hide) understandably didn't quite fit her parents' idea of an ideal partner for their well-bred daughter, but Cat certainly captured the heart of my mother.

There was, however, a major problem. As a foreigner, she could only stay in South Africa for limited periods on a tourist visa that had to be regularly renewed in the UK. So it kicked off as basically a long-distance romance, a mixture of sad departures and joyful reunions. Strangely, it worked.

When Cat was with me, she helped out in the bush, and it was great having her by my side. She also loved Zingela, who returned the attachment to some extent, but generally he was so devoted to me that he didn't pay anyone else much attention.

After about a year at Untamed, I decided it was time to move on. I enjoyed working there but felt there was not much room for growth and I needed new challenges. And sure enough, one soon came along in the form of an advert in the local newspaper for a job in an anti-poaching unit (APU) on a Mpumalanga game reserve. Although the reserve was not named, the advert grabbed my attention right away as the escalating situation against poaching was becoming a dominant theme of my life. But to win against this ever-increasing threat, I was convinced that dogs would be key combatants, particularly highly intelligent, loyal and insanely brave animals such as Weimaraners. This core belief, first sparked by the assassination attempt at Mthethomusha where Zingela had saved my life, was now a burning conviction. In fact, it was fast becoming an obsession. But first I needed to get onto an anti-poaching strike force, rather than being a ranger where patrols were just one of many other duties.

As a result, I put in an application and waited to see what would happen.

A week or so later, I got a reply. I was asked to go for an interview at the Wimpy restaurant in Nelspruit. Still not knowing which reserve was involved, coupled with the fact that a chain diner-type Wimpy was a somewhat humble venue for an interview, I was prepared to be disappointed. So, imagine my delight when the guy who met me at the restaurant was the APU manager at Sabi Sand Wildtuin, one of the most prestigious wildlife areas in the country and part of the greater Kruger National Park biosphere system. Many call it the Sabi Sands Game Reserve, but its official name is Sabi Sand Wildtuin – Wildtuin being the Afrikaans word for game reserve.

We spoke at length, and afterwards he said he would contact me soon. I was on tenterhooks for the rest of the day. I really wanted this job.

I didn't have to wait long. Good as his word, the manager phoned the next day and said the position as second in command of the Sabi Sand Wildtuin APU was mine. I was ecstatic and also humbled to find out that there had been more than two hundred applicants.

Another excellent omen as far as I was concerned is that the Golden Meridian longitudinal line – 31° 14' east – runs directly through the reserve, just as it does at Bongani. The geographic centre of the earth's landmass had intensely fascinated me during my San rock art discoveries, as the San shamans considered it sacred, mirrored above by the Milky Way.

Once again, my faithful old Land Rover was packed with all my worldly possessions, and with Zingela perched on the front seat, I was ready to go.

Sabi Sand Wildtuin is a massive wildlife area, spanning fifty-five thousand hectares, and is owned by numerous proprietors who have either built exclusive game lodges on their grounds or kept their land wild for private use. It also incorporates some of the most famous and luxurious reserves in the country, including Singita, Ulusaba and Londolozi. All owners contributed to the APU costs, which at that time consisted of about thirty staff, and we regularly had to cover distances of up to two hundred miles a day. I was based in the north near the Gowrie Gate, and it would take me an hour and a half just to travel across the reserve.

While it seemed almost impossible to keep a constant eye on such an enormous stretch of bushveld, rhino poaching was still sporadic in those days so most of the poaching problems were still related to bushmeat. However, we also had to deal with security issues such as theft from the lodges or private homes, which had also been a major headache at every other reserve I had worked at.

With such vast distances and small staff, Zingela soon proved his worth. We were a slick, cohesive unit – something my new boss noticed right away. We worked together day and night, tirelessly tracking wounded animals and poaching gangs. In fact, one of Zingela's first jobs was to find a hyena that had been hit by a vehicle. He picked up the bloody spoor immediately and tracked it to a drainage pipe under the road. Unfortunately, the hyena was critically injured and I had to put it out of its misery with a bullet.

As with Untamed in the Mdluli Concession, there was also an ongoing problem with rabid dogs. Most of the western fence of Sabi Sands is bordered by villages, and local dogs often burrowed their way under game fences and drainage lines. We regularly came across them, many already frenzied and foaming at the mouth, and I must have shot close on a hundred dogs during my time there. As a dog lover, it broke my heart. Fortunately, the problem today is not as serious, due to intensive inoculation programmes.

I soon realised the true enormity of what we were up against. The most pressing problem was not wounded animals, snares or rabid dogs. It was, once again, the human factor – and it was happening right under our noses. The biggest culprits were those we should have been able to trust the most.

I found that out quickly. During my first week at work, I was outside my house at Gowrie Gate when one of the assistant wardens, who has since passed away, arrived with several twenty-five-litre plastic buckets on the back of his vehicle. His house was next to mine, and initially I thought nothing of it.

But not Zingela. He immediately started sniffing the air, looking at me then pointing with his nose at the containers. To me, that meant one thing. Poached meat.

I approached the assistant warden warily. He was, after all, my senior.

'My dog is indicating that there is meat in those drums on the back of your vehicle.'

He barely blinked. 'Oh, *ja*,' he said with a shrug. 'One of my cows died outside the reserve and I had to go and cut it up and take the meat to some people in the village.'

I was highly suspicious. Why had he brought the meat into the reserve when it had died outside? But as I had just started the job, I did not check the containers to see what type of meat it was.

That was a mistake. Not long afterwards, one of our informers – known colloquially as *impimpis* or sources – quietly told me that particular assistant warden was allegedly the biggest poacher of all in the reserve, ably assisted by a sergeant in my APU. Both were from the same village and, according to the *impimpi*, this had been going on for years. He claimed they were selling bushmeat at R4.50 (about 20 pence) per kilogramme to the expanding communities along the western border and it was a highly lucrative business.

A few months later, Sabi Sands's chief warden and the APU manager both left the reserve and I was made acting head of anti-poaching patrols until a new manager could be appointed. One of the first things I did was call in the *impimpis* for updates.

It paid dividends. The sources told me most of the poaching activity was currently being handled by the sergeant, now my second-in-command, mainly because the more senior official was deliberately keeping a low profile. This was probably due to the fact that his house was too close to mine, and also I think he got a fright when Zingela scented the meat on his truck.

Armed with this information, I decided to mount a sting operation. I called the sergeant in for a meeting and told him that I would be away for a week working on a project in the Kruger Park. He would be in charge of the APU rangers in my absence. The man's eyes lit up.

However, unbeknown to him, I had attached a tracking device to his vehicle so all his movements could be monitored. I left my house, ostensibly to go to Kruger, but instead set up camp in the bush where I settled down to watch and wait. Every trip the sergeant made was tracked on the monitor in front of me. For the first two days there was nothing suspicious and I began to wonder if my *impimpi*'s information was correct.

Then … bingo! On the third day the monitor showed the vehicle leaving through the Manyeleti Gate in the far north and heading for Makrapine, a notorious shebeen in the nearby village where it was rumoured criminals and other assorted riffraff gathered.

Since the tracker showed that the sergeant had driven out of the reserve without stopping at any house or staff accommodation, I was certain that he had his company-issued firearm with him. This was illegal – no company firearm can be taken off the reserve – and the sergeant had already been subjected to a disciplinary hearing for contravening this ironclad regulation.

I then called Mark, the warden of Manyeleti, who asked me to come to the gate where we would confront the sergeant. We waited for several hours before he eventually arrived back from the shebeen with two other field rangers. All were drunk.

We searched the truck and found the three men's firearms behind the seats. Not only that, there were several bloodstained drums on the back that presumably had been used to store poached bushmeat.

I formally charged the three rangers with leaving the reserve carrying company-issued firearms, itself enough to get them dismissed. However, we couldn't charge them for the bloodstained buckets, although it was pretty obvious what those had been used for.

Suddenly all hell broke loose. With a roar, the drunk sergeant grabbed Mark around the neck and started throttling him, while one of the field rangers also became extremely belligerent. I rushed up and locked my arm around the sergeant's neck in a chokehold, trying to force him to let go of Mark.

As I tightened my grip, I felt a sharp pain, followed by the warm flow of blood. The sergeant had clamped his teeth tightly onto my upper left arm, biting like a wild animal. The more I squeezed, the harder he bit, and at one stage I thought I would lose a chunk out of my arm. I started hammering the side of his head with my free hand as hard as I could. After about fifteen hefty wallops, he let go.

We stood panting and glaring at each other with bloodshot eyes. Fortunately, Mark and I had confiscated the men's firearms before the brawl, so it was now a standoff. We had weapons and they didn't. The three men then left, cursing us.

But for me, it was not over. Most alarming was that we knew the sergeant was HIV-positive as he was receiving antiretroviral treatment at the nearby clinic. To have been bitten deep by an AIDS carrier could be a death sentence.

I rushed off to the clinic and was immediately put on the maximum possible dosage of antiretroviral drugs for a full month. The side effects were horrendous: blinding headaches, continuous nausea and extreme debilitation. It was an intensely scary time and I had to return every three months to be tested, which fortunately all proved negative. Scars of the bites are still visible on my arm.

The next day I went with a police captain to search the sergeant's rooms. We found excess ammunition, snares, biltong hooks, and other poaching equipment, confirming his guilt. He was fired from his post.

Sadly, this incident was merely a snapshot of what was happening in some sections of the wildlife community. Those people who seemed the most honest, those we thought were genuinely on our side, were often involved in the biggest betrayal.

It was indeed a bitter pill to swallow.

12

No Tigers in Africa?

After the brawl and the dismissal of my second in command, I became a marked man. Several *impimpis* warned that the disgraced sergeant had hired a team of assassins to ambush me along the northern fence of the Sabi Sands reserve. I was number one on the hit list, they said.

It was a repeat of the Windy Ridge tragedy more than a decade ago.

Consequently, for the next few weeks I avoided the northern boundary, always changing my movements at the last minute and never repeating a schedule. I also wore a bulletproof vest at all times and each night Zingela and I slept in a different room of my house.

Then we got the news that the sergeant had died from AIDS. Apparently, he had stopped taking antiretroviral drugs after being dismissed and the assassination squad disbanded as they were no longer being paid. Zingela and I were free to patrol in the north again.

Zingela was also singled out by poachers, so I made sure he never left my side. But it wasn't only poachers after him – there are hundreds of lions and hyenas in Sabi Sand Wildtuin, especially in the north where I lived, and of course leopards consider dog meat the ultimate delicacy. The yard of my modest house was fenced, but the poles and wire had been weakened by burrowing warthogs, porcupines and honey badgers. I doubted if it was strong enough to withstand a determined predator.

I was soon to find out. One evening, after a long day in the bush, I parked outside the house, stretching and thinking of a long cold beer to wash the dust from my throat. I patted Zingela standing next to me, who no doubt was also looking forward to his drinking bowl.

Suddenly I heard a low growl, and a split second later a massive lion crashed into the fence, trying to get at Zingela. The wires bulged like a balloon, but by some fluke didn't snap. I rushed Zingela into the house, slamming the door as the dazed lion stood glaring from the other side of the flimsy barrier, its eyes glowing red in the dark.

That night, every door was locked, every window bolted, and I did some hasty reinforcing of poles and fencing the next day. And not a moment too soon as a week or so afterwards, another seven lions arrived, prowling outside and trying to get at my dog. All of this, of course, was a hockey-stick learning curve for Zingela, and from then on, he always warned me well in advance when lions were around.

Well ... almost always. Once, while patrolling the northern boundary fence near Dixi Village, we skirted a clump of magic guarri bush and walked straight into a pride of lions. I have seldom been more surprised, not to mention alarmed. For the first and only time, Zingela had completely missed their scent. The single thing that saved us was that the big cats were all fast asleep under the bushes and – incredibly – had also missed our scent.

I subtly hand-gestured to Zingela to retreat and we literally tiptoed backwards. Most dogs would have barked and perhaps even charged the lions, but Zingela was so attuned to the bush and my commands that he didn't make a sound. It was simply unbelievable for any dog to have that level of intelligence, training and intuition. I could not have been prouder of him, as even a squeak would have had potentially dire consequences.

Another valuable lesson learnt from this was that whenever Zingela and I came across lions, I would divert his attention and we would pretend to ignore the pride before moving off in another direction. This seemed to confuse them, as if they were wondering why we had the audacity to snub them, and, as we didn't retreat or back off, the big cats concluded we did not pose a direct threat.

But the main point was that if Zingela could hold his nerve, not uttering a sound when surrounded by lions, imagine how silently he could track poachers. Once again, I knew that dogs would be our ultimate allies in the looming full-scale wildlife conflicts ahead of us. If only I could get the authorities to see that.

Fortunately, there was one other ranger who agreed with me. Richard Sowry, a Kruger section ranger at Kingfisherspruit, owned a Belgian Malinois, and he also believed that dogs were the way forward for APUs. We joined forces and slowly, through demonstrations and real-life situations, started showing what well-trained, smart dogs could do in the wild.

We also teamed up with Henry Holsthyzen, a dog trainer from Pretoria who owned a security company called K9 Security Solutions. Henry regularly came to Kruger and Sabi Sands to train with our rangers and donated a Malinois called Ingwenya to Richard. Richard soon had the first major success, arresting rhino poachers at night in Kruger using Ingwenya and her handler.

It was an invigorating time as I was now mixing with other service dog teams and there was much cross-pollination of ideas and methods in developing skills and abilities. Up until then, I was purely self-taught, just me and Zingela out in the bush, but now with Richard and Henry, the drive to create a service dog section gathered momentum. We outlined our plans to anyone who would listen and we believed we were making good progress in getting converts to the cause. It was not a hard sell as the benefits are obvious. A dog is trained to track down poachers without fear or favour and cannot be bribed. It runs far faster than humans and does not give up until its quarry is caught. And it bites – hard. For this reason alone, poachers who have little fear of the often-hamstrung forces of law and order are terrified of dogs.

In fact, I was so convinced that we were on the right track that I thought it was just a matter of time before the Sabi Sands APU, along with most other reserves, would be using anti-poaching dogs.

I was wrong. As fate would have it, a new warden at Sabi Sands took office who decided to outsource APU duties to a separate security company. As a result, the in-house unit that I worked for was disbanded and staff given the option to join the private company, subject to signing new contracts and a three-month probation period, or be made redundant.

It was a harsh blow. After all the work we had done and arrests made under some harrowing conditions, many in our APU considered it to be a slap in the face. Some resigned in protest, while others, like me, decided to wait and see. Ever the optimist, I hoped my new bosses might see the light in using service dogs such as Zingela.

No such luck. The incoming private company made it clear they had no plans for that. Consequently, the work Richard, Henry and I had done took a sharp step backwards. No matter how often I spoke of previous successes in the bush, or how even corrupt staff members had been nailed by Zingela, my words fell on deaf ears. For all intents and purposes, my dream had gone up in smoke.

One thing that cheered me up considerably was that Catherine was back in the country. She now had a job with Wild Earth Productions, a reality TV production company. Her work was unpaid as she did not have a work permit, but it did mean we would be able to spend more time together. Even better, Wild Earth Productions was based at Sabi Sand Wildtuin, just ten minutes down the road from my house. As far as we were concerned, she had come home.

It was also hugely beneficial for me to be able to vent my frustrations about the lack of interest in anti-poaching canines, and Cat was the perfect sounding board. She believed in my plans as much as I did, something that was to prove invaluable in the near future.

Coincidentally, my immediate dog family was now growing as I had just been given another Weimaraner, a rescue dog named Adi. She was a pretty little thing and Zingela immediately fell in love, with the inevitable result that Adi fell pregnant.

Three and a half months later, I was driving home from the south of the reserve when I saw a group of game drive vehicles stopped ahead. This invariably means tourists have spotted something interesting and, sure enough, there was a leopard in the road. As I switched off my engine, I heard a squealing noise from the back of the pickup. Glancing through the rear window, I saw a tiny, squirming body. Adi had just given birth to the first of the litter – and there was a leopard just fifty yards ahead.

Expecting to see a big spotted cat leap into the truck at any moment, I hurriedly restarted the engine and squeezed past the tourists, getting home just in time for Adi to deliver eight more puppies.

A few days later, I had to go on patrol, again in the southern area of the reserve and, as Catherine had flown back to the UK, I had no option but to take Adi and the puppies with me.

The next evening, sitting around the campfire with some rangers, a hyena loped into the boma. Fiercely protective of her litter, Adi jumped up to chase it out of the enclosure. In her adrenalin rush she didn't notice a splintered tree stump sticking out of the ground. There was an agonised scream as she impaled herself on a needle-sharp sliver of wood, and blood and gore gushed like a spigot from her chest.

One of the rangers wanted to shoot her and put her out of her misery, but I yelled at him to stop. I rushed off to get cotton swabs from the medical kit, shoved the wads into the gaping hole and wrapped bandages around her. Then, with my foot flat on the accelerator, I sped off to the White River Animal Hospital fifty-five miles away, where vets were standing by. They managed to remove the shards of wood and stitch her up, leaving a small drainage hole in her chest to get rid of discharge. Weimaraners are a hardy breed and Adi not only survived the ordeal, she managed to continue feeding her puppies. However, it was a tough time for both of us as I had to look after her, supplement the puppies' feed with bottles and still do my APU duties.

I kept one of the litter and called him Landa, sending him to Pretoria to be trained by Henry, while the rest were placed in good homes.

Then something happened that should have proved the immense value of working dogs in the bush beyond doubt to anyone involved in conservation. It had all the newsworthy ingredients for a good story: dangerous wildlife, police searches, fortune tellers, psychics, charlatans – and even a potential man-eater prowling in populated areas.

It was on a winter's day, about eleven o'clock in the morning, when Henry phoned from Pretoria saying that a seventeen-month-old pet tiger called Panjo was on the run. Could I help track it down?

I paused for a moment. A tiger? In Africa? Was he serious?

Yes, said Henry. In fact, Panjo belonged to a Groblersdal farmer, 'Goosey' Fernandes, who owned several Bengal tigers. He had been taking Panjo to the vet for routine booster injections when the animal escaped from his cage on the back of a truck somewhere on the R25 motorway between Groblersdal and Bronkhorstspruit. The juvenile tiger had now been on the loose for two days in a farming area surrounded by densely populated townships. Search parties were using helicopters as well as police and army trackers, but Panjo was nowhere to be found.

The story was splashed across national newspapers and TV with reward offers bandied about, each amount growing larger the longer the tiger was missing. The massive publicity of an exotic Asian tiger on the run in Africa had totally captured the public's imagination. So much so that the media bunfight was now becoming a circus, with psychics and astrologers 'predicting' where Panjo was.

But aside from the hype, the real concern was that Panjo had not eaten for forty-eight hours. He would be mighty hungry – and in an area with a lot of humans. Someone then told 'Goosey' Fernandes about a ranger and his Weimaraner from Sabi Sands who'd had great success in tracking predators in the bush.

'Find that guy,' he said.

That would be me and was the reason for Henry's call.

I got permission from the chief warden to offer Zingela's services, then set off for the six-hour drive to a forest outside the town of Verena where recent paw prints had been spotted. It was getting dark as we arrived, and Zingela was taken to Goosey's truck to get Panjo's scent and sniff some of the young tiger's droppings that had been placed in a plastic bag.

I then took him to the freshest prints and gave the command, '*Soek e bubes*', which Zingela understood as 'find the predator'.

It was chaos, with people scrambling around the forest flashing searchlights, shouting Panjo's name and putting out chunks of meat to entice him out of the woods. Zingela ignored it all. He put his nose to the ground and less than an hour later 'pointed' to a copse of black wattle trees, indicating the tiger was there.

Indeed, it was, and Goosey's son, Justin, managed to collar Panjo and take him home. Zingela and I left in my pickup. Job done – no fuss, no frills.

Of course, the promised reward money did not materialise. I never considered asking for it because as a public relations exercise for canines in conservation, the benefit of this high-profile rescue was far more valuable than mere banknotes. Zingela was now a hero, featured prominently in the local press as well as on international networks such as the BBC and influential global newspapers. He had achieved in one hour what human trackers, helicopters and psychics had failed to do in two solid days. The positive publicity was priceless.

Sadly, the security company I was on probation with didn't see it that way. Dogs still had no meaningful role in their future plans. I shook my head, exasperated. If even the Panjo incident that had the whole county applauding couldn't change their minds, nothing would. So, with cold-minded clarity, I decided it was time to move on and start what I had been planning to do all along: launch my own anti-poaching dog unit. I even had a name for it: K9 Conservation.

With Cat's unflagging encouragement and help, we started setting the wheels in motion and sourced a potential investor who was keen to establish a venture in KwaZulu-Natal. Coming with me would be my right-hand man at Sabi Sands, Elmond Kunari Ndlovu, and a Malinois called Giant that belonged to Henry. The three of us would form the nucleus of the new company, with Cat handling the office work, while Elmond and I would be out in the field with our dogs.

I could not think of a better partner than Elmond. A committed, highly skilled ranger, he was not only a colleague, but also one of my closest friends, and we had run countless patrols in the bush together. We were a constant thorn in the side of the poaching syndicates, even if I say so myself, and Elmond had the uncanny gift of being able to squeeze information out of suspects without threats of violence. He also was a natural dog handler and bonded tightly with Giant – in fact, I was not sure who loved who more.

As far as I was concerned, Elmond and I were ahead of our time in working with dogs in the wild. It was not only in the bush; I remember getting a callout one morning to follow up on a theft from one of the game lodges. We let Giant sniff around the crime scene, and then he took off like a rocket, nose to the ground, with Elmond running behind and me trying to keep up. This continued at a cracking pace and I was wondering what was going on, until Giant unerringly led us to a room at another lodge five miles away. We opened the door and the Malinois lunged at the man inside as Elmond hung tightly onto the leash. In the room was the pile of stolen goods and the terrified thief howling with fright. So much so that the rest of the staff thought he was being attacked by some wild animal.

Suffice to say, all theft in that part of the reserve abruptly halted.

Elmond and I had many other escapades in the bush, even once solving the mystery of an impala wandering around with an arrow through its abdomen. The obvious conclusion was that a poacher had shot it, but for both Elmond and me, something didn't ring true. So, we did some investigating and found the culprit. It was no rural poacher – instead, it was one of the owners of a luxury lodge on the reserve.

We named him in our report, but perhaps for political reasons, no action was taken. However, I was extremely impressed at the way Elmond thought out of the box and didn't take anything purely at face value. From that moment, I knew what an invaluable partner he would be in our new company.

Then, just before Elmond and I resigned, a rhino was killed at Sabi Sands, its horn hacked off and sold for a fortune in the Far East. It was the first to be poached on the reserve, and that shot reverberated around the country, shocking the conservation community to the core. Cat, Elmond and I were embarking on a new adventure called K9 Conservation just in time.

Or so I thought. Two weeks after I left Sabi Sands, Elmond suddenly took ill and died of meningitis.

I went into shock when I heard the news. It was simply unbelievable. He had been healthy just a month or so beforehand, laughing, energetic, full of life and excited to be on the cusp of a new career.

Now he was gone. I would never see him or be out in the wild with him again. I struggled to come to terms with the loss.

Then, a few days later, I was told that Giant had also died.

Within the space of a few days, my world had literally crashed. My entire business plan was in ruins. I had lost my right-hand man and half of the dog team. I also had no job. The future looked bleak in the starkest way imaginable.

Then another tragedy struck.

13

Death of Zingela

The old adage that a dog is a man's best friend could not ring truer for me. Zingela was not only that, he was also my soul companion. It was the purest unconditional love one can get.

After nearly seven years together and numerous hazardous encounters with both wild animals and bad people, we were a well-oiled and effective team in the bush. We had saved one another's lives on several occasions and we were now on the cusp of starting a new career. We would still be chasing poachers, but on our terms within the law.

After working out my notice period, I left Sabi Sands and headed south to Nelspruit to stay with my cousin Brandon on the small Havemann family farm just off the Barberton road. I planned to be there for a few weeks, catching up with the training courses I needed as qualifications to start my new company, now tragically without Elmond, and also to upgrade my firearms competency certificate. This is a strict legal stipulation if one is involved in any kind of security work, and upgrades are required every five years. I normally did mine at Aim Training Academy in White River, about forty-five miles north of Nelspruit.

My test was booked for Thursday, 9 June 2011, but I could not take Zingela as there were other students writing exams at the centre. I left him at the farmhouse, thinking he would be safe as the yard was enclosed by a wire fence.

I was halfway through writing my test when my mobile phone buzzed. I stared at the screen. It was not a number I recognised.

'Hello? Who is this?'

The woman on the other end was crying. 'Your dog is dead. Hit by a car head-on.'

'What? Where?'

'On the Nelspruit road. I got your number off his collar tag.'

I went cold, my heart racing. I could not believe what I had just heard. My mind would not accept it was true, even though I knew with absolute dread that it was. How else could the caller have got my number?

I jumped up from my desk and ran over to Chris, the owner of Aim Academy.

'My dog has just been run over.'

Chris knew of my relationship with Zingela and waved towards the door. 'Go now! Quickly. You can finish the test later.'

Hightailing it out onto the motorway in the Land Rover with emergency lights flashing and my foot flat on the accelerator, I sped past some traffic cops. They tried to flag me down but I ignored them, going even faster. Arriving at the turnoff to the Havemann farm, I saw Zingela's broken body lying on the side of the road.

Choking back a sob, I pulled over and jumped out of my car, hoping against all logic that a spark of life still burned.

He was gone. I picked him up and could feel rigor mortis setting in. Tears from the depth of my soul gushed out. I did not try to stop them. The only tiny consolation was that I could see by the damage to his head that death had come instantly. He had not suffered.

The driver of the car that struck him did not bother to stop. The Good Samaritan who phoned me was another motorist who had showed utmost compassion by moving my best friend's body off the busy road. My gratitude to her is infinite.

I called my mother, who knew more than anyone exactly what Zingela meant to me. She told me to wait for her; she was leaving her house right away. When she arrived, we ran towards each other and hugged, our foreheads touching and our hands on each other's shoulders. Neither of us could speak. My mother later said I gave a guttural cry that sounded sub-human with pain. I lifted my head skywards and shouted, 'Why? Why?'

I placed my loyal friend in the back of the Land Rover, and my mother and I drove to the main farm house. We stopped at *Oupa* Havemann's tree, a knob thorn, that had been planted in the family garden on the day he died twelve years ago. I fetched a pick and spade and started digging. *Oupa* had been my much-loved mentor, instilling in me a passion for the wild almost before I could walk, while Zingela was my soul brother.

My chest heaved with sobs as I dug his grave at the base of my grandfather's tree. The winter ground was cold and hard. About a yard down, I struck a batch of verdite, a semi-precious, soft stone used by African sculptors over the centuries, and put one of the rocks in my pocket. I then carried Zingela from the Land Rover and gently covered his wounded head with his velvet floppy ears. I laid him to rest the ancient San way, facing east towards the rising sun, and shovelled the earth on top of him.

My mother and I gathered more verdite rocks from the grave and made a circle around the newly dug earth. In the centre we placed a metal bird to watch over him. I said a prayer of farewell, but no words could ease the ache in my heart. It was as if something had been ripped from my soul and all that remained was a massive gap. I was inconsolable.

That evening, when I got to Brandon's house, I found a slit in the fence that had been cut by burglars some time back. That was where Zingela had broken out. I cursed myself. I should have checked the fence before leaving, as I knew that Zingela hated it when we were apart and would do anything to find me.

I later found out he had first headed to the main house where he was seen but, to my intense disappointment, this had not been reported to me at the time. Being a top tracker dog, Zingela then followed my smell and the familiar Land Rover tyres to the road about four hundred yards away. He had been so engrossed in tracking my scent that he was oblivious to anything else. As he ran onto the tar road, he was hit by a vehicle and somersaulted into the air.

The evening beforehand we had been at the stream at the bottom of the farm, where I took some carefree pictures of him playing in the water looking for fish. He loved doing that. I still have those photos, and when I look at them or hold the verdite stone I pocketed from his grave, vivid memories flood back. They always will.

African shamans say death is always stalking you, and now my soulmate had gone to the other side. There was no calling him back. Whatever part the universe had played in this tragedy, the only thing I could do was hope that there was some reason behind it, something to make sense of it all. It could not have come at a worse time – just as I was about to start a new phase of my life, a radical change where I would be the boss. I had chosen a path where I would make the decisions. But I would be doing so without my faithful partner.

As Zingela was famous for finding Panjo the tiger when everything else had failed, his death was reported in newspapers and on radio. To honour him, the local station played Johnny

Clegg's international hit, 'Spirit of the Great Heart', which was also the theme song for the 1986 movie *Jock of the Bushveld*.

It was a fitting eulogy, for the spirit of Zingela did not die. Of that I have no doubt, and for me, living proof of it came two weeks later.

Catherine had to return to England a week or so before the tragedy to renew her visa, so could not be with me at this terrible time. However, before she left, we were visited by a friend who would also be in London in the coming weeks. Cat, the born-and-bred Londoner, suggested he join her on a night out with some of her English friends to show him the city.

Two weeks to the day that Zingela died, the friend phoned Cat saying he was in London. She invited him to join her at a music event that another good friend of hers was organising in Old Street, Islington. Sharing a love of similar music, he agreed. They met up later that evening in a large warehouse-style building off the busy main road.

The music event was a big hit. There was a large turnout with more people arriving by the minute. As the music played and cocktails flowed, Cat danced and milled around with the crowd, chatting to friends that she hadn't seen for some time and enjoying the vibe. But, having spent so much time in the African bush over the past few years, she let her guard down, making the cardinal error that any big city girl knows only too well – NEVER leave your drink unattended. For make no mistake, there are far more evil predators in the city than in the bush. And the weapon of choice for these creeps is date-rape drugs.

When she turned back to reach for her glass and take a sip, the damage was done. Suddenly the world began to spin. She felt woozy, nauseous and disorientated, her legs turning to rubber as she struggled to walk.

She turned to her friend. 'I don't feel right. I think my drink has been spiked. Stay here, I'll be back.'

Before he could answer, she somehow weaved her way through the gyrating crowds to the cloakroom, where she violently threw up, almost passing out.

The one spark of clarity was that she knew she had to get back to the table where her friends were waiting. Only they could get her home safely, as no doubt the drink-spiking weirdo would be watching and waiting to pounce. However, she was now barely able to stand, holding onto the cloakroom wall to prevent herself from collapsing. How would she get through the boisterous throng of stomping dancers, let alone find the table where her friends were?

Totally disorientated by blurred vision, extreme nausea and the distorted thumping of blaring music, she slowly made her way out of the cloakroom into the mass of heaving humanity.

She then felt a bump and looked down. There was Zingela on her left-hand side. She blinked hard, trying to focus. Now her world was truly surreal. Was she dreaming? Was she hallucinating?

She put her hand out and touched his head. It felt real. He started walking off and, reassured by his presence, she followed him. He took her straight through the crowd to the table where her friends were waiting.

With tears streaming down her face, she said, 'Zingela! Zingela is here!'

Her friends looked at her in astonishment. They had no idea what she was talking about.

'Are you alright?' one asked, deeply concerned.

'Zingela is here,' she repeated.

But he was gone.

Seeing how shaken and sick she looked, one of her friends immediately took her home.

She woke the next morning feeling horrendously ill, but at least she was safe. Making straight for the shower, she vigorously soaped and scrubbed herself, symbolically washing the awful memory of the nightmare away. While doing so, she felt a slight indentation on her left thigh. She looked closer. There was a zigzag mark. It was definitely not a cut or a bruise. It was as if the flesh had been sucked in, dimpling a clear 'Z' into the top of her leg.

Later that day, she phoned to tell me the story. I was shocked speechless, six thousand miles away, feeling utterly powerless that I had not been there to help her.

But Zingela had. For us, there was not the faintest doubt. We both knew that the spirit of Zingela was with Catherine that night. He had been standing guard, faithful as ever on point duty, saving her by showing her the way to safety.

The Z imprint remained on her thigh for almost a year and then, as quickly as it had appeared, it vanished.

14

White Lions and Shamans of the Cave

The southern hemisphere autumn of 2011 was the lowest ebb of my life. I had resigned from Sabi Sand Wildtuin, my great friend Elmond Ndlovu had died and Cat had returned to England to renew her visa for another year.

And Zingela was gone.

Thankfully, the rumour that Giant, Elmond's dog in our new venture, had also died was false. He was alive and well, but without Elmond and Zingela, there was no APU team left.

I was now not only without work but fast running out of money.

Then came a glimmer of hope. I received a call from Linda Tucker and Jason Turner of the Global White Lion Protection Trust asking me to check out a lion-breeding farm in Free State province. They had concerns, particularly as some of the big cats there were white lions, a unique, endangered sub-species that is almost extinct in the wild. Sadly, those bred in captivity have often been killed in canned hunts where sick trophy seekers get to shoot them like fish in a barrel. So, whenever Linda and Jason heard about white lions bred in captivity, the trust thoroughly investigated the breeder.

Of huge personal interest for me is that white lions originated from the Timbavati region of Mpumalanga, which is directly on the Golden Meridian. In fact, in the Xitsonga language, Timbavati means 'the place where something sacred came down from the heavens', so I was more than keen to help out.

In this case, the deal was that the breeding farm in question would be donated to the Global White Lion Protection Trust, provided it took over full responsibility for everything happening there, although the owner would still have a vested interest.

But what was happening behind the scenes? The trust wasn't exactly sure, so my brief was to go undercover to establish that this was not a disguised canned hunting operation and that the owner was a reputable person. The last thing the Trust wanted was to be part of a tainted deal.

As I would be in the Free State for several weeks, I decided to fetch Landa, Zingela's son, who was to become my new canine companion. Although Landa was now about seven months old, he barely knew me, as for the past three months he had been at Henry's dog training centre in Pretoria. That was about to change, as he would now live with me permanently and this trip would be us forging a new bond. The heartache of losing Zingela was still fresh, but having his son with me might ease it a little.

We arrived at the farm, enclosed by high lion-proof fencing, and I was buzzed in through multiple electric gates to the house. As I stepped out of the vehicle, I was surprised to see that I was surrounded – literally – by hundreds of caged lions, as the farm house was in the centre of the big cat enclosure.

Landa, never having seen a lion before, stayed close to my side as I introduced myself to the farm owner. He knew I was from the trust, but not that he was under scrutiny. He believed I was there to help out prior to the farm being handed over.

Conraad with Bamba at Windy Ridge game reserve, his first post as a game ranger.

Aaron Nkuna, 'a huge, powerfully built Shangaan with an encyclopaedic knowledge of the bush' at Ship Mountain, Kruger National Park, Limpopo.

Con on bush patrol in Thanda Game Reserve, KwaZulu-Natal, with Landa (left) and Manzi.

Rock art in the Stolzneck wilderness section of the Kruger National Park showing depictions of a roan antelope and a giraffe.

'I saw an old nyala bull standing motionless in the overhang. I could see it was old and emaciated and had obviously come here to die.'

A bushmeat poacher with snares and wearing a stolen police shirt. Animals are massacred wholesale, either shot or snared. Kudu and giraffe meat is openly sold door to door in villages.

A sculpture of a rhino made by Con from snares, spears, cables and wires collected during anti-poaching patrol missions over five years. The sculpture stands outside K9 Conservation's headquarters outside Hoedspruit in the Limpopo province of South Africa.

Con with the wounded leopard that he'd had to shoot when it charged. The second barrel of his shotgun went off as it hit him and killed the leopard. They were attempting to dart it and return it to the game reserve from which it had escaped as it was killing livestock and people were afraid for their children.

Zingela at Singita Game Reserve in Sabi Sand Wildtuin (also known as Sabi Sands Game Reserve).

Zingela watching lions feeding on a giraffe at Sabi Sands Game Reserve.

An impala wounded by an arrow fired from a hunting bow and arrow. A local lodge owner was suspected.

Con with Landa, one of the nine puppies sired by Zingela.
(Photo: Anke de Rosner)

On a night patrol in Singita Game Reserve in Sabi Sands. 'Eventually we owned the night.'

'One of our biggest successes was a raid that took out a notorious poacher and the most malicious person I have ever met, Mthobisi Lenox Ngwenya.'

Landa persisted in indicating that there was something hidden in the rafters: it was the rhino poacher's rifle.

Walking the dogs at home in Liverpool rural district near Hoedspruit.
(Photo: Johan 'Vossie' Vorster)

Con, Anke and their dogs: Landa, Anubis, Manzi, Kalandra and Nsimbiti on patrol. (Photo: Wojtek Koziara)

Anke's dog, Jock, part Canis Africanis, has more in common genetically with a poacher's dog. Anke rescued him at five months when his mother was run over, shielding him, on the motorway in front of her.

Dehorning rhino in Selati game reserve with Anke in the foreground. Dehorning is much debated as it still leaves a baseplate and two-inch stub of horn, and poachers increasingly indiscriminately kill whichever rhinos they can.

Con and Anke were married on 3 December 2022, in a handfasting ritual, a centuries-old Celtic tradition in which hands are tied together to symbolise the binding of two souls.

With parents at our wedding (from left) Elaine Bell, Con, Anke, Cesere and Willie Smith.

The next few days were interesting, to say the least. Whenever I went outside the house, the lions, both white and tawny, hungrily stalked Landa from behind the fences. The farm owner warned that if one hooked him with its claws through the cage, Landa would be a goner. I made sure to keep him well away from the wire.

I counted one hundred and forty lions in the enclosures, which obviously meant a lot of meat was required. Every day some workers and I would go and fetch carcasses of horses, cattle and other livestock that had died on surrounding farms. Many of these animals had been treated with antibiotics while sick and I was concerned what effect these powerful drugs in the carcasses would have on the lions.

As this was an undercover operation, a lot of information remains classified. However, it rapidly became apparent that not everything was above board, and one of the first things I noticed was that a significant number of the lions were squint-eyed and radically obese, which is a sure sign of inbreeding. Bizarrely, there was also a dead white lion stored in the walk-in freezer. When I casually asked what was to become of it, I was told that the bones would be harvested. That meant one thing: it was destined for the illegal Far East market.

That was just the start, and over the next few weeks I became increasingly uneasy about what was happening on the farm. As a result, when I began compiling my report, I strongly recommended that the protection trust stay away from this operation. Despite the obvious inbreeding and other discrepancies, there were too many question marks over what the animals were being bred for, and who the owner's clients were. It was also obvious that the breeder was becoming ever more suspicious of me.

It came to a head one afternoon when I was at the back of the house and he stormed over, abruptly instructing me to pack my stuff and leave. The game was up. He now knew the true reason for my visit and I was escorted off the premises by a newly appointed security detail, which alone seemed to indicate there was something to hide. But I had seen enough to make up my mind, so was happy to hit the road.

The final outcome was that the Global White Lion Protection Trust heeded my advice, particularly the concerns about white lions, and did not take over the farm.

As I was already in the area, there was one other thing I wanted to do – for me, an ultimate bucket-list wish. So instead of going home, I headed into the foothills of the Maloti Mountains where an ancient traditional healers' settlement nestles inside the second largest cave in the southern hemisphere. A friend had told me about it – a breathtakingly spectacular grotto about eight hundred yards long and close on a thousand feet high in places.

I drove as far as I could, then Landa and I trekked up a winding path deep in a craggy valley along a river with crystal clear water flowing over rocks. Hundreds of red-winged starlings flew between the sheer cliff faces, while the faint herbal scent of *impepho* drifting in the breeze told me I was getting close to the settlement. *Impepho* is an indigenous African plant that, once dried, is lit and smoulders in order to communicate with the spirit world. It's considered sacred by *sangomas*.

Then I saw the cave. It was truly stunning – a waterfall cascading directly off the high overhanging roof creating a surreal cloud of mist. I could just make out the blurred forms of the healers' huts within.

In visiting a holy place of shamanism such as this, it is essential that ancestral culture is strictly observed, otherwise entry is denied. I sat down and waited on the far bank of the stream where a goat sacrificed to appease the spirits lay at the bottom of a small pool.

After about an hour, an old man dressed in the traditional red, white and black garments of a *sangoma* emerged out of a haze of *impepho* smoke. I cupped my hands, clapping them and respectfully greeting him with the words, '*Makosi, Makosi*' (Chieftain).

'What is that?' he said, pointing at Landa. He had never seen a blue-grey dog with yellow eyes before.

I explained that I had come from far away to pay my respects to this great place and that Landa was my trusted companion.

'Is this a spirit dog that is accompanying you?' the *sangoma* asked.

I nodded. 'He is a golden dog from royalty, not a normal dog.'

The old man asked me to wait and walked back into the cloud of smoke. A short while later he returned with several other healers, all gawking at Landa. The old man said that I could enter the cave, but he didn't want the dog to kill the cats inside. Many Africans consider cats to be magical creatures, so I assured him that the dog was my spirit brother and wouldn't harm anything in the cave.

Wading across the stream above the sacrificed goat, we passed through several tight passages into a labyrinth of clay huts and then turned into a vast chamber. It was surreal, with hundreds of felines slinking ghostlike in the shadows. I commanded Landa not to chase them and he listened, as loyally obedient as his father had been.

In the middle of the chamber were some old wooden stools, and the *sangomas* beckoned me to sit. They gathered around me, scrutinising Landa and saying this was the first time a dog had been allowed into the cave. They then wanted to hear my story.

I said I had come from a dwelling of many lions and that I was a child of Africa and its wild places. I said I also, in the traditional African way, needed to get on my feet again as I had been through much heartache and loss. I needed to find a path forward with the help and advice of these wise healers.

Pointing at Landa, I told them I wanted to create a dog team to catch evil people who were killing Africa's wild animals for the sake of greed.

By now, more *sangomas* started materialising from the depths. They also wanted to see the spirit dog with its yellow eyes. Their body language was a mixture of apprehension and reverence as they tentatively stroked Landa's soft fur. He was magnificent, aloof as always, but showing no aggression whatsoever.

Then one of the younger *sangomas* approached me.

'There is a reason that you came here,' she said. 'You must now go into the deep chamber. It is dark and your eyes will not see. Go in alone with the dog. There your path will become clear as there have been many troubles in your recent past. Only you will know when it is time to come out.'

They started singing, chanting and clapping as Landa and I were guided into the pitch-black chamber. There was not even a pinprick of light, and I held Landa's lead tightly as we walked deeper and deeper into the bowels of the earth.

To be honest, nothing spectacular happened. There was no bolt of lightning or epiphany. It was instead something more obscure, almost incomprehensible. It was as though a load had almost imperceptibly been lifted off me. As if the still raw deaths of Zingela and Elmond were harbingers of a new life path.

After spending several hours in blind blackness, I felt as if the darkness had drawn out my sadness and pain, so I rose and headed towards the light. As I emerged, a shrunken old woman with decades of wisdom etched as crevasses into her face looked me deep in the eyes. I blinked under her withering gaze.

'You have called your dog *Ulanda*,' she said. (*Ulanda* means 'to fetch' in Zulu.) 'You will always be fetching something and you must be aware of many dangers to come in your life. As you become more of a warrior hunting the hunters, so too will your enemies become more.'

I stared at her. She spoke in a riddle, but I understood perfectly. She unerringly prophesied what I had set out to do for the rest of my days.

I spent the next few hours exploring the ancient and mysterious village inside the giant cave with these remarkable people. As I was about to leave, the old man who had first come out to meet me took my arm.

'You are on your path and you must never stray from it,' he said. 'There are different directions that can be taken, but all paths lead back into each other again.'

We shook and clasped hands and Landa and I went back down the mountain. As I said, there was no sudden Damascene insight. It was rather a long-term life lesson. The visit to this holy shaman cave had given me the guidance, support and affirmation I needed.

I spent another month working for Linda and Jason doing anti-poaching duties for the Global White Lion Protection Trust, which was also superb training for Landa. Most of the work involved clearing snares, while at night we tracked meat poachers.

One night I switched off my flashlight on hearing a slight fidgeting, snuffling sound ahead. Stopping dead still, Landa at my side, I waited, barely daring to breathe. Then, in the cold light of a half-moon, a shape loomed and moved slowly towards us, seemingly unfazed by our presence. Closer and closer the blob came, but still I could not make out what it was. Eventually, almost on top of us, it stopped. In the gloom it morphed into a massive aardvark.

This wonderful animal with a protruding pig-like snout, long pointed ears and thick, tapered tail feeds mainly on termites, licking them up as it probes nests with its extended tongue. It is strictly nocturnal and seldom seen by humans.

It looked at us calmly; we looked at it. It sensed we posed no danger. For a long minute or two we stood motionless until the aardvark gave a sniffling grunt and slowly moved off, continuing its nightly business. So seldom encountered, it was a rare privilege to share the quiet night with this magnificent creature. I was sure it was a good omen at this desolate time of my life.

A week later I left for KwaZulu-Natal to start a new venture. My dream of perfecting the training of dogs for wildlife anti-poaching was in tatters, but it was still alive.

It was, after all, what the *sangomas* had told me in the sacred cave.

15

Rhino Poachers and Zombies

The trusty old Land Rover double cab was once again loaded with my worldly goods, and I headed south with my dogs to KwaZulu-Natal. This time it wasn't just my possessions riding on its bundu-bashing suspension, but my hopes and aspirations as well.

The goal was simple: to try and persuade as many game reserves as possible that the future of wildlife protection hinged on well-trained service dogs and handlers. In other words, boots and paws on the ground.

I now had three dogs, Landa and Manzi, another Weimaraner that had been given to me and Cat, and a Malinois called Makhulu. I was also going to fetch Cat as she had her visas in order and would be working with me as cofounder of our new K9 Conservation business. Not only did she give me total support emotionally, but the pounds sterling she had saved in England helped our financial situation enormously, particularly with the abysmal rand exchange rate. She committed whatever she had to the project, and her enthusiasm and belief in me are largely responsible for this dream eventually becoming a reality.

With much optimism and high hopes, but not much else, I picked up Cat at King Shaka Airport north of Durban and we set off on our new journey in life. At first, we lived like nomads, rattling along in the old Land Rover with dogs and goods piled in the back and sleeping under Africa's megawatt stars. But we had more than enough idealism and determination to carry us through the tough times.

And they were tough. We had very little success until I contacted the director of Nyati Anti-Poaching based at Phinda where I had done field-guide training. Nyati had an excellent reputation protecting rhino in KwaZulu-Natal's private reserves, and I offered our services for free to show what we could do.

After spending a few weeks with the Nyati anti-poaching teams, I heard that the nearby Thanda Private Reserve was looking for an APU manager. As our proposed company, K9 Conservation, was still little more than a pipedream, Cat and I decided I should apply for the job in the interim. Apart from my work at Bongani, Sabi Sands and two Kruger Park concessions, I also had references from Grant Tracy, a top game capture specialist, and David Havemann, who I had worked with at the Jock Safari Camp. So, I fancied my chances at Thanda, which was also a prestigious Big Five park.

The interview itself was a classic example of perfect timing. I had barely sat down to discuss my credentials with Alwyn, the reserve's manager, when an emergency call buzzed through. An armed poacher was on the reserve. Alwyn, still a good friend after all these years, suggested we go and catch him. It was surreal … one minute I was trying to impress him, saying what a hotshot I was – the next I was told 'prove it'. It was that sudden. I don't think many job applicants have been tested in earnest quite so quickly.

We rushed to where the poacher had been sighted and I let Landa loose. Within minutes he was on the scent and the chase took off at a blistering pace along a drainage line cutting through dense vegetation. Unfortunately, it was almost evening, and in the sub-tropics of Africa the sun sets faster than a falling curtain. There is no true twilight.

This posed two problems for me. Firstly, I didn't know the terrain well and the poacher could turn the tables and ambush us in the thick bush. My instincts, which I always trust, told me to back off.

'I don't like this,' I said to Alwyn. 'This guy's armed. There's a good chance he could backtrack on us in the dark.'

The other even bigger problem was that I hadn't been formally appointed by the reserve. I had to bring this up now before any shots were fired.

'Alwyn, technically I'm still a civilian. There could be major legal issues if I'm involved in a gunfight at night where everything could go south very quickly.'

Alwyn considered this for a moment, then looked at Landa. I could see he was impressed at how quickly and efficiently my dog had picked up the poacher's scent, how he listened to me and how quietly he tracked.

'Okay, the job's yours,' he said. 'We'll sign the paperwork when we get back to the office.'

We resumed the chase the following morning and Landa soon followed the scent to the reserve's border. The poacher had broken out of Thanda and into community lands during the night and we would not have caught him anyway. But the main thing was that I was now back in frontline anti-poaching operations with my dogs. Things seemed to be looking up.

Cat and I moved into the APU manager's accommodation high on a hill in the south of Thanda overlooking vast stretches of rural Zululand. It was called Bukanda House, and despite its panoramic view, it was a cold, menacing building that we disliked immediately. We soon found out why – it was haunted by the ghosts of two former residents. Both had been murdered: one shot in the back of the head by his wife while sitting on a couch in the lounge; the other ambushed by disgruntled staff armed with shotguns. In the case of the husband, the bloodstained couch was still where his brains had been splattered. We hurriedly moved it into a spare room.

Whether one believes in the supernatural or not, there definitely was some weird stuff going on in Bukanda House. Both Cat and I noticed cold eddies of air swirling around at night accompanied by the sound of footsteps. There were other spooky noises, including groans and scrapes that were certainly not caused by us. We also often felt we were being watched walking from one room into another.

Adding to the chilling atmosphere was the incessant rasping squawks of a pair of crows nesting in a high gum tree outside our bedroom. This was not helped when one night a wind howling like a banshee blew a chick out of the nest and it was killed by our dogs. The cantankerous crows now upped the volume even higher, screeching for vengeance as they dive-bombed Landa, Makhulu and Manzi.

I have lived with the supernatural for much of my life and accepted the unhappy spirits that could find no rest at Bukanda, but it was awful for Cat. She never settled in that dark and brooding house on the hill.

Then serial rhino poaching, which had already kicked off in Mpumalanga, flared up in Zululand. Among the initial victims was our immediate neighbour and part of the greater Thanda system, the Mduna Royal Reserve. It was a community-owned project that had been given a couple of rhinos by KwaZulu-Natal's flagship reserve, the Hluhluwe–iMfolozi Park. Poachers struck swiftly and brutally, killing and dehorning one within two months of its arrival. Although rhino poaching around the entire country was going ballistic, the locus in KwaZulu-Natal was where we were.

Ominously, at this crucial time I once again inherited a 'trusted' sergeant in Thanda's APU as my right-hand man. I had doubts about him from our first meeting. It was nothing concrete, just a gut reaction … a sixth sense honed from years in the bush. Something was not right; his smile was phony, his body language shifty, his eyes darting when I spoke to him. He reminded me of the sergeant at Sabi Sand Wildtuin who turned out to be the reserve's most prolific poacher. I decided to be on high alert whenever this guy was around.

My misgivings increased when the first rhino on Thanda was poached. It happened during my first weekend off, and as I had a friend visiting from Durban, we spent the Saturday morning riding motorbikes down the valley leading to the river on Mduna Royal Reserve. Consequently, my sergeant was in charge of rhino monitoring duty. We soon discovered one was missing.

Two days later, we found the animal's maggot-infested carcass. Rigor mortis had set in and its horns had been hacked off. I called the reserve manager and it was a bleak moment inspecting the gory crime scene. While I might have been overly suspicious in my distressed state, to me it seemed a little too coincidental that we lost our first rhino the moment I was out of the way. And on my sergeant's watch.

Then, to my astonishment, I was fingered as the chief suspect. As my friend and I had been riding bikes close to where the rhino had been killed, the blame was directed at me. And the person spreading the malicious rumour was – surprise – my right-hand man. The sergeant.

Knowing that I was about to be called into a management meeting, I took the initiative and demanded that both I and the sergeant be polygraphed immediately. Bizarrely, that didn't happen, so the black cloud of suspicion hovered. The intensely hostile mood so rampant in conservation circles as the horn crisis escalated meant even the flimsiest accusation of rhino poaching could – and invariably did – destroy careers. It was a case of trial by rumour and this accusation followed me for years.

Knowing full well that my closest colleague was knifing me in the back, I had no option but to carry on doing my job as best I could. The most damning way to silence detractors is to get results, and the key factor in my favour was that our APU was doing effective work by anyone's estimate. After multiple clashes, we were incrementally winning the battle against poachers on Thanda.

One of the more unusual 'punch-ups' happened at night when I heard a shot in the valley below Bukanda House. I could see the lights of the vehicle from where the gunfire had originated, and luckily Jason, a Thanda ranger, was with me. We sped off in a Land Rover with Jason driving down the rutted dirt roads like a Grand Prix champion and me in the back gripping a R4 assault rifle. As we got close, I fired several warning shots, but the vehicle, a Hyundai pickup truck – or bakkie, as we call them – with a closed canopy, did not slow down.

I then shot out the two back tyres. However, the driver sped off on bare metal rims with sparks flying off the stony track, only swerving to a halt after crossing an iron cattle grid earmarking the border of tribal community land.

Jason drove the Land Rover up tight against the back of the bakkie so those inside the canopy could not open the door, while I ordered the driver and his female passenger out of the Hyundai. I did a quick search and found a pistol under the front seat.

Inside the canopy were nine people, eyes wide with terror. To my astonishment, the poacher was also a pirate taxi driver and these were innocent paying passengers who were merely getting a ride from the nearby town of Hluhluwe to their village. Jason and I had absolutely no knowledge of that and I obviously would never have shot at the vehicle otherwise.

As we had no jurisdiction in the tribal lands, I called the police. They arrived two and a half hours later and instructed the traumatised passengers to push the battered Hyundai off the road before releasing them. I thought there would be questions about the bullet-riddled tyres, but none were asked.

The police then arrested the driver and his accomplice and confiscated the handgun. It was later found to be a stolen weapon that had been used in a farm murder a few months previously. The driver, a hardcore criminal, was sentenced to eight years in prison.

That chase and arrest of a poacher who was also implicated in a grisly farm murder further boosted Thanda's APU reputation, and although rhinos were being taken out on other reserves, the poachers grasped that the odds of them being caught by our dogs were not in their favour. Few other reserves were using tracker dogs as effectively as we were at the time. Also, one of the area's most notorious lion poachers was killed in a shoot-out with rangers close to Thanda, which sent shockwaves throughout the poaching community. We took no pleasure from the death of anyone, but if the poacher hadn't fired at rangers, he would probably be alive today. I later found out that this was the same poacher Alwyn and I had tracked – and lost – on the day I was being interviewed for the Thanda job.

In the intensely volatile situation, the consequences of success can backfire, and along with the growing list of people we were bringing to justice with our tracker dogs came increasingly vicious death threats. This is to be expected in rural Zululand where there is a warrior ethos and blood feuds run deep. But even so, the list of sworn enemies vowing vengeance grew by the day.

However, one of the scariest incidents while I was at Thanda had nothing to do with armed poachers, car chases, haunted houses or dangerous animals.

It was a fight with actual zombies.

In South Africa, addiction to *nyaope*, one of the most toxic and dangerous street drugs on the market, is soaring alarmingly. It's a virulent mixture of HIV antiretrovirals, skunk marijuana, crystal meth, mandrax (quaaludes), detergents, bath salts and whatever else is available. Even rat poison. It creates intensely contrasting highs of euphoria and violence.

In America, it's called flakka; elsewhere, it's known as whoonga. But the most apt name for it is the zombie drug, as addicts live in a state of acute stupefaction. It also imbues a user with superhuman strength, and even the bravest think twice about tackling a person who is high on *nyaope*. The madness is terrifying.

It was Christmas Day and I had driven to the outback of the tribal lands on my motorbike to meet an informer about potential rhino poachers. On my way home, I stopped at a cattle kraal alongside a small shebeen. It opened for business at 4.30 p.m. and I decided to wait as I wanted to buy cigarettes. There were about thirty other people outside as well.

I stood admiring some Brahman bulls in a kraal and chatting with the owner when I heard a scream. Startled, I looked up and saw two skinny youngsters, about nineteen years old, dragging a small girl by her ankles into some bushes. She was about to be raped. But what was really strange was that everyone outside the shebeen simply stared. No one made any move to help the struggling child.

Her screams intensified, and I ran towards the youths, shouting at them to let her go. They dropped the girl, then turned to face me. I could see straight away from their dilated, bloodshot eyes and crazed look that they were addled out of their minds. *Nyaope* smokers. That's why the rest of the crowd was hesitant to get involved.

The youths stared at me for a moment. One drew a ratchet lock-back Okapi knife while the other smashed a pint beer bottle, transforming it into a jagged-edged weapon. Then they came for me.

I drew my pistol. This galvanised the crowd and about ten men formed a barricade to block the addicts' way, shouting to them, 'Leave this white man alone. He will shoot you.'

Infused with zombie-like supernatural strength and impervious to pain, the stoned youths charged the human barricade. The bottle flashed, the knife slashed, bricks, rocks and metal pipes flew like missiles as a full-blown street brawl erupted. I watched as a man smashed a thick plank over the head of one stoned youth, which would have knocked any normal person comatose, if not killed them. Blood gushed from the addict's skull, but in his madness he barely flinched.

I had three magazines of ammo on me, and every time the crazed youths attempted to stab someone, I fired a warning shot over their heads. As a deterrent, it failed miserably. In fact, it only served to inflame them even more.

By now the crowd, some of whom were injured, pleaded with me to shoot the wannabe rapists, but I was extremely reluctant to do so. With South Africa's fraught race relations, a white shooting a black will automatically be considered guilty of a racist hate crime.

I ran around the back of a building to reload. I had already fired off two magazines of warning shots and the fight was still raging, with stabbed people screaming and blood spilling in the streets. With a single magazine left, I had to stop this frenzied brawl soon.

Emerging from behind the building, I noticed the zombie with the Okapi knife was about to stab a helpless man lying on his back. I shouted at the addict and he looked up, forgetting about his victim and instead coming for me. That was what I wanted. Aiming at his lower leg to disable rather than kill him, I fired. The bullet sliced through his flapping trousers and passed within a fraction of his skinny limb. He stopped, looking down with surprise at his torn pants.

Then someone shouted, 'Behind you!'

I spun around as the second youth swung a galvanised pipe at my head. I quickly sidestepped and now had both zombies in front of me. Still with murder in their inflamed eyes, I could see they were going to charge again.

'Come one step closer and you will get a bullet in your heart,' I shouted in Zulu.

Miraculously, in the heat of their drug-induced rage, some spark of sanity penetrated their scrambled heads. They stopped. It dawned, at last, that I meant what I said.

As they seemed to calm down, one of the senior community members ran up to me. 'Get out of here,' he wheezed, gasping for breath. 'Now is your chance. We will take action against these youngsters.'

I didn't need to be asked twice. Backing away cautiously, I jumped onto my motorbike and sped off. The devastation was horrendous; people sprawled bleeding in the dirt, screaming and retching in pain. I did not know if anyone had died, but I had done what I could.

The police arrived and tried to make sense out of what had happened. They also visited me at Bukanda House and, although I went to the station to make a statement, as far as I know, no case was filed. The cops, however, did tell me that a woman Cat and I employed was the sister of one of the youths. She never came back to work.

A few days later, I was heading back to the same shebeen and saw one of the addicts walking down the road. Pulling up next to the now sober young man, I got off my bike and confronted him. Without the drug, he was just a scrawny youngster, barely able to hold his own in a normal fistfight. Yet that day he had been an evil incarnate superman. The ferocious strength of madness and savagery defied all logic. I berated him at length, asking how he could respect himself for attempting to rape a child. His response stunned me – instead of appearing contrite, he asked if I could give him a job. He even had his CV on him, proudly holding it out for me to read. My answer to that is unprintable.

The *nyaope* brawl was, albeit indirectly, the final straw at Thanda. Neither Cat nor I were happy there and I was finding it ever more difficult to do my job. On top of the threats on my life from poachers, I had a traitor in my ranks – my right-hand man. I was certain that he was the brains behind the poaching operations at Thanda, but I didn't have enough evidence to get him.

All I knew was that I now had to make some big decisions. Cat and I had come to KwaZulu-Natal to create K9 Conservation, but that had been put on hold by my job at Thanda. No longer. It was now time to shift our own fledgling anti-poaching dog unit into top gear. To do what we had planned to do all along.

I handed in my resignation.

That wasn't the last I heard from Thanda. Three or four years later, the managing director phoned to tell me that the sergeant I had always suspected was indeed the chief poacher on Thanda.

'You are exonerated,' he said.

'How did you find out?'

'One of his relatives was running with a gang of horn poachers and was shot dead in a gunfight with rangers. That opened up a huge can of worms. To cut a long story short, we now have evidence directly linking him to local poaching gangs, just like you always said.'

I clicked off my phone. The apology was too little, too late. The malicious rumours had persisted and the damage to my reputation done.

But it reinforced my belief that, sadly, in conservation it is all too often the most trusted person, the one who works closest to you, who thrusts the dagger the deepest.

16

The Birth of K9 Conservation

K9 Conservation was at last a reality. The paperwork was through and Cat, co-founder, and I registered it as a private security company as I did not want to become part of any NGO structure, dependent on begging and handouts to keep going. We were going to do things our way.

There was still one thing missing, though. Clients.

Then, almost overnight, that changed when a call came from Dave Wright, ecology manager of Singita Sabi Sands. Dave had heard about my efforts to create an anti-poaching unit with dogs and was aware of what Zingela and I had accomplished during my time at the Sabi Sand Wildtuin, which incorporates Singita. He got straight to the point.

'Con, we have big problems up here. Poachers are targeting the reserve and there is trouble all around.'

I had already got wind of this, so waited to see where this conversation was going.

'We're planning on making a significant investment in protecting Singita's rhino population and ensuring the safety of our guests,' Dave continued. 'Would you be interested in taking on a contract?'

Would I? Heck yes!

We submitted a quote for a four-person APU with a three-dog capability. It was accepted. I had my first contract. Not only that, it was with one of the most prestigious conservation organisations in the country – the iconic Singita brand. Singita fittingly means 'place of miracles' in the Tsonga language, and the company operates game lodges in South Africa, Zimbabwe, Tanzania and Rwanda.

Cat and I left Thanda, piling Landa, Manzi and Makhulu with our other worldly belongings into two double-cab Land Rovers and heading north. While a little sad that our dream of KwaZulu-Natal being the base of our operations had failed, if I was honest with myself, I always felt most at home in the spectacular bushveld of Mpumalanga – particularly along the Golden Meridian. So going back with Cat beside me was a wonderful sensation, and we first stopped off at a farm in the Barberton valley belonging to good friends, Dirk and Nicole, to prepare for the new contract at Singita. I was determined that this fantastic opportunity would not go to waste.

Before taking up my new position, I had to undergo an exhaustive polygraph test, and from then on it was all systems go. Singita provided us with a camp hidden in the bush, and for the first time we had a proper base where our dogs had protected kennels and we could start building on our already crack canine team.

Rather like my interview at Thanda where Landa and I were tracking poachers before the ink dried on the contract, Singita was white-hot action from the word go. We were still unpacking on the first night when gun-shots were fired near our base camp. This gave me a good point of reference of where poachers were busy, and the next day I visited nearby villages to make contact with my previous network of Sabi Sand Wildtuin informers.

I always paid for good information, which the *impimpis* in the area remembered and were happy to work for me again.

However, new intel coming in revealed that the situation was far worse than I imagined. Rhino poachers were swarming everywhere, including the Kruger National Park, which shares an open border with Singita, and all reserves right up to Manyeleti in the north were basically combat zones. Demand for horn was insatiable and the syndicates had ordered their gangs to shoot rhino wherever and whenever they could to fill orders. The game reserves in the area were losing several a day in Mpumalanga alone, and this was happening week after week. The poachers were able to disappear into villages that extend up to the reserve's fence line and no one would give them up. The gangsters' grip on local communities was all-pervasive.

There was a security unit already in place on the greater Sabi Sand Wildtuin – the same one I had previously worked for as second in command – so strict rules had to be implemented to prevent 'friendly fire' or what we called 'blue on blue' incidents. But it was obvious that much more work needed to be done to lock the area down. And it was equally obvious that the poachers were using mind games to play both APUs in the area off against one another, fuelling suspicion with carefully targeted rumours. I first realised this when the Sabi Sands APU drove onto our base and their patrol leader grimly strode up to me.

'A rhino has been shot close to your camp. We're coming to look for it.'

The unspoken implication was that we might have had something to do with this, no doubt due to poachers spreading rumours saying exactly that. Hiding my initial shock, as we had only been at Singita for a week, I replied, 'That's not possible. We would know about it – especially if it happened near our camp.'

However, I knew the APUs had to investigate all reports, so said I would accompany them. I watched as they exhaustively searched our new base and the surrounding area without finding any trace of a dead rhino. It was just as I had said.

But it didn't end there, as two days later, a Singita field guide found the rotting corpse of a dehorned rhino in a drainage line some distance away. It seemed likely that it had been killed shortly before the Sabi Sands APU came searching our base. Although poachers also tried to pin that killing on my small unit through disinformation spread by fake *impimpis*, the fact that the carcass was so far from our headquarters meant that the evidence simply didn't stack up. It was nothing more than a psych-ops ruse run by the syndicates to discredit us before we had even started work in earnest. If anything, it signalled they were not happy that I was back with a crack team of tracking dogs. We had clashed before, so these poachers knew of my single-minded obsession in hunting them down.

We wasted no time in making our presence felt, running dog patrols day and night, tracking the rhino herds around Singita like the San hunters of yesteryear as they had followed the antelope migrations. If we weren't patrolling, we were lying low in the bush, silently watching from the shadows. It was hard going in those early days, covering large areas in the middle of a raging poaching war with such a small team and only three dogs. Landa, Makhulu and Manzi were magnificent, and soon afterwards I got another puppy that I named Anubis after the half-man, half-jackal deity in ancient Egyptian mythology. He was a pitch-black German shepherd that Cat had sourced from a highly reputable breeder, and he showed his pedigree right away: tough, fast, tenacious and loyal. I knew I had a winner and Landa immediately took him under his wing, teaching by example tricks of the bush that we humans could not.

We worked long, exceptionally hard hours, as we were such a small team. I always made sure that the dogs were rested during scorching sunshine, but as the poachers mainly operated in darkness, increasingly so did we. We became creatures of the night, catching quick naps during the day and venturing deep into the bush as the sun went down.

Night patrolling in the wilderness is like being on another planet. It's tantamount to putting on scuba gear and plunging into the ocean where you're instantly immersed in an alien environment. At night, birds, bugs, insects, reptiles and rodents come to life that most people have never seen before. It's a dark, vibrant world you wouldn't know existed without experiencing it. It became my world.

Ideally, patrolling at night should be done in pairs, but with our small team, I often had no option but to go out alone with my dogs. I would select a listening or observation post close to where most of our rhino had gathered and hide in nearby bushes with either Landa or Anubis – or increasingly both as Anubis matured. Landa was my conservation dog that I used to detect animals killed or injured by poachers, whereas Anubis, who was learning fast, was my man-tracker. Much of the time was spent as still as a gecko, scanning the bush through night-vision goggles and thermal camera imagery. At times I hastily cocked my rifle, seeing a poacher a mere twenty yards away, only to find it was a termite mound with the same height and thermal temperature as a man.

But most of all, I listened to my dogs. Dangerous game poses an even more lethal threat in the dark than it does in daylight, and Landa and Anubis were my frontline alarm systems – particularly as they too were vulnerable. All predators consider dogs a delicacy, and the biggest worry in this regard were hyenas, as there were scores of them on Singita. A hyena will first go for a dog but will also attack humans. I've heard of three cases where hyenas ripped the faces off sleeping people, one at a lodge where a staff member fell asleep in the TV room with the door open. He woke with a hyena's jaw around his throat, bleeding out and dying before a fellow staff member found him. I'm told the hyena returned later that night for its prey.

Hyenas are extremely cocky at night, and once, patrolling along the old Selati railway line built during the gold rush in the late nineteenth century, I turned around to see a whole row of them following me. The closest was barely two yards away and I blasted him in the face with pepper spray. He gave a sort of weird chuckle as he and the rest of the clan ran off.

Another close call was when I was with Anubis and Makhulu and we heard poachers' gun-shots near the reserve's southern fence. While tracking in the dark, we walked right into a pride of lions. They glared at us, but strangely seemed more curious than alarmed as we hastily backed off. We continued tracking, and to my eternal relief the lions didn't follow. However, that interlude gave the poachers time to escape with a ladder over the fence.

Another big problem is elephants, as despite their enormous size they move so silently you only know they're around when you're surrounded. That's when you need to hightail it – and fast. Fortunately, dogs will almost always alert you to the presence of elephants, as well as buffalo, but you need to be constantly alert. I have lost count of how often I have been warned in the nick of time by Landa and Anubis. Without them, I'm not sure that I would be around to tell this story.

Dogs also have far superior night vision than we do. Although colour blind in our terms, as they only see tonal combinations of yellow and blue, their secret weapon is the part of the canine eye called the *tapetum lucidum*. This is a special layer of reflective cells behind the retina that magnifies visual sensitivity under low light conditions. Dogs also have a much larger pupil than humans, allowing more light to enter the eye. Combine that with their superb sense of smell and hearing, and you have no better ally in the wild at night.

So, take it from me. When a dog lifts its muzzle or cocks its head, you had better pay attention or else have a good life insurance policy.

Equally, dogs rely on us to save their lives. It works both ways. They tell me if a hyena is nearby with full confidence that I will handle the situation. When a pride of lions is around the corner, they stick with me. It's a symbiotic relationship in the purest form.

Another key indicator of danger in the bush is the plover or lapwing, which we call a *kiewiet*. This is one of the few birds that chirp when they see people, but not animals. If I hear the croaky 'krueeet' of a *kiewiet* at the same time Landa or Anubis indicate humans, I know there is going to be some action.

As we started recruiting more rangers and handlers, we expanded our dog units to become a wider rapid reaction force, hitting poachers wherever they were. Each unit has a minimum of two people, and although patrols operate around the clock every day of the year, the most active poaching periods are between half-moon waxing and waning. In other words, four days either side of a full moon, which is still called a poacher's moon in bush circles. However, most syndicates now avoid a full moon as although they can see their target animals almost as clearly as in the day, they know we can spot them just as easily.

The worst night of all is New Year's Eve as every Tom, Dick and Harry in the surrounding villages seems to think it's their solemn duty to let off as many firecrackers as possible. The result is that even the dimmest poacher knows any gunshot is likely to be drowned out by chaotic pyrotechnic displays, so this is the ideal time to let rip at any nearby rhino. No ranger anywhere in the Lowveld celebrates New Year's Eve. We're all out in the bush.

Also, due to the proliferation of villages and rapidly expanding populations around the reserves, there is an increasing amount of ambient light and particularly what I call 'government lights'. These are bright lamps mounted on high towers, presumably erected by the government to deter crime. That may well be the case, but they certainly assist poachers who use them as marker points. Now we do so as well and have actually caught a rhino poacher that way. Early one morning we heard gun-shots ringing out through the bush and another APU radioed through that they were chasing a horn gang who were fleeing in four different directions. We hid in some thick scrub in a direct line with one of the tower lights and grabbed a poacher who ran straight into us using the beacon as a marker.

There is no doubt that spending every night in the wild honed our anti-poaching skills like nothing else. We lived in a world without sun, becoming true nocturnal beings. Our senses adapted to this unlit cosmos; our eyes focused on the changing shades of twilight and dawn, the tar blackness of storms or megawatt full moons, and our ears tuned to the whispers and echoes of sounds in the murk. The darkness became a friend. It was no longer alien. The cover and protection and stillness it provided for poachers was equally available to us. And we were just as expert, if not better, at using it.

It also elevated our dogs to new skill levels as this was repetitive training at its best. Every night would see them doing the same thing the same way, responding and reacting to hazardous situations just as we showed them again and again. Our dogs quickly learnt what to do no matter what happened, and one of the highlights of this was the effective way Landa trained Anubis, which paved the way for the next generation.

Even with the nocturnal proliferation of hyenas and other predators – including gunmen – I always kept Landa and Anubis off lead. But even so, we were in constant communication and they obeyed my every command. A mere sucking in of my lips, sounding like a rat's squeak, would have them instantly by my side no matter what the danger was. I dared not whistle in the bush as the enemy would hear that like a siren.

We became better and better at outwitting the horn gangs. After all, we were in the bush every night and they weren't. One trick was to drive our vehicles into a specified spot and then switch off engines and headlights. As soon as the night became still, we would quietly drive off, this time without lights. The poachers would believe we were where they had last seen us, so avoided that area. Meanwhile, we were waiting for them elsewhere.

They also soon found out that their silenced weapons were ineffective, as our listening posts were so strategically placed that we could hear almost all gun-shots. They tried to modify their suppressors, but it's impossible to totally silence the distinctive 'crack' of a .458 or a .375 and, of course, our dogs were all trained to detect – 'imprint', as we call it – the acrid smell of gunpowder. We knew whenever a rifle had been fired, suppressed or not.

We also used Sirenco strobe lights to confuse them. These were strapped magnetically onto the roofs of our vehicles like a police light, but as we had more lights than vehicles, we sometimes would leave three or four flashing in the bush. These could be seen from miles away, and although the poachers knew some were decoys, they weren't sure which, so it was safer for them to go somewhere else. It was a cunning plan, as Blackadder's sidekick Baldrick would say.

All this eventually started to pay dividends. Singita was now locked down. Rhino were no longer targeted or poached in our area, as the gangs increasingly avoided us and our dogs. They continued hitting other sections of the reserve but left us alone. That is true to this day.

The biggest irony is that when K9 Conservation arrived at Singita, all private reserves in the Greater Kruger National Park system were referred to as 'buffer zones'. Today the situation is reversed. There are so few rhinos left on Kruger that the main congregations are now in the private reserves, with poachers increasingly focused on areas where metapopulations still exist. Kruger is still being infiltrated on a regular basis, as are provincial reserves such KwaZulu-Natal's Hluhluwe–iMfolozi Park, but the poachers are finding it more difficult to locate rhino due to diminished numbers.

Those years that I spent in the bush at night affected me profoundly. I love nights in the wilderness with a passion: the vibrancy that defies the stillness, the tranquillity that can mask extreme danger, the buzz of the cicadas, the sky alive with meteorites and shooting stars so bright that it's almost daylight. However, it has seriously messed up my internal clock. Even today, for me to get to sleep before midnight is almost impossible.

Once we controlled the night, the primary battle for our contracted area of the Sabi Sand Wildtuin was won. But it was a mere skirmish. Rhino poaching was not over by any stretch of the imagination.

However, in Africa you take what wins you can. And in this case, the win, to a huge extent, had been achieved by our dogs.

17

The Ngwenya Gang

Not long afterwards, K9 Conservation was awarded the APU contract for the Othawa section on the north side of Singita. We now had two high-profile contracts and managed to lock down this new protected area relatively quickly, thanks to the extraordinary synergy developing between our handlers and their dogs.

Cat was superb, managing the administrative side of our expanding business, as well as having to spend even more time worrying about me in the bush every night with the dogs. We all lived on the edge in those exciting but extremely stressful days.

I knew we were making good progress when death threats against us started escalating. It was a mirror image of what had happened at Thanda; the more arrests we made, the more intimidation and aggression we faced. The threats mainly involved phone calls on 'unknown' or 'private' numbers, and if I or any of my team answered, there would be vicious abuse, direct death threats or just heavy breathing. This was not only an attempt to spook us; it was also strategic. Poachers often phoned to find out where we were merely by listening to background noise. If the caller heard a vehicle engine or the crackle of a handheld radio, he knew I was driving and probably on patrol and had dogs with me. If he could hear a TV in the background, he knew I was at base. The frightening thing is that with all the new mobile phone apps, callers could also identify which area we were covering. Consequently, I instructed my team that under no circumstances should an unidentified call be answered.

Death threats are par for the course in the poaching world. If you let them get to you, you have no business being here. So, we continued taking the fight to them.

One of our biggest successes was a raid that took out a notorious poacher and the most malicious person I have ever met, Mthobisi Lenox Ngwenya. He looked the part with abnormally wide-spaced eyes that made his vacant, malevolent stare even more disconcerting. Although not a big man, he had a demonic presence and the hairs on my neck stiffened whenever I saw him.

We knew Ngwenya well, as he regularly came through Sabi Sand Wildtuin, either poaching or on his way to Kruger. He often hired Mozambicans from the dirt-poor shanty towns across the border to do his dirty work, and once they had poached a rhino and handed over the horns, Ngwenya would shoot them rather than pay out what he owed. His gang then chopped up the bodies, dumping the pieces into the river to be devoured by crocodiles. Ironically, the Zulu word for crocodile is *ngwenya*.

He was certainly right up there on the most wanted list, and eventually we had the breakthrough I was craving. Our sources told us that Ngwenya's gang had poached a rhino a day or so previously and the police's Provincial Stock Theft and Endangered Species Unit as well as Kruger and Mpumalanga Tourism and Parks Agency rangers planned to raid his headquarters in a nearby village called Mahushu. I was invited along as they knew Landa was one of the best dogs in the area. I also had a recent photo of Ngwenya snapped by a trail camera on our contracted property.

Landa and I met up with the joint operation strike team outside Mahushu as the sun set. The plan was to search Ngwenya's and his five closest henchmen's homes one after the other, using speed and surprise to overpower them, hopefully without shots being fired. All Ngwenya's men had distinctive gang tattoos, either a scorpion, dragon or spider, so would be relatively simple to identify.

The Kruger rangers were led by the legendary Don English, considered one of the toughest wildlife warriors in Africa. This was the first time I had accompanied Don on a rhino horn bust, but I had worked closely with his father, Mike English, documenting San rock art sites in the Stolzneck region of Kruger a decade or so earlier.

The first house we hit was Ngwenya's, but he was not there. Instead, we found him in an outhouse where he was asleep with his girlfriend. We grabbed him, and although he fought back, the policeman in charge of investigations 'persuaded' him not to be so rude.

We then went into Ngwenya's main house and I put Landa to work. Within minutes he had indicated a hidden bowsaw used to cut off rhino horns as well as some bloodstained shoes.

Next stop was the second suspect's house, and we parked about a hundred yards away before storming the property. Landa immediately went ballistic, indicating that bone and blood scent was all over the place. The ground in the yard was also muddy, so it was obvious that the syndicate had recently been washing off any gory evidence from their clothes and equipment.

The suspect, a tall, well-built man who was also in bed with his girlfriend, was extremely aggressive, so the police investigating officer slapped him with an open hand. This was not considered excessive in subduing violent suspects, but I have never seen such an effective slap. The big man went flying onto a glass coffee table, smashing it to smithereens. He decided not to resist physically after that but remained uncooperative.

I called Landa into the main bedroom and he immediately sniffed out a hidden compartment with an opening concealed behind the bed board. Once we had opened that, Landa again went crazy, indicating virtually every section of this secret room was tainted with blood odour. We then found a sophisticated lever-system compound bow with arrows capable of silently killing a rhino and rolls of tinfoil to cover poached horns. Many rhino horns are microchipped and the poachers use tinfoil to prevent homing signal emissions. We also found bloodied shoes, knives, and – crucially – some high-calibre bullets. This was the evidence we needed most. But we needed the rifle as well.

Don English held up a bullet inches in front of the suspect's face. 'Where's the *isibhamu*?'

The man, still recovering from the slap, shook his head. 'No gun.'

Don repeated the question. The suspect repeated his denial.

While this was happening, I noticed that Landa was indicating something on the brick wall of the room. Basically, everything in the house seemed to be contaminated, but Landa was specifically concentrating on the wall. I looked up to the roof. There was no ceiling, just rafters. Nothing could be hidden there.

Landa persisted, eagerly indicating that there was blood scent on the wall.

'Don,' I said. 'I'm pretty sure someone climbed up the wall here.'

Don looked over. 'Is it? I don't see anything.'

I shone the flashlight upwards at a twenty-degree angle. Then I saw it. A faint foot scuff.

'There's definitely something in the roof,' I said, pointing to the tiny mark.

Don nodded and looked at me quizzically. He's a big, beefy man, and I couldn't see him shimmying up the brick wall in a hurry.

'Okay, I'm going up,' I said, pulling myself onto a cupboard and then jumping up to the roof rafters.

While the room we were in did not have a ceiling, the bedroom next to it did. And there lying on the boards were a rifle and two silencers. It was a .340 Weatherby Magnum – an extremely unusual calibre. I know rifles well but had never seen a .340 before. How these poachers got hold of such a rare weapon, I have no idea.

At that exact moment, I heard the suspect again repeat what was now becoming a mantra. 'There is no gun here.'

I shouted down, 'Hey Don, I've got the rifle.'

There was silence.

'What?' asked the police officer.

'The firearm is up here,' I replied. 'A Weatherby and two silencers.'

The cop grabbed the suspect's shirt.

'So, you are lying!' he said, and gave another of his epic open hand slaps.

There was not much the suspect could say to that.

'Pass it down,' said Don.

'I don't have gloves.' The last thing I wanted to do was taint evidence, so the men below threw a pair up. I then handed down the rifle, making sure the barrel was pointing away as I didn't know if it was locked and cocked.

What had happened was that the poachers had killed a rhino the day before and had been standing around the carcass while sawing off the horns. Consequently, the gang member who had climbed up the wall to hide the firearm and silencers had blood on the soles of his shoes. He had left a trail as clear as daylight for a tracking dog as skilled as Landa.

As I handed over the weapon, I received the only compliment I have ever received from the legend Mr Don English, and probably ever will. Even so, it wasn't exactly glowing.

'Well done, Con.'

I had to smile. Coming from Don, who's not the most effusive person around, that's the equivalent of winning the Academy Award of accolades.

From there we went to the next three houses, arrested another two guys, and concluded the operation.

To our intense frustration, Ngwenya and his gang were let out on pathetically lenient bail conditions when they appeared in court, this time with tragic consequences. Some may argue that in this case the judicial system has blood on its hands.

About a week afterwards, the policeman leading the investigation into Ngwenya's rhino poaching activities left his office to drive home after work. As he pulled up to his house, Mthobisi Lenox Ngwenya emerged from the darkness and shot him seven times with a 9mm pistol at point-blank range. The cop, a lead investigator and hero in the anti-poaching struggle, died horribly in front of his wife and young children.

The gloves were now off and an intensive manhunt launched. Ngwenya was captured and charged with the murder of a policeman. While awaiting trial, he allegedly hung himself in his cell.

That was the end of the Ngwenya gang. As far as I know, only one is still alive. Of the three other members we arrested, one was shot dead while poaching in Kruger, another was killed in a car crash and the third was murdered, we think by the community taking the law into their own hands. Local communities are not always on our side in hunting down poachers, whom they sometimes consider to be Robin Hood-type characters, so this guy must have done something diabolical to incur their wrath.

I was not surprised. To give an example of the breed of person we were up against, any sane person need look no further than another prominent poacher in the area, whom I'll call Jackson.

Like the Ngwenya gang, Jackson was high on our most-wanted list, and one night one of my rangers, Morné, reported a hole cut in a fence in the area he was patrolling. Morné had been a nightclub bouncer and debt collector before joining K9 Conservation and was a good guy to have on your side in a fight. However, he often said to me that he 'had done some bad things' in his life and was sorry. I just remarked that he was now doing good things for conservation, and so should rather regard himself as a good man.

I hightailed it to the fence but was in such a hurry I didn't have time to call my dogs. Instead, I radioed another APU company at Sabi Sands to come and assist.

Morné was waiting for me and soon afterwards two other security men arrived. We walked along the breached fence when suddenly one grabbed my arm.

'Hear that scuffling in the grass?'

I suffer from tinnitus, having been around firearms for so long, so shook my head.

'Listen,' he whispered, pointing directly ahead. We crept to where he was pointing and I saw the grass move slightly. It was a man.

There's big trouble here, I thought. We were all cocked and loaded – one bullet in the chamber – and I hissed to Morné and the backup guys. 'Stay down, stay down!'

We eased forward cautiously, ready for the inevitable firefight, when a man crawled out of the chest-high grass.

'Don't move or we'll kill you,' I shouted. He immediately obeyed, and as I put handcuffs on him, I smelt urine. He had wet his pants in fright.

I then saw his rifle. It was lying in the grass, cocked and pointing in our direction.

'Why didn't you shoot us?' I asked.

'I was too scared,' he said.

Indeed. His soaking pants told the story even more graphically.

His rifle was a .270 Winchester Magnum, usually too small for thick-skinned game like rhino, but even so, he admitted he was with the horn poaching gang we were after. The rest had fled when they heard us coming, but Jackson had been too terrified to stand in the tall grass and got disorientated, crawling instead towards us.

We called the police, who arrived at about 2 a.m. and took him to the cells. However, I forgot to give the cops my handcuff keys, and the next morning I got a call from an irate police captain.

'Conraad, come and fetch your handcuffs. I had to wrench the bloody things off the suspect myself.'

When I next saw Jackson, he still had bandages on his wrists. The handcuffs had not come off easily. In fact, when I got them back, they looked as though they had been worked over by the spoon bender Uri Geller.

To the surprise of no one, Jackson was released two days later, paying chicken feed for bail. I then heard that while awaiting trial, he allegedly raped a seventeen-year-old girl in Hazyview, one of the main towns on the south-western border of Kruger.

I'm not sure what happened after that. All I remember is putting handcuffs on a coward who peed in his pants and then went on to allegedly rape a teenager.

As I kept repeating, we might live in paradise, but at times we deal with hell.

18

A Sad Farewell

After almost two years at Singita, we were getting to where I wanted the company to be. We had a reputation for doing our jobs efficiently and getting results.

Also, our dogs were regarded as being among the best in the business, while our handlers were level-headed and followed the letter of the law – despite syndicates knowing how to work the system by using every cynical trick in the book. We only fired in self-defence, but that didn't stop poachers from always claiming we were the aggressors, or that in any arrest we had used 'excessive force'.

However, a key factor in our success rate was without doubt our links to the underworld through an ever-expanding network of informants. Accurate intelligence is crucial in winning this war, so we put a huge amount of energy and money into information gathering. Without that, we would be on a hiding to nothing.

Running an effective spy system is a vastly different skill to chasing criminals in the sticks. It's basically a game of chess in a maze, made even more intense as both sides have *impimpis* providing strategic information. Whenever we made a tactical move, the syndicates responded with a counter-move. And vice versa. They were watching us as carefully as we were watching them.

The result of this is that it is often almost impossible to know who to trust. Some seemingly reliable sources often turn out to be double agents – or, even worse, triple agents, working for multiple poaching syndicates.

To counter this, we initially treat every source as questionable, feeding them deliberate misinformation or doing false flag operations to see if anything trickles back to the syndicates. If it does, we know who the traitor is.

In any event, all *impimpi* information is double checked, and we assess which is most accurate and work on that. We also take extremely good care of our trusted sources, for obvious reasons, rewarding them well and reimbursing all expenses. Their safety is paramount and only a source's handler has access to his or her file that is kept in a locked vault. These people live on a knife's edge and, if caught, they will be tortured and die a horrible death – just as any spy would.

This combination of accurate intelligence and a rapid canine strike force paid off handsomely and K9 Conservation got another prestigious contract at Makalali Private Game Reserve, a Big Five park outside Gravelotte in Limpopo province. I couldn't handle that one personally, so luckily for me, my old friend Pete agreed to take over management of the APU on this twenty-five-thousand-hectare registered protected area. He had been the former game ranch manager at Bongani and it was he who had advised me to leave after I had been in a brawl with a Mthethomusha ranger almost ten years ago. When I heard he had left Bongani, I snapped him up.

We now had three prominent contracts, and poachers knew that if they came into our spheres of control, we would set highly trained dogs after them. The odds were too high that they would be caught. The clearest indication of this was when we noticed that rhino from the other parts of the reserve started congregating in areas we patrolled, sensing it was safe for them. We had, so to speak, got a vote of confidence from the rhinos themselves. For me, that was the most satisfying yardstick of how successful our dog teams and their handlers were. It was also good for the game lodges, as visitors were assured of seeing these magnificent, highly threatened creatures in their natural habitat.

However, rhinos were dying elsewhere in alarming numbers, some with international repercussions for South Africa's tourist industry. For example, in July 2012 two game vehicles loaded with foreign guests excitedly drove up to view a large rhino bull on a reserve east of Singita. Unbeknown to the trail guides, the bull had earlier been shot by poachers and proceeded to collapse and die, agonisingly, in front of the traumatised tourists.

In another incident, also outside our contracted areas, tourists were avidly watching a pride of hunting lions circling something in the long grass. Suddenly a poacher in a full ghillie sniper suit stood up, pointing his heavy-calibre rifle at the big cats. The lions had actually been stalking him.

Seeing the poacher's weapon, the guides hurriedly reversed their vehicles, which distracted the lions, and the gunman escaped. That's how cocky these guys are.

Consequently, even though we were getting the upper hand in our areas, the poaching epidemic still raged around us. This meant we could not for an instant relax or cut down on patrols. On the contrary, we had to be even more alert. If we lost what we had fought so hard to gain, it could be irretrievable. Needless to say, the stress of night work, stake-outs and endless vigilance continued.

This never-ending grind of conflict was physically and psychologically gruelling for all of us, but particularly so for

Cat. On most nights, she had to wait anxiously at base camp while I was on patrol, not knowing whether I was in a firefight or being eaten by a lion. Sometimes I would be gone for thirty hours at a stretch with no communication as I didn't want to alert poachers. Just as it is often harder for a combat soldier's family than for the soldier himself, so it was with Cat. She lived with this soul-sapping, unrelenting uncertainty every day.

Apart from that, the hassles of managing a security company and the myriad arcane rules and regulations that have to be complied with are overwhelming. Paperwork is not my strong point, so the huge responsibility for the smooth running of the business sat squarely on Cat's shoulders. And it was horrendous, as any security company will attest. Every day she had to wade through an Everest of red tape, from updating firearm licences to writing laborious legal reports outlining every miniscule detail of any shot fired on a patrol, no matter how inconsequential. It is extremely worrying that people on the right side of the law are the ones subjected to mindboggling bureaucracy while the criminals play the victim card.

Cat always had a hot meal ready no matter what time I came home – invariably filthy, fatigued and jittery after run-ins with armed poaching gangs. She also regularly took coffee out to our exhausted teams patrolling in the bush. There is no doubt that we would not have been able to operate as effectively as we did without this amazing woman.

But the cost was high. Too high. No one can live like that without eventually burning out. The constant strain started to take its toll on both of us.

I had hardened and become distrustful and cynical, which I suppose is logical when fighting what is basically a continuous insurgency. As a result, I made up my mind that I didn't want children. I considered it to be irresponsible as the risk was too great that they would grow up without a father. The dangers weren't only the obvious ones of being killed in a shoot-out or by a dangerous animal. I'd already survived an assassination attempt by fellow rangers at Mthethomusha, as well as a rabid dog attack. I had been bitten by a man in a fight who had full-blown AIDS and was probably only saved by an intense course of antiretroviral drugs.

Cat, on the other hand, wanted to settle down with a firm commitment for a more stable life. She had been with me for five years – four of them under huge stress while at Singita – and now wanted a family. She wanted a stable home. She had totally immersed herself in my life's dream in Africa, so understandably in return she expected some compromise. I am the first to accept that her wishes were completely reasonable and justified. The question boiled down to this: would it be too difficult for me to marry and have children and live half of the year in England and the rest in South Africa? Was that asking too much?

In my case, it was. With the best will in the world, I simply could not live in England, even if it was only for six months at a time. I am African; I belong here and nowhere else. This is my home; this is my life. I simply could not give up and leave my path. If I did, I knew I would be chronically miserable. Even worse, I would make Cat miserable. It just would not work.

We both gradually started to realise that, sadly, there was no middle ground. We decided to separate. It was one of the most painful decisions of my life. The simple reality was that our two worlds could not come together.

I drove her to the airport in Johannesburg, shedding several buckets of tears along the way. We hugged for the last time and I watched as she walked off. Elegant, beautiful … then she was gone.

I headed for home with a heavy heart.

19

Owning the Night

The phone rang at 12.30 a.m. It was Pete. He told me to move my butt quickly. They had just been in a firefight with rhino poachers on a reserve west of Hoedspruit and one of the gang had been shot in the gut.

'We've arrested another and paramedics are on the way,' he said. 'But the rest are on the run. So, get here fast.'

We had been after this horn gang for some time. They had killed several rhinos in the Harmony Block area, a rhino breeding enclave between Hoedspruit and the small mining town of Gravelotte, but had consistently evaded us. Then we had a breakthrough. Acting on intel from a trusted source, Pete had taken a team out the day before to wait near one of the reserve's game fences where we believed the poachers planned to enter.

But this was no ordinary fence. It was heavily fortified with sensors and other detection technology, forcing poachers to tunnel their way under it. That's what gave them away, and Pete's team moved in on the sounds of scraping and picking. They waited until the group emerged from under the fence and blocked them in a half-moon arc.

'We shouted at them to drop their weapons,' said Pete. 'Then all hell broke loose as they opened up on us.'

I scrambled out of bed, kitted up quickly and jumped onto my Yamaha XT660. This was the fastest way to get to Harmony Block, some thirty-five miles away. Dodging a few cattle and donkeys that were almost invisible on the tar road, I arrived at the firefight scene minutes after the paramedics.

Peering inside the ambulance, I saw the wounded suspect struggling to free himself from the stretcher straps as medics inserted an IV drip into his arm. He was writhing in pain, but I had no sympathy. This guy had just tried to kill my men and was shot in the stomach when they retaliated. The other suspect, who had to be physically subdued, was groaning on the ground, hands cuffed behind his back.

As the paramedics rushed the gut-shot suspect to hospital, where he died two days later from gastric infections, the police arrived to take over the investigation. In the interim, we called in support from another APU team with a pack of free-running hounds. These tracking packs consist of about nine unleashed dogs, mainly blueticks and bloodhound crosses, that first compete with one another to pick up the target scent and then work together as a cohesive unit, giving chase at top speed. There is no way in hell any person will keep up with them, which was another reason why I had bought the XT660.

The backup APU arrived with their hounds, and Craig, the unit's leader, split his team into two; one to assist the police at the crime scene and the other to track down the remaining three poachers on the run.

We first had to cut through the electrified fence to get the dogs on the trail, and then they were off into the night. It's awe-inspiring to watch a baying and yelping pack in full flight as the sprinting animals howl if they lose or overshoot the scent, then bay like a maniacal choir as they find it again. The bush was too thick to use the bike, so we had no choice but to run behind the pack. It was about two miles to the nearest tar road and the dogs were charging in that direction.

Unfortunately, we were too late. When we arrived at the road, the pack was circling aimlessly, as the poachers had just been picked up by a getaway vehicle. It had been close, and all credit to the dogs.

Free-running hounds can be extremely effective, particularly in the Kruger Park as there are no interior fences and their well-financed APUs use helicopters to follow the dogs, closing the gap fast. However, in the private sector we do not have ready access to choppers, so the chase is an exhausting, hot and sweaty slog through thick bush. There are far more fences on the smaller private reserves, which slows us down considerably, and hounds have been seriously injured charging full tilt into the wire. Also, free-running packs are susceptible to poisoned meat that fleeing poachers throw down. The meat is usually laced with pesticide, either aldicarb or cutworm bait, and is sometimes wolfed down by the chasing hounds. It's lethal stuff – we refer to it as 'two step' because that's how long it takes to kill a dog. Poachers almost got Anubis that way when we were after a gang one night, but luckily I spotted the poisoned meat in the moonlight and hurriedly called him back.

Although we didn't get them all, news of the gut-shot gunman dying and another captured went viral among poaching gangs. Our reputation was spreading throughout the area – not just on our contractually protected reserves.

We decided to capitalise on that, so our units initiated a new strategy. We would now go on the offensive and take the fight directly to the rhino syndicates. We would be proactive, apprehending poachers *before* they killed animals, rather than the old reactive system of catching them afterwards. We were able to do this for several reasons. Firstly, we had one of the best spy network systems in the area, and secondly, our tracker dogs made us one of the most feared APUs in the Lowveld.

But the third reason was even more crucial. We finally had permission to operate outside game parks on joint operations with police wildlife crime investigators. Thanks to good relationships with the cops, we formed a team that could target poachers in their homes or vehicles – in fact, wherever they were – and not only when they came into protected wildlife areas. That was the biggest game changer of all. In fact, this cohesive team, consisting of members from different units working together, was now for the first time catching more rhino poachers *outside* game reserves. In the old days, that would have been unheard of.

It's difficult to prove that even serial poachers have killed a rhino unless caught red-handed with either a horn or blood on their gear, so we instead got them for illegal possession of firearms. In many cases that's better, as not only does it mean we don't have to have a mutilated carcass as evidence, but possessing an unlicensed big-calibre weapon sometimes carries a stiffer sentence.

After a couple of years, we had the highest arrest rate of poachers in the Mpumalanga and Limpopo provinces for a private security company. Just as important, by going on the offensive we were grabbing more horn poachers on their way to kill a rhino rather than having just done the dirty deed. That alone saved the lives of many animals.

However, I always had to keep in mind that the lives of our people and dogs were paramount. It's easy to forget that in the heat of a chase, particularly when rapidly closing in on these wildlife killers that we detest with a passion. This was a lesson we learnt when chasing a particularly brutal gang in the bush just west of the Kruger National Park.

Once again, the emergency call came from Pete.

'Con – get here now! The gang we're after is on the move. We've identified the vehicle. The TRT and several other APUs are on their way.'

I whistled. The fact that the police tactical response team were involved meant this was serious.

'Where?' I asked.

'At the bridge north of Acornhoek village.'

'See you there.'

I was breaking in a Dobermann cross bloodhound called Hashtag, and this would be his baptism of fire. He seemed to sense that, as his tail was spinning like a 'copter blade when I called him into the Land Rover.

Things did not go as planned at the Acornhoek bridge chokepoint and the poachers escaped by doing a screeching, rubber-burning U-turn, almost running over a police captain in the process. The TRT opened fire, and after a high-speed chase the suspects' vehicle was forced off the road at the junction leading to the Kruger Park's Orpen Gate.

Police then swooped in, arresting one of the gang who had been shot in the hip, while the others fled into the bush. We hastily formed a five-man tracking team with Hashtag as the lead dog. Hashtag immediately took the scent, and any doubts about my new dog's tracking skills were dispelled when I saw a woollen cap on the ground. A branch or thorn had ripped it off a suspect's head, confirming we were right on their trail.

However, it was painfully slow going, the bush so clogged by razor-sharp sickle bush thorns that it was almost solid. I couldn't see more than a couple of yards ahead, relying exclusively on Hashtag's phenomenal sense of smell. But we had no choice other than to barge through that thorny hellhole if we wanted to catch the fleeing gang.

What made it even more scary was that the virtually impenetrable scrub forced us to track in single file, which meant everyone's locked and loaded firearm was pointing directly at the rear end of the person ahead. Usually we track in a Y formation to prevent this, and I cautioned the team to have safety catches on and shield their trigger guards with their hands to prevent a branch or thorn snagging the triggers.

We stopped a few hundred yards further on, and as I turned to consult with the group, I saw everyone's face and arms were ripped and bleeding from multiple thorn scratches. To make it worse, it dawned on me that the suspects would be bleeding just as profusely.

That was another scenario altogether – and even more frightening. What if one of them was HIV-positive? If so, his infected blood would be smeared over the same thorns that were ripping us open as we were following directly in their footsteps. It's no secret that AIDS is rife throughout Africa.

I had a quick discussion with the ranger directly behind me and we agreed it was madness continuing the chase. We knew the three suspects on the run were armed and there was an extremely good chance we would be ambushed at close quarters in the dense bush. Add the possibility of someone being accidentally shot in the butt or catching AIDS from blood-soaked thorns and it was just a disaster waiting to happen.

'We're calling it off,' I said. There was no argument from the rest of the guys, despite our extreme disappointment.

Hashtag had done exceptionally well on his first major assignment in some of the worst terrain imaginable, but I think even he was happy to crawl out of that thorn-infested thicket. Sometimes we win, sometimes not, but it was with careful consideration for everyone's safety that we took the right decision that night.

In any event, one suspect was already in custody, who had to have a bullet removed from his hip at taxpayers' expense. Not long afterwards, the TRT rounded up the rest of the gang. Not much surprises me these days, but I must confess I was a little bemused to hear that the gang leader was a preacher at a local church. That was his day job – a classic case of praise the Lord and pass the ammunition.

He was let out on bail on his first court appearance and I'm not sure what happened after that. Maybe he is still a man of the cloth.

But one thing is for sure, he's responsible for creating a bit of hell in a dwindling wildlife paradise.

20

Caught in a Snare

Isn't Liverpool supposed to be in England?

With three large areas to patrol, as well as accompanying police by taking the fight outside the reserves, we now faced a major staff shortage. From starting out in 2012 with four people, two Weimaraners and a Malinois, we had grown beyond my wildest dreams. We now urgently needed more handlers, dogs and equipment.

However, finding good staff is no easy task as top-level handlers and trained dogs are in high demand. This shortage was aggravated by the increasingly intense poaching battles and the high turnover, as well as burnout, of both dogs and handlers. Anti-poaching dogs have a working life of perhaps ten years as they operate in extreme heat and hard terrain, and the handlers and rangers we employ have to be exceptionally trustworthy. Poachers continuously attempt to bribe our people, so we're constantly on guard for internal as well as external threats.

To overcome this skills deficit, we needed to start training dogs and handlers for our own needs. But this was expensive and time consuming, and might detract from our core business of catching poachers and conserving wildlife.

I then had what I considered to be a brainwave: to pay for this, why not take it further and train dogs and personnel for the wider anti-poaching industry as well? An expert tracking dog costs about R150,000 (about £6,150), so it would be good business and a natural extension to K9 Conservation's area of expertise. It would also work both ways as we would not only be catering for our own requirements, but creating a new generation of dogs and handlers specifically primed for counter-poaching operations.

We couldn't do this at our busy Singita headquarters, so I started looking around for a new base. I knew exactly what I wanted: a small farm where I could build kennels and training facilities, but also large enough to accommodate our retired animals. We never got rid of any dog just because his or her working life was over.

An ideal property soon came up. It was a twenty-one-hectare smallholding in a rural district called Liverpool near Hoedspruit, a bustling adventure-tourist town in the heart of classic big game country. Foreigners come to Hoedspruit from around the world to experience this magnificent bush haven and many have built luxury eco-homes in the surrounding wildlife estates. One of Hoedspruit's warthog families has become so accustomed to humans they saunter in and out of high-street shops.

Hoedspruit is also central to one of the most scenically phenomenal areas of South Africa. The Kruger National Park is just over forty miles to the east, while the Blyde River Canyon, a valley carved by the gods below the Drakensberg escarpment, provides a breathtaking western backdrop. The sixteen-mile-long Blyde is a green canyon dominated by subtropical bush – unlike Arizona's arid Grand Canyon – and is considered to be one of the world's most outstanding natural sights. And the property I was interested in had arguably the best view of all, nestling on a ridge overlooking this majestic range. With some financial assistance, I was now the proud owner of a small bush farm.

This meant I would have to leave Singita, so I asked Rory Guthrie, a respected anti-poaching expert and safari operator, to manage our operations there and at Othawa. Rory was already working for K9 Conservation at Singita Lebombo in Kruger, so this was essentially a transfer. He's a former professional hunter and has walked deep along Africa's bush trails. It is those hunting skills, honed in the most demanding environment, that make him such a formidable anti-poaching operator. Our paths had crossed many times over the years and the opportunity to work together has been one of my most satisfying moments in conservation. We formed a partnership agreement on a profit-share basis where he could also pursue interests in another company he owned, Eastern Wildlife and Security Services.

Pete was currently managing the APU contract at Makalali, so with two excellent men running our flagship contracts, I moved onto the new base at Liverpool to set up the next phase of K9 Conservation.

Why is there a district called Liverpool right in the middle of an iconic expanse of big game bundu? Good question, and the answer is shrouded in imperial quirkiness rather than geography. More than a century ago, the old transport ox-wagon trails zigzagging precariously down the Drakensberg Mountains ran through this area, and as it was so sparsely populated, the colonial administration handed out expanses of land to pioneers from Britain. The new owners named their farms after their hometowns, resulting in wild bush somewhat incongruously being called London, Derby, Portsmouth … and Liverpool. As the years went by, these properties were subdivided and sold off, but the original names remained. However, Africa being Africa, my home in bushveld Liverpool is as far removed from the birthplace of the Beatles as a tabby cat is from a lion.

Being used to living in massive ranges of wilderness, I initially felt a little claustrophobic with only twenty-one hectares, but the plan was to secure further contracts and expand into more virgin bush. However, there were far more pressing problems in the interim – mainly the severe problem of bushmeat poaching on our doorstep. Commercial bushmeat poachers use many barbarous killing methods, but wire or cable noose snares set across game trails near water sources is the most common and brutal. These bush garrottes kill indiscriminately, and an excruciating death comes fast or slow, depending on which part of the body is caught. 'Lucky' animals snared around the neck are strangled relatively quickly, but if a limb is snagged, the struggling creature invariably dies agonisingly from thirst.

I was called into action soon after moving into my new home when a neighbour phoned one night saying he had seen poachers on the next-door game farm.

I jumped onto my motorbike and sped into the bush. It was a poacher's moon, bright and full, and I saw the intruders heading north for the Olifants River. I needed to catch them before they crossed the river, so got off my bike in the thick bush and started sprinting.

The next thing I knew I was flat on my back, yanked so violently that I thought a leopard had grabbed me.

'What the hell!'

Then I saw it. It was no leopard. Instead, a cable snare had clamped around my ankle like a steel jaw. For the first time in my life, I was trapped like a wild animal.

These nooses are constructed in such a way that two interlocking knots crimp into each other and are impossible to loosen by hand. The more you struggle, the more the knot tightens. Cursing, I got out my Leatherman, a ranger's most valuable tool, and spent the next half-hour painstakingly cutting myself free.

This was it. No more Mr Nice Guy. The battle lines were drawn and I decided to do what I do best. I would go all out for the bushmeat poachers with the full resources of K9 Conservation.

Although the poachers escaped, I knew exactly where they had come from. It was a village called Finale, the centre of the meat poaching industry in a ten-thousand-hectare community-owned area on the northern side of the Olifants River bordering Liverpool. The fact that the criminals had been running for the river was enough indication.

The next week I paid a visit to the village headman. It's vital to have good relationships with leaders of settlements in rural Africa, and anyone who ignores this does so at their peril as many are no-go areas for white people. Their vehicles are stoned, burning tyres are set up as roadblocks and those foolish enough to venture uninvited or without massive backup are lucky to come out unscathed.

The headman was friendly enough and we spoke about the health of his family, the forthcoming rains, how the crops were doing and other formalities that precede any conversation in the outback of Africa. I then got to the point, saying that there had been poaching incidents in Liverpool that we needed to address.

The headman looked suitably surprised, but we both knew that was just theatrics. However, he agreed to call a meeting the next week and 'interested parties' – in other words, the bushmeat poachers – would be invited to attend. This was a significant concession on his part, but I don't think he was too worried about any meaningful outcome as I would be severely outnumbered. The meeting had also been sanctioned by Kruger to Canyons, a non-profit biodiversity company promoting sustainable use of natural resources on which people's livelihoods depend, and their representatives were there to assist.

As it turned out, about eighty villagers pitched up for the meeting, and to show I meant business, I also brought Anubis along. As black as night, he certainly looked menacing, and I could see the suspected poachers eyeing him warily.

I introduced myself and K9 Conservation, saying we were an anti-poaching security company and it was our duty to protect wildlife, as well as the land and the people in the area.

'Okay,' I then said. 'Now you know who I am, my message is simple. From now on, the wholesale slaughter of bushmeat has to stop. Immediately.'

This might sound confrontational, but these hard men knew I was not there to be their buddy. There was no point in pretending otherwise, and showing fear or hesitation is considered weakness. In these rough neighbourhoods, the meek do not inherit the earth. You have to put your case forward with unshakeable self-confidence.

Although I kept my tone friendly, I did not mince words. I said that my company would now be patrolling the area regularly, and those caught killing wildlife would be arrested and jailed.

'Especially if we catch anyone killing animals to sell for bushmeat,' I warned. 'That will be a big problem for them.'

This was a crucial point, as we would be more lenient on those who hunted only to put food on the table for their families. But most – if not all – of the audience that day were commercial bushmeat poachers. Very, very few in the village were purely subsistence hunters.

Consequently, I stressed that if poachers ran into our rangers in the bush, they should immediately drop their weapons, as any aggression would trigger a proportional response from my well-trained men.

'My people are armed with semi-automatic rifles and will not hesitate to defend themselves,' I said. 'I cannot say that strongly enough.'

I paused for a moment. Then added, 'And they have dogs.'

Throughout my short speech, Anubis was superb. Whenever a poacher raised an arm to ask a question, the German shepherd lifted his upper lip, baring his fangs.

Pointing to him, I said, 'If anyone thinks it is wise to run away from an arrest, I hope they can run faster than a dog or can climb high trees.'

My final message was more amiable. 'My friends, we all live here. We have to coexist together. I am sure we will all get along well with mutual respect towards each other.'

Before I left, I gave those present my unregistered mobile phone number and said anyone assisting with accurate information in apprehending poachers would be financially rewarded. I needed local *impimpis*, and addressing a gang of poachers was as good a place as any to start.

The game was on. And boy, did things get interesting from there on.

21

Showdown with Bushmeat Poachers

I returned home to wait and see what would result from the Finale village meeting. I had played my hand and it was now up to the poachers to make the next move.

I wasn't sure what to expect but was pleasantly surprised to find that illegal hunting suddenly went quiet in the district. I was not naïve enough to think that this was anything more than a lull in the storm, or that the bad guys were cowering in their homes. These men are some of the toughest I know – bloodied bush veterans of numerous clashes with Farm Watch and police anti-stock theft units.

Instead, we were in the eye of the poaching storm – a period of eerie artificial calm as the gangs tried to figure out how our dog patrols operated and how to evade us. Just as we used *impimpis*, so did they, getting information from rogue rangers and threatening labourers or cattle herders. They were watching us, just as we were watching them. When they were ready, chaos would reign once again.

During the lull, I focused on building up my own list of sources as well as completing dog training facilities at our Liverpool base. The kennels, generously sponsored by

Kwikbuild Cement's CEO Brian van Aswegen, were now ready and I believe the best anywhere in the country. They were huge, consisting of six twenty-seven-yard runs and eight times roomier than almost any other similar facility. I wanted to keep our canines happy, as five Weimaraners, four German shepherds and a Malinois were already on the property, with more to come.

Then suddenly the uneasy truce was over. It was late one night when Anubis, lying on the floor next to me, gave a low warning growl. I knew that particular pitch only too well. He had caught a whiff of human scent. A split second later, Landa, Zingela's son, also looked up, the hackles on his back bristling. He too could smell humans.

That was all the confirmation I needed. I switched off the inside house lights, put on body armour and grabbed a rifle before slipping outside and melting into the darkness. Both Landa and Anubis at my side indicated that the intruders were north of us, about two hundred yards away on the border of my property. The border facing Finale.

I motioned them to be quiet and, listening intently, heard muffled voices. Definitely *nagloopers* (night walkers), our word for trespassers with evil intent. They had come to test my alertness and see what I would do.

They soon found out. Shouting that I was about to shoot, I emptied two magazines of warning shots, firing at a forty-five-degree angle into the ground in the general direction of the unwelcome visitors.

The crackle of gunfire echoed throughout the valley, then everything went silent. Even the toads in my koi pond stopped their incessant croaking. The *nagloopers* had dispersed. I quickly sent out a WhatsApp message informing the Liverpool Farm Watch group that the gunfire was merely warning shots and there had been no contact.

I knew the *nagloopers* would be back. And sure enough, several nights later I got an urgent call that some men had broken into a farmhouse about three miles to the east. Bushmeat poachers are opportunists, just as happy committing armed robbery as they are killing wild animals.

I whistled for Anubis and called a field ranger, then drove down the mountain to a gate on a property that I figured would be the gang's most likely escape route. The three of us hid in the dark.

Soon afterwards, four men came stealthily down the dirt track. I could see them silhouetted in the moonlight and they also had a scrawny *Canis Africanis* with them. Definitely poachers as well as housebreakers.

I fired a warning shot, shouting at them to stop. They immediately bomb-shelled, splitting up and bolting in different directions. I let Anubis off his lead and the big dog was off like a wolf. A minute or so later he cornered a suspect who had dived into some thick sickle thorn bushes.

'If you move, I will set the dog on you,' I said. He remained dead still.

'Okay, now come out,' I ordered.

As he emerged, I saw to my astonishment that he was wearing a K9 Conservation T-shirt. These are only issued to our staff and I quickly shone my flashlight in his face. He was definitely not one of our employees. I angrily ripped it off him.

'Where did you get this?' I demanded, holding up the torn shirt.

The answer was the last thing I expected. Instead of some elaborate explanation, he merely pointed to my field ranger.

'What the … ?' I turned to face the ranger.

'We are neighbours,' the ranger said, giving me the man's name. 'He must have taken it from my house.'

I turned back to the suspect. 'Is that correct?'

He nodded. I briefly wondered if that was purely coincidental but pushed the thought from my mind.

As I interrogated the suspect further, the field ranger suddenly squashed his burning cigarette out on the man's bare chest. I wasn't sure whether this was to make the suspect talk or because the ranger was angry about his stolen shirt, but I quickly pulled him off. The last thing we needed was to be accused of torture, resulting in the suspect going free and us in jail.

Although we had only captured one, it was enough. I wanted information more than anything else. But we'd struck it lucky as the guy we got was a prominent poacher in the area.

'Okay,' I said. 'I know your name. Now tell me the names of your friends.'

He stared back sullenly. That was going to be my biggest problem – getting this guy to talk. Even an extremely painful cigarette burn was not enough to make him spill the beans and any more physical 'persuasion' was not an option. All we had on him was that he had run away while I was investigating reports of a burglary.

I then noticed he was no longer looking at me. Instead, he was watching Anubis straining on his lead. I let the dog get closer.

'Tell me who your friends are,' I repeated.

The man took another look at Anubis's bared teeth barely a yard away, glinting in the moonlight.

'Or would you rather have a talk with my dog?' I asked.

That, more than anything else, tipped the balance. With eyes as wide as Frisbees, the verbal floodgates opened and he started singing louder than the proverbial canary. I quickly scribbled down names and addresses in my notebook, and the suspect also confessed that he and his friends had just tried to rob a house nearby. From what he was saying, I suspected he belonged to the same group I had chased a few weeks earlier when I was caught in a snare. This was a big fish, all right.

'I now want the names of the important poachers in Finale,' I said. 'Every one of them. I want to know where they live.'

He continued talking as if his life depended upon it and, with Anubis nearby, he probably thought it did. When we had pumped him for all the information I could get, I handed him over to the police.

On the way home, I said to the ranger, 'Why did you stub your cigarette out on the man's chest? He's your next-door neighbour. He'll come to your house and slit your throat when you're asleep.'

The ranger just grinned. He didn't seem worried at all, which was curious. Crossing the poaching gangs was not conducive to longevity, particularly when you live in the same village.

I later found out why. My field ranger and the suspect were not only neighbours, they were also first cousins, and there was much suspicion that both were connected to the same gang. I never could pin anything concrete on him as far as poaching was concerned, but later fired him when he was caught smoking the toxic drug *nyaope* on duty.

Thanks to Anubis scaring the living daylights out of the poacher, I now had a wealth of data on the local poaching hierarchy and started cross-checking how accurate this was. It didn't take long to find out that it was spot-on. My information was gold dust.

Piecing everything together, it seemed almost certain that a group of nine men controlled the various Finale gangs. Now that I knew who they were, the next move was to initiate a sting-style operation. It cost a lot of money, but I tasked various sources to get GPS readings of each poacher's house as well as names and identity numbers of all living there. Of particular importance was how many old people were on each property, as the elderly always sleep outside and could raise the alarm during a raid. This is not some elaborate lookout system, it's instead a traditional belief that it's bad *muti* to have someone die inside your home. If that happens, the entire family has to vacate the building permanently or even burn it down. Consequently, grandparents or the terminally ill always sleep outside on porches.

After about two months, I had collected enough data to justify a police raid, along with the names of suspects, GPS locations and head counts. My information was that these guys were so cocky it was likely they would also have poaching equipment, such as snares and machetes, and probably gutted carcasses on their properties. All that was needed was for the cops to go in and I would show them exactly where to look.

To my dismay, the police refused. They said the case was not solid enough. As Finale poachers were 'only' after bushmeat, unless we caught them in the act, any case would be thrown out of court. It wasn't the police's fault. It was just the way the judicial system worked.

Although rhino horn poaching is the country's most high-profile wildlife crime and likely to result in the first extinction of a large mammal since the woolly mammoth, in our view, illegal bushmeat hunting is in fact more serious due to the sheer number of animals slaughtered – far more than anyone thinks. We know this for a fact, as unlike armchair observers, we are right there where it's all happening. We destroy wire snares, gill nets, nooses and traps and see animals killed in the most barbaric ways imaginable every day of our lives.

Sadly, the South African judiciary doesn't agree with us. The courts do not view bushmeat poaching as a major crime and culprits are either fined a pittance or released with a warning. All a meat poacher has to say is his family is hungry and he is basically let off. That's despite hard evidence that the majority hunt bushmeat on an industrial scale to sell at the many wet markets. What also works against us is that meat poaching is not considered 'organised crime' so it is investigated by overworked and under-resourced police anti-stock theft squads, a far cry from the well-equipped wildlife crime units that specifically target horn or ivory syndicates.

My rangers vigorously pursue rhino and bushmeat poachers and, believe me, both are extremely dangerous. Even though meat poachers might not be armed with the heavy-calibre rifles that the rhino cartels carry, they are just as deadly. Some have firearms, but everyone carries either machetes, axes, bows, spears or knives. These men butcher animal carcasses daily and are expert knifemen. They know exactly where the carotid, jugular and vital organs are. They will gut you in a blink, but even a scratch can be life-threatening as poachers' blades are infested with putrefied bacteria from field dressing slaughtered animals. Every ranger is keenly aware of the twenty-one-foot rule made famous in the frontier days of the American Wild West. It's a simple calculation: if a knifeman is within twenty-one feet of you in a fight, you're dead. You won't have enough time to aim and fire a rifle.

Without the police, my proposed raid was a non-starter. Frustrated, I had to put it on hold. There was no other option. I didn't know it then, but that wait would be three long years as poachers continued to run rampant.

In the interim, something far more interesting came into my life.

I met Anke.

22

Meeting Anke

My wise father, Zoltan de Rosner, whose spirit will always be with us as his ashes are scattered in the mighty Olifants River bordering our property, often said to me that those whose paths cross with their soulmates are blessed. He said it might only come about once in a lifetime and you may not even be aware of it. But if it happens, you are truly fortunate.

My path had crossed and parted from Cat's about a year earlier, and I was not looking for a partner. We had split due to different lifestyle choices.

Then I crossed paths with Anke Kruger and I knew from the first instant that she was my soulmate.

I first heard of her when she moved into the area, studying in Klaserie to be a wildlife practitioner and conservationist. It was not just the news that an attractive woman was living nearby. As I said, with Cat gone and the wrench that had caused, the last thing I wanted was another relationship. But a rather intriguing comment that sparked my interest was that she had flaming red hair like the Valkyries of old. She also practised archery from horseback, so closely resembled a warrior goddess. The warrior soul in me had detected the spirit of a warrior woman and I was interested in finding out more about her.

I sent her a WhatsApp message saying 'hi', and then on impulse called her later that evening. We hit it off immediately. The phone call ended at five the next morning.

It would be a few months later, after several lengthy telephonic conversations, that our first date was arranged. The plan was to meet in Hoedspruit on one of her rare days off from studying, and as she was one of the small handful of women in her class, she had plenty of big, beefy fellow students around. Take it from me, Anke does not need guardians, but due to a fairly large age gap, these self-appointed 'protectors' were intensely interested in who this older male suitor was. Most likely, several of them also had the hots for her.

Knowing all eyes would be on me, I arrived armed with copious amounts of beer and cider – literally cases of it. Her brawny protectors' eyes gravitated to my arsenal of bribery and corruption and set about consuming it. The attention shifted from me to the booze, just as I had planned, and I whisked her off while they were distracted. My aim was to show this stunning goddess my Liverpool farm and, of course, the dogs. She did not know that I was the boss of K9 Conservation and I did not tell her. As far as she was aware, I only trained dogs for counter-poaching operations.

Traveling down the dusty road to Liverpool, we passed two sable antelopes. I slowed the Land Rover and remarked, 'What beautiful animals.'

She looked at me as if I had thrown cold water in her face. Then laughed.

I didn't know what to make of this strange response. It was only about a year later that she told me a Bulgarian shaman living in Pretoria had prophesied that she would soon meet a man and when he pointed out a 'beautiful animal' to her, she would recall the shaman's words in that precise moment and recognise him as her soulmate. Those were her exact words. Sable antelope still play a symbolic part in our relationship today.

After showing her the farm and taking the dogs for a walk, Anke got a call from her best friend Carli, who was on the same ranger course, urging her to get back to Hoedspruit. After consuming my gifts of bribery, her 'protectors' had got into a bar scuffle and the Hoedspruit Farm Watch was out looking for them. I quickly called my friends in Farm Watch and told them everything was under control and I would take responsibility for the students. Lucky I did so, as Anke's protectors, burly as they were, would be no match for the even brawnier guys on Farm Watch.

We returned to Hoedspruit and had dinner at Sleepers, the local hangout, and I mentioned to the student rangers that I had just saved their asses from a *pak slae* – the Afrikaans understatement for a serious hiding. All was good between us from then on.

Anke has a deep connection with conservation and is an 'old soul', highly intuitive and believing in the karmic cycle of life. Her first profound connection with wildlife was on a friend's farm when she found an impala ewe trapped in a wire snare. She was about twelve years old and wanted to give the exhausted buck some water that she poured from her bottle into her hand. The friend's father and the vet said she was wasting her time as the animal was too traumatised to drink. Ignoring them, she held her hand under the ewe's mouth and the buck immediately drank, her tongue licking her hand. That awakened something deep and spiritual in her. Although she was not sure what it meant at the time, it was a defining moment.

In 2017 she enrolled in a two-year course to start her conservation career. The key aspect was the anti-poaching section, and that was the job that she really set her heart on and identified as her true calling. Hoedspruit became her heart home.

But to try and get work in anti-poaching units was another story. Everywhere she applied, it was the same answer: the position was for men only. One guy did offer her a job but said she would have to shave her hair off to be 'one of the boys'. He also made it clear he wanted a relationship. When she turned him down, all job offers dried up. It was a male-dominated society, but Anke is stubbornness personified. Ironically, several organisations that turned her down offered her employment in later years. But Anke has established her place in the conservation industry and her loyalty lies with K9 Conservation.

When I met her, she had just rescued a puppy that she planned to train as her companion for anti-poaching. Joining a K9 unit was not part of her original plan, but the universe has an amazing way of steering one in the right direction. Fortuitously, as soon as we met, our parallel paths came together in a remarkable way. It was as if we did not have a choice in the matter. We shared the same adventure gene and warrior spirit. By warrior, I mean a bush warrior. Anke and I work together as a cohesive unit in some very hectic situations. We have total trust in each other. We always have each other's backs. As far as I am concerned, women are just as capable as men in the bush because they use their brains rather than brawn. The crucial reason why Anke and I make such a good team is because of the balance of male and female energy.

However, to say that the beginning of our relationship was all roses would be a lie. In fact, it was more like Guns N' Roses with a dram of gunpowder. The two of us had to learn about a life together and how to balance our fiery personalities. I, for one, have become a lot more hardened since the spiritual days of Bongani as constant battles against rhino and bushmeat poachers have taken their toll. I have inadvertently become a bush warrior dedicated to a life set against the killing of wildlife. Anke feels exactly the same. Having come from a very interesting upbringing – including three armed home invasions when she was only nine – she is as tough as nails, and we happily managed to get our sometimes heated arguments out of the way at the beginning of the relationship.

It takes someone like Anke to not only survive the lifestyle demanded by this environment, but to thrive. She moved in with me in December 2018 and that New Year's Eve, just as we were getting ready to patrol in the bush, we got nasty death threats over the phone from a disgruntled staff member I had just fired.

Welcome to Liverpool.

23

Action Stations Around Hoedspruit

When I first moved to my new base in Liverpool, I offered other game farms in the district our services for free as it would be an extension of what I was already doing: clearing poachers off my own land.

However, I obviously could not keep this up indefinitely, and when K9 Conservation started charging the landowners, many signed contracts with us as they had seen the results first hand. Those who didn't were soon targeted by poachers, and so most eventually came on board. Any unprotected stretch of bush with wildlife today is a magnet for meat poachers.

Farmers are just as vulnerable as game reserve owners, as almost all have wildlife on their land. On one cattle ranch we intercepted poachers' tracks that led straight to the herders' camp where we found several hidden carcasses of butchered impala. We arrested the herders and when we told the shocked farmer, he immediately signed an APU contract with us after firing his staff.

As a result, we were kept busy, but with Rory's and Pete's APUs pretty much clearing out horn poaching in our rhino protected areas, we could concentrate more on the bushmeat problem escalating alarmingly on our Liverpool doorstep. At the time of writing, we have not had a rhino poached on Singita for almost eight years, which even our most ardent critics say is impressive. In fact, today Singita and the central portion of Sabi Sand Wildtuin is one of the finest examples of conservation success in keeping poachers at bay. Our unit based there under Rory Guthrie is incredibly effective and poachers stay well clear of him and his crack team. He is one of the most professional men in the industry, as sharp as a razorblade, and I respect him immensely for his knowledge, efficiency and sheer dedication. Just about every time I call him, he is out in the bush training dogs and handlers. That alone is why this man is so on top of his game.

At Liverpool, we are contracted to protect forty-five thousand hectares of wild bush and farmland on the southern side of the Olifants River. The northern river bank encompasses a stretch of tribal trust community lands, but thanks to a deal with local leaders, we now are able to pursue poachers across the river. Getting that permission was a game changer, as the local community is also badly affected by these criminals, with villagers regularly losing cattle to snares. But even so, it involved countless meetings with the three area chiefs culminating in a contract permitting K9 Conservation to patrol their lands as well as ours. In return, they get our protection for free and it allows us to better safeguard the entire area.

However, just as we are continuously adapting and perfecting our operations, so too are the meat poaching syndicates. As I have said before, it's like a game of chess; as one side makes a move, the other tries to counter it. The more effective we are, the more reactive they become. For example, as we start to get the upper hand in various areas, gangs that formerly operated independently now run a type of roster system. If one gang has a successful hunt and takes a break for a few days, another moves into the temporary vacuum.

Also, beforehand when the Olifants was in flood, poaching would die down as the gangs dared not cross the raging river. No longer. Poachers are now dropped off in syndicate vehicles that cross bridges several miles away.

As a result, there is no respite. The poaching war is incessant. We are continuously removing snares from the bush, and on average, our APUs have some form of contact – whether a firefight, skirmish or chasing gangs with dogs – at least once a week. The true extent of the problem came to light when Anke started keeping diligent records, something that hadn't been done effectively by previous APU managers. Every incident, every shot fired at us, every snare found, every animal killed or maimed, was documented on a spreadsheet, and during one particularly soul-destroying period, we removed six hundred snares in eight hectic weeks. That's an average of eleven a day. When she started sending out these highly detailed reports, the conservation and farming community reeled in shock. We knew we had a big problem, but not how massive it actually was. Without APUs, there is little doubt that much of the magnificent bushveld around Hoedspruit would be devoid of wildlife.

Another ominous trend was some poachers were training their semi-feral *Canis Africanis* hunting packs to attack us. We discovered this on a nearby game reserve one night when an APU cornered a gang at a game fence breach. As our guys apprehended them, the poachers shouted at their dogs to attack. Within seconds, the APU was surrounded by the snarling pack, and while one ranger was frantically fending off the animals, a poacher wielding an axe rushed him. The ranger was unable to defend himself, so shouted at his colleagues to intervene.

However, although the sergeant in charge of the APU had an AK-47, he was standing to the side and legally could not shoot as the axeman was not coming directly at him. If he did so, he could face a murder charge. What to do?

Showing remarkable presence of mind – not to mention rock-steady aim – the sergeant thought to hell with the consequences and shot the axe-wielder in the leg to stop but not kill him. He saved the field ranger's life, but even so, an attempted murder docket was opened as the poacher claimed he had been running away.

Not only were the poachers now setting their packs of dogs on us, but they also once even kidnapped one of our dogs. It happened while patrolling a dam where illegal immigrants from Zimbabwe were gill-netting up to six hundred and fifty pounds of fish a night. We caught them in the act and, as they fled, one of our Belgian/Dutch shepherds called Makhulu was chasing so hard that his handler lost his grip on the lead. Makhulu, now free-running, caught one poacher and bit him on the butt. However, in the wild melee, we lost track of him.

The rest of the gang then grabbed Makhulu's lead and, as he was trained to respond to commands on lead, he thought the poachers were now the good guys. As a result, he calmed down and they took him to their village.

A trained dog is worth a lot of money, but besides that, Makhulu was on loan to us from Pete and there was no way I was going to let these men take him. We were all devastated and I called Pete to tell him the bad news.

We had information that the man Makhulu had bitten was one of the leaders of the fish syndicate, and we knew where he lived. The next day, with the headman's permission, I went into the village with Pete, Anke and a couple of rangers. The suspect was fast asleep when we knocked on his door, which was not surprising as he had allegedly been out poaching all night. However, we couldn't arrest him as we had no concrete proof of this even though he had a bit of a limp, probably from Makhulu's bite. But I had a far more powerful threat. Most Zimbabweans in the village live there illegally.

'You have our dog,' I said to the man. 'We want him back. Now.'

He denied it. I didn't have time to play games. For all I knew, Makhulu might be dead.

'Okay,' I said. 'This is what we are going to do. We have already called the police and if we don't have our dog back by tomorrow, we are coming here with immigration officials. Every Zimbabwean in this village without a work permit is going to be arrested and deported.'

I could see his eyes widening. That was the biggest fear, that they would be deported to Zimbabwe. That news spread around the village faster than a tornado. Many Zimbabweans in the village, illegal or otherwise, had put down roots in the area and were not poachers. The pressure on the syndicate from their neighbours to return our dog would be huge.

Later that day I got a call from one of my sources, who gave me the worst possible news.

'Your dog is dead. The Zimbabweans killed him.'

I clenched my fists and vowed to follow up on my threat. Luckily for the innocent Zimbabweans living in the village, this proved to be unnecessary.

As I was driving to Hoedspruit the next morning, a citrus farmer who lived close to us rang my mobile phone.

'There's a dog tied to a drainage pipe in my orchards,' he said. 'The workers think it's one of yours.'

I swung the car around.

'They've found a dog,' I said to Anke. 'It could be Makhulu.'

We sped back to the farm. Sure enough, roped to the pipe was Makhulu. He was overjoyed to see us. But not as much as we were to get him back, especially Pete who, like us, thought his loyal dog was dead.

However, one of our closest shaves was when our dogs bizarrely *didn't* perform as required. They literally saved Anke and me from being shot by refusing to take a scent – the exact opposite of what a tracker dog is trained to do. I still am puzzled, not to mention grateful, about it to this day.

It was mid-afternoon when a callout came through that a gang of poachers had been spotted on a reserve in the Greater Kruger National Park system, and we took two of our crack dogs, Jock and Hashtag, to beef up the police and APUs giving chase. Anke now came with me on all raids as not only was she one of my most skilled rangers, I trusted her skills more than just about anyone else on my team.

The first thing we noticed when we arrived at the reserve was a shiny Porsche 911 parked at the boom gate – not exactly a common sight in the bush. Even more incongruous was the driver emerging from the vehicle dressed in bling and designer clothes with the price tags still dangling. We immediately thought he was one of the poachers.

I told him we were a security company doing routine searches and asked if he had any weapons in the Porsche. Expecting a denial, this guy casually nodded as if it was totally normal to have firearms on a game reserve. We found two handguns, both cocked and locked, and a rifle in the car.

'Where are your licences?' I asked.

'At home. In Johannesburg.'

'You know you have to carry a licence with a weapon?' I asked.

He shrugged as if he couldn't care less. I was amazed at his nonchalance as he was now in serious trouble. He was not only a suspected poacher, but for all intents and purposes, his weapons were unlicensed. I called the police, who did some checking, and to our surprise, the 'blingster' turned out to be the owner of a game reserve in the area. He got his people to text photos of his firearm licences, so was off the hook.

We then entered the reserve and almost immediately picked up tracks indicating that an elephant bull had chased the poachers and then crashed through the fence, pulling it down. This is where we thought the poachers would be hiding and, as a helicopter was on standby, Pete went up to provide aerial surveillance. There was a lot of odour for the dogs to follow, and with a chopper in the sky, it should have been a slam-dunk capture. It was also late in the afternoon and getting cool, ideal conditions for the dogs to track at speed.

Yet for some inexplicable reason, Hashtag and Jock refused to take the scent. We tried everything, looping them back and forth, putting them directly on obvious tracks, but they simply would not respond. This was completely out of character as when our dogs pick up a trail, nothing distracts them. Yet on this occasion they were not interested. It soon got too dark to use the helicopter and, with the dogs not cooperating, we called the chase off.

It was extremely fortunate that we did. We later heard from a source who had been with the heavily armed gang that day that they had been lying low in the bush barely a hundred yards from us. As they couldn't escape with the chopper circling overhead, they decided their only option was to kill us if we came any closer. They could hear us talking – even saying a woman (Anke) had been there – but couldn't see us in the thick foliage. We didn't know they were almost within spitting distance, and if the dogs had led us to them, Anke and I would have walked directly into an ambush. We would have been shot.

I am not sure what unusual forces of nature were at play on that day. All I know is that both Hashtag and Jock had never before nor since refused to take a human scent.

Although that chase was not successful, it does emphasise the amount of teamwork needed. The call goes out, we respond with Farm Watch and police are there to jail the suspects. To be effective in this line of work, it's not a game of egos. In fact, the complete opposite. We don't care who takes a poacher down –

as long as he's taken down. And one of our biggest partners in this regard is the Hoedspruit Farm Watch. This highly effective organisation was originally formed as a rapid reaction unit to combat crop theft and robberies on farms, but now are involved in multiple other anti-crime operations as well as providing invaluable support during natural disasters such as floods.

I've mentioned below that these guys are also elite bush drivers and would give any professional racer a run for his or her money. In fact, one is an actual rally driver, and the souped-up Hilux bakkie he uses for Farm Watch raids probably goes faster than anything you'll find at white-knuckle events such as the Dakar Rally.

So yes, he's a world-class driver, but even so, Anke and I are always a little hesitant about going on a bust with him, mainly because bouncing around in the back of his bakkie is even more hair-raising than confronting poachers. But on one raid we had no option.

It started with a tipoff that a suspected poaching gang from Gauteng province on the Highveld was driving down to shoot rhinos in the Greater Kruger National Park system. Our information was that they had an illegal AK-47, which would be enough for an arrest. We alerted the police and the Hoedspruit Farm Watch, and about ten vehicles got ready to give chase if necessary. We even had a wildlife investigator on the highway tailing their car, so everything was in place for a clean swoop.

Then the suspected poachers got a flat tyre not far out of Hoedspruit and pulled over to the side of the road. As cool as anything, the investigator stopped to ask if he could help. The suspects looked relieved. Did he have a wheel spanner?

He did, and he helped them put on the spare tyre. He then offered to follow them to make sure the spare was okay and the suspected poachers gratefully accepted, thinking this was normal Lowveld hospitality. Meanwhile, the investigator was busy radioing through to us exactly what was going on. A few miles later, the poachers turned left at a split in the road, and rather than raise suspicion by following them, our man hooted and waved as he drove off. They waved back.

Farm Watch now needed to take over the pursuit, so we raced to where the vehicle had turned off. However, as fate would have it, the suspects blew out another tyre. But now without a spare, they had no option but to get the puncture repaired at the nearest garage. The driver and one man remained with the vehicle, while the other three flagged down a local farmer transporting his workers in a truck.

We arrived to apprehend the five suspects but found only two at the vehicle; they were arrested by the police and their unlicensed rifle was seized. Pete, Anke and I jumped into the back of the Farm Watch rally driver's Hilux to grab the other three before the alarm was raised.

We soon realised this was a ... well, debatable move on our part. At times, our driver was reaching speeds of one hundred and fifteen miles per hour, hitting potholes, roaring past anything in front of him, wheel-spinning around corners and generally having the time of his life. Not so much for us in the back – in fact, we were going so fast we couldn't put our heads out of the side of the vehicle for fear of being scalped by the wind. We just kept low, clinging desperately onto the roll bars and every now and again peeping through the cab's window to see where we were going. A sign at the side of the road warning there was a T-junction one hundred and fifty yards ahead flashed past – which at the speed we were going was perhaps a second away. I closed my eyes – this was it. We would never stop in time.

No problem for our driver. He barely touched the brakes as he took the right-angle turn. We skidded down the road, snaking like a turbocharged mamba, and nearly smashed into another truck, which our fearless driver had no option but to overtake as he was going too fast to stop. That was bad enough – but now we were directly facing oncoming traffic with our driver's foot flat on the accelerator. Somehow, he managed to squeeze between the truck we were overtaking and the stream of cars hurtling directly at us with barely an inch to spare. Anke says that in those few seconds she converted to every religion on offer.

We arrived at the garage in a cloud of smoke and dust and our driver boxed the bewildered farmer in just as he was about to leave. Pete, Anke and I jumped out with AK-47s at the ready and ran towards the suspects who were trying to hide among the farm workers.

'You drive like a pig!' the shaken farmer shouted at us.

'We don't want you,' Pete said. He pointed to the three suspects. 'We want those guys.'

The open-mouthed shock on the farmer's face was priceless. He had no idea he had been a Good Samaritan to suspected horn poachers.

Equally comical was the feigned nonchalance of the suspects, who were trying to blend in with the workers in the back of the truck. Anke pointed her AK at the nearest one and barked, 'If you move, you die!'

She didn't need to say anything else. We handcuffed the men and put them in the back of the Hilux.

As our driver stamped on the accelerator with a vengeance, the suspects' nonchalance was replaced by undisguised horror. I know we were scared, so I'm pretty sure they were even more relieved than we were when we finally screeched to a halt outside the Hoedspruit police station.

24

Profile of a Poacher

Who are we up against? Who are the villains in the struggle to save Africa's increasingly threatened wildlife?

There is no blueprint of a typical poacher. Some are barely literate with limited employment opportunities; others run business empires and are virtually untouchable due to their powerful political contacts. Some have no idea of the harm they are doing; others cynically see the looming extinction of a species as a golden opportunity to hike prices. Some are villagers in tattered rags; others are wheeler-dealers in designer clothes operating from air-conditioned offices. There is no classic psychological profile.

What we do know is that the rhino poaching syndicates operate on five different levels. Level one is where the action takes place: the killing of the animal, hacking off its horns and handing them over to a level-two receiver. This second-level operator is someone who has the contacts and logistical ability to get the horn from the bush gangs and fast-track it to level three, the actual buyers of the raw product. These guys control the supply chain from the moment the rhino is shot until they receive the horn. From there it goes to level four, the men who fund the lower tiers and smuggle the horns out of the country. That's where the big money starts rolling in. The key outlets for smugglers are OR Tambo International Airport in Johannesburg and the Maputo airport and harbour in Mozambique. Many of these operatives are highly placed, and it is believed that horns have even been sneaked out in diplomatic pouches. Level-five operatives are the buyers in south-east Asia who get the product to the end users. Like a Mexican drug cartel, few people at one level know who's in the next. It's a truly multifaceted operation, ranging from sprawling shanty towns to smooth-talkers in suits bribing their way past border controls. That's why it is so hard to cut the head off the snake.

But one thing operators at all levels have in common is that they are hard, extremely dangerous people. To counter that, those fighting them have to be equally ruthless. That's why my days as an eco-idealist discovering ancient rock art and marvelling at the spiritualism of San shamans ended. I still believe in the essence of Africa and that the soul of the San, the world's original environmentalists, lives on in people like me, but I am now a realist – a bush warrior. I have to be. Both my wife and I, as well as many close friends, are said to be on the syndicates' hit lists. I never go anywhere without a firearm, unless I am getting onto a commercial flight or crossing international borders.

The poachers we encounter are mainly level one and two, the low-hanging fruit of the poaching tree. They are the gunslingers, the people in the field who are paid the least and are the most likely to get caught or die in shoot-outs. They are at the criminal frontline, the most expendable, and they are as tough as humans come. They can track animals for hours in blasting sub-tropical heat on a gulp of boiled muddy water. They can live in the bush for days with no food. They sleep on rocks and under thorn bushes. They can carry nearly their bodyweight in rucksacks of poached meat and horn on their backs while on the run.

On top of that, they do not have powerful contacts and multimillion-dollar financial empires to protect them, like the fat-cat criminals on the higher levels. At best, their bosses will hire lawyers to stall any court case and get them bail − pretty simple in the current judicial system − but for many, their firearms are their primary defence. They are not afraid to use them.

I have chased and caught hundreds of poachers, but two stand out: Okubi and Ishi. Okubi, in particular, had been a thorn in my side for ten years. *(NOTE: Both are pseudonyms.)*

When I returned to Singita to set up K9 Conservation in 2012, I immediately activated the group of sources I had used before as second in command of the Sabi Sand Wildtuin APU. One of the first things I noticed was that in my absence a new name − Okubi − kept cropping up. He lived in a village barely a hundred yards from the southern border of Sabi Sands, which meant he could literally walk to work. His particular MO was to use lightweight folding ladders to climb over the game fences of the reserve, avoiding the electric strands. Simple and undetectable, it was incredible how active he was. Rampant poaching was already off the charts, but even so, little seemed to be happening without his name or one of his accomplices being mentioned. For example, we would get a report that Okubi had been spotted buying stuff at a local shop. A day later, food wrappings or packets from that particular shop would be found at a poaching scene. Another snippet was that he regularly wore All Star trainers with distinctive tracks that were regularly spotted inside game reserves − suspicious, even though other poachers wore that brand as well. Also, several sources told us he was hiring out a heavy-calibre rifle to Mozambicans coming across the border. We knew the gun was stashed inside a reserve in our area, but no matter how hard we looked, we couldn't find it. All of this was circumstantial evidence, but it certainly created an incriminating picture.

Then suddenly Okubi disappeared. We didn't hear of him for a couple of months, which was strange seeing that up until now he had been active almost daily. Had he given up poaching to pursue the quiet life?

No such luck. Instead, he had been shot, allegedly by a fellow poacher, and was taking time off to recuperate. Apparently, his gang had been tracking rhino and the designated shooter carrying a .458 Win Mag had an accidental discharge, the bullet smashing into Okubi's leg. Fortunately for him, if not the rhino population, it had been a flesh wound. If the .458 slug had hit a bone, he could have lost his leg.

After recovering, he allegedly continued poaching rhino on an industrial scale, and we heard he had built an underground bunker covered with cinderblocks at his house to stash rifles, machetes, axes and other equipment to slaughter and dehorn the animals. If true, this was the evidence we were after, but unfortunately we didn't have enough proof to get a search warrant.

All we could do was to keep him under close observation – perhaps too close, as he suddenly bolted to another district along the western fence of Sabi Sand Wildtuin simply known as Area. As various other horn syndicates were also said to operate from there, he fitted in well. Through our sources, we learnt that several former rangers from both Sabi Sands and Kruger were also heavily involved in Area's poaching gangs, but to my infinite relief, none of them had been our staff members.

However, Okubi must have got wind that he was on our radar as he was jumping all over the place trying to evade us. Some people are easy to catch and make basic mistakes, but not Okubi. He was the Scarlet Pimpernel in our reserves.

Then one day his luck ran out. He and his gang were allegedly hunting rhino on the eastern side of Sabi Sand Wildtuin and ran into a Ntomeni Ranger Services patrol. These crack rangers are highly trained, and in the ensuing gunfight, Okubi was shot in the shoulder and arrested.

He was released on bail a few days later and took a forced break while his bullet wound healed. From what we were told, he then allegedly started another 'business' scamming bank cards at automatic teller machines in the Area district. We were hoping that we had seen the last of him, but locals got wind of him swindling their life savings and unsurprisingly were unimpressed. He had to flee for his life and allegedly returned to his 'career' of rhino poaching.

Once again, he was on our radar. Catching him became one of my company's obsessions, but I suppose I say that about all poachers. I next heard he had been killed on the Zimbabwe border and that we were rid of him for good.

Or so we thought.

Late one night, K9 Conservation rangers at an observation post at Singita heard gun-shots ringing out across the stillness of the night. Definitely poachers. Rory Guthrie and his team gave chase and soon were hot on the tracks of three men. As they closed in, one of the suspected poachers started shooting at them with an elephant rifle.

Rory then put up a thermal imaging drone to follow them. The men split up and Rory made a quick decision to follow the guy running south-west. It was the right decision.

Drones only have a limited battery life and our one ran out of juice before rangers could catch the suspect. Luckily, another APU also had a drone, so that went up to follow the fleeing man while Rory changed the battery of the first one. They then started leapfrogging drones with the other security team to make sure the suspect on the run was always in sight.

The chase continued for five miles at a blistering pace, an indication of how fit one has to be in the bush. Eventually the suspect reached one of the reserve's lodges and climbed into a water storage tank, thinking his pursuers would not find him there. However, the thermal imaging drone soon picked up the man's body heat and the APU teams surrounded the tank, ordering the suspect to surrender. As he climbed out, Rory thought he looked familiar. Then, to his surprise, he realised it was Okubi. Reports of the wanted man's demise were somewhat wide of the mark.

Unfortunately, one of Okubi's alleged accomplices got away with the elephant rifle. In this game, retrieving a high-calibre weapon is almost as important as arresting the shooter, so we are still looking for it.

But, at last, we had caught Okubi. There was much jubilation, although sadly not for long. At his first court appearance, Okubi was released on a pitifully low bail and walked out of jail as, basically, a free man for the second time. He remains so today, as it is unlikely that his court case will come up within at least five years. That's how backlogged the wildlife judicial system is. But we are still waiting and watching.

Another memorable bust involved one of the biggest alleged poaching gangs in the Lowveld, led by a particularly hard-nosed individual I'll call Ishi as he still has other cases pending against him. For us at K9 Conservation, this was personal as Ishi had allegedly killed four rhinos in a reserve we were protecting. We had chased his gang relentlessly for more than a year, always getting close, but just not catching him. Consequently, the board told us that they were not going to renew our contract.

Then, just before the contract ended in January 2022, we had a breakthrough when a source told us that Ishi and his gang had a rhino horn and were on their way to a village called Mica, not far from Hoedspruit. I was about twenty minutes away with

Pete and Dirk Meyer, another of our managers, and requested Hoedspruit Farm Watch to stop the vehicle. When we arrived, the Farm Watch guys told me that they had searched Ishi's car and it appeared to be clean.

'There're no signs of weapons or rhino horns,' one said. 'Just some meat in the back, which might be eland meat. Should we release them?'

I shook my head. This was one of the first times we had Ishi and his gang in our grasp, and there was no way I was going to let them walk free until we had searched every inch of the vehicle.

'We're keeping them here until the police arrive. Then we'll do a comprehensive search,' I said.

Ishi and his people – who included a woman who said she was an innocent passenger – were lounging around without handcuffs and seemed pretty confident that they would soon be released. Ishi continuously glared at me with a cold, devilish stare and I swear I could see the reflections of dead rhinos deep within his eyes.

As soon as a police official arrived, Dirk and I did another search of the vehicle, going through every compartment, nook and cranny we could find. Once again, we found nothing. However, my attention kept being drawn to some loose spanners strewn on the plastic firewall between the engine compartment and windscreen. Why were they there?

'This looks dodgy,' I said to Dirk. 'Is this a toolbox, or are they trying to distract us?'

Dirk prised open the plastic covering beneath the spanners.

'Nothing. There's just a coconut underneath,' he said. Then he paused. 'No, wait – shit! It's a bloody rhino horn!'

Our reaction was instant. I drew my pistol and shouted at Ishi and the others sitting around the vehicle to lie face down on the ground. We handcuffed all five of them.

This was happening close to the main road in Hoedspruit and a lot of motorists were watching as they drove past. The Provincial Stock Theft and Endangered Species Unit arrived soon afterwards, and so the arrest of one of the most prolific alleged poachers in the Lowveld was very public.

We then went with the police to Ishi's house and found unlicensed rifles and pistols of all calibres, piles of ammunition, animal skins as well as butchered eland, sable and warthog meat. Ishi was allegedly a prolific bushmeat and horn poacher and was also said to be involved in the theft of critically endangered Lillie Cycads, one of the most protected plants in the world. This species of cycad only grows on the slopes of a single granite hill in Limpopo province.

Apart from this treasure trove of evidence, we also found several tortoises cooped in a pen. There's a belief in the area that if you eat the heart of a tortoise, you will never die, supposedly due to a tortoise's lifespan of up to one hundred and fifty years. Thankfully, the reptiles were still alive, so were later released into a safe reserve.

A big win for us here was that unlike Okubi, Ishi had been convicted of rhino poaching in 2014 and given a suspended jail sentence. Consequently, as soon as police re-arrested him, the suspension was automatically rescinded and he will be behind bars for the next five years, which is probably around the same time as this case will take to get to court. We also later learnt we had made a mistake in letting the woman go. She was no passenger; she was in fact said to be one of Ishi's most trusted accomplices.

But at least Ishi is out of the way for a long time.

Another sidebar to this raid was that the package of eland meat found in Ishi's vehicle was actually a gift for two of his alleged horn buyers. The first, Petros 'Mr Big' Mabuza, died six months later just as he had lived – by the sword. He was murdered in a hail of bullets while parked outside a shopping centre in Hazyview. The assassination, thought to have been carried out by a rival syndicate and captured on the shopping mall's CCTV, was a true Wild West shoot-out, with people screaming and scattering in every direction.

The other suspected horn buyer was a former policeman who has faced multiple poaching charges dating back to 2010 and is alleged to be the biggest rhino poacher of all.

His name is Joseph 'Big Joe' Nyalungu. Our paths would soon cross.

25

The Dark Side

It's not just the poaching syndicates we are up against. Sadly, a significant number of rangers and others involved in conservation also end up turning to the dark side.

This remains one of our greatest headaches. We know the poachers are the bad guys, but what about the enemy within?

It goes without saying that finding and employing staff with the right experience, temperament and skills who are not compromised by the poaching syndicates is absolutely vital. Many of our rangers and dog handlers are the finest humans I know, and it's a privilege to work with them. But unfortunately, some aren't.

It's a hard life for rangers who operate daily in what is increasingly becoming a highly armed conflict zone. Not only are the battle lines in the bush blurred, but our people often live in the same villages as the poachers. Or, if they don't, their relatives do. In some cases, they are related by blood or the close-knit ties of extended African families. We have even had a situation where one of our rangers lived next door to a prominent poacher. The result is that they often know each other and maybe even grew up together. So, the opportunities to entice good men to work on the dark side are, regrettably, prevalent.

A typical work schedule for a ranger is twenty-one days on duty in the bush and seven days off. It is on those off days, when rangers are relaxing at their homes with their families, that the syndicates make their approaches. Usually it is through bribery, but sometimes it is through threats. A ranger who has given evidence against a poacher in court may suddenly find a group of gunmen paying his family a 'visit' in the village. We are acutely aware of that. Just as we take every precaution to safeguard our sources, we do the same for our staff.

Either way, once the poaching syndicates have got a man on the inside of a security company, all hell breaks loose. Reserves suddenly start haemorrhaging rhino or other wildlife and, at first, we have no idea who's to blame. By the time we find out, and we always do, much damage has been done. In at least two game reserves where I have worked, the chief poaching culprit has been my second in command. I say this with great sadness, embarrassment and despair but unfortunately, it's a frequently occurring reality and one of the biggest threats to conservation worldwide.

To counter this, we use an exhaustive system of background checks, social screening, as well as polygraph 'lie-detector' tests that are done on a regular basis. Everyone takes them – including me – and anyone failing the test is temporarily relieved of active duty while we investigate further. If the investigations are not resolved conclusively, we usually dismiss the person concerned by ending their contract or through disciplinary hearings. Harsh as it seems, there is no alternative as the stakes are too high. We are talking about the future of South Africa's wildlife and, by extension, much of the tourist industry.

The enemy within, the spy in our patrol units, the traitor in our midst is what I fear the most. I can handle firefights, stake-outs in pouring rain and on cold mountain tops, high-speed chases through thorn bush, wading crocodile-infested rivers, or even stumbling into a pride of lions at night. But not knowing whether the guy fighting by your side is compromised is the worst nightmare for any ranger.

The biggest disappointment of all for me was when one of my top people went over to the dark side.

His name was Godfrey, a big guy with bulging weightlifter's biceps and a ready smile. Out of all the field rangers, he was the most efficient at catching poachers, and within a year he had the highest arrest rate in the company.

'It's what I do,' he often remarked, whenever someone praised him. With his powerful physique and imposing presence – not to mention his somewhat heavy-handed interrogation techniques – he acquired such a fearsome reputation that many poaching gangs from the nearby Finale village dared not put foot on the southern Liverpool farms. They feared all of our rangers, but Godfrey most of all.

However, what we weren't aware of was that, despite his impressive record, his life was spinning out of control. I think it all started when he crashed his uninsured car then bought another one on credit. It was the start of the slippery slope into a morass of debt, and soon he was selling information of our movements and how we operated to poaching gangs. He then took it further, setting up a 'security company' of his own that provided protection for rhino horn syndicates operating on other reserves. But by now, he was not running with the syndicates just to pay off his debts. On the contrary, he had developed an insatiable appetite for the loads of extra cash he was getting – working for me for three weeks each month, then riding shotgun for poaching gangs on his days off.

Matters came to a head when he and another ranger were driving along a dirt road one evening and were stopped at a routine Hoedspruit Farm Watch roadblock. Godfrey was on AWOL and had just finished doing work for the syndicates, so he panicked, doing a spinning U-turn and accelerating away. You don't do that with the Farm Watch guys, most of whom have souped-up pickups and are the Mad Max elite of off-road drivers. They soon cornered Godfrey and the other ranger, searched them and found two of my company shotguns in the vehicle. Farm Watch called me as Godfrey had not only removed a company firearm from the premises without permission, he was also supposed to have been on duty. I fired him on the spot.

I also fired the other ranger but he pleaded so desperately for his job, saying he had to feed his family, that I decided to give him another chance. But as they say, no good deed goes unpunished, and not long afterwards one of the local *indunas* complained to me that the ranger had attempted to kill two farmworkers by forcing them to cross a flooded, crocodile-infested river. I again fired the ranger, who responded by taking me to the workplace dispute arbitration court, and I was fined R59,000 (about £2,440) for 'unfair dismissal'. I would have been interested to hear what the two farmworkers who had narrowly avoided being eaten by crocodiles had to say about that.

After his dismissal, Godfrey spiralled further into a life of crime from which there was no return. As we now knew he was providing protection for the poaching gangs, we were pretty sure he would try and break into our armoury as he needed extra weapons. I doubled our security measures, while Anke kept tabs on him in her usual thorough way to see what he was up to. She found his name popping up everywhere in an interconnected web of crimes linked to poaching and horn smuggling. It was obvious he was now one of the most dangerous men in the area.

It got worse. We heard through our sources that apart from working for syndicate bosses, he was also said to be trafficking in human body parts.

This climaxed during an armed robbery in a nearby village called The Oaks that went wrong, and irate residents cornered Godfrey and two accomplices. Godfrey then grabbed two children as hostages, shoved them into his vehicle and made a run east towards the remote Sekororo valley below the Drakensberg Mountains. Grabbing child hostages is the last thing one does in those frontier-style villages, and soon the entire area's taxi association was giving chase. Most taxi drivers are armed due to blood feuds over passenger routes, and they set up a roadblock, cornering Godfrey and his accomplices. In the ensuing gunfight, Godfrey fired his revolver until he ran out of ammunition, then drove into the bush until he could go no further. When he emerged from his wrecked vehicle, he clutched a *sangoma*'s sarong, probably believing that this *muti* would save him from superstitious villagers.

It had the opposite effect. Shouting that Godfrey was not only stealing their children but was also a 'witch', the mob stoned him, killed him and burnt his body.

They then torched the vehicle with one of the accomplices inside. However, the diesel engine wasn't flammable enough for the mob's liking so they dragged the man out, built a bonfire around him, and also set him alight. The third accomplice was beaten to a pulp but survived. Several bystanders took mobile phone videos of the brutal murders, which went viral.

There was no way this story could end happily. Godfrey had gone down such a rabbit hole of crime that there was no escape.

But it still saddened me. It was a terrible waste of a potentially talented ranger.

26
Heroes of the Wild

On most Big Five game reserves, rangers do not interfere with naturally injured wildlife that is an intrinsic part of the food chain.

It's a brutal environment and many animals are hurt or maimed in the daily struggle to survive. Predators quickly remove any creature that cannot fend for itself and, like it or not, that's the natural cycle of life in the wild. It has been so since time immemorial.

However, when wild animals are injured by humans – usually poachers with snares or guns – that's a different scenario. It's certainly not part of the natural cycle and veterinarians, assisted by rangers, will almost always intervene, sedating and nurturing sick animals back to health.

It was while helping wildlife veterinarians, whom I consider to be among the true heroes of conservation, that I discovered how incredibly useful our dogs could be in tracking and darting wounded game. A darted animal can travel some distance before the anaesthetic kicks in and, as a result, is extremely difficult to find in thick bush. Also, a significant number of injured animals are first spotted by field rangers or tourists on game drives and move off before a vet arrives. Big problem for the vet – but not for our dogs.

So, just as dogs track a poacher, we now also use them to help wildlife vets in particularly difficult terrain and challenging situations. Today, our dogs have become as useful to the veterinary profession as they are to law enforcement.

When working with vets, we normally use Weimaraners, who are superb at blood-scent tracking, and Zingela was exceptional at this job. Once an injured animal has moved off a road or dirt track, it has to be located on foot, which can be particularly 'interesting' when it involves darting big game. It didn't take long for the vets to see first hand how crucial an experienced dog is, not only in finding a wounded dangerous animal in long grass, but also in giving enough warning when getting close. This is particularly true with lions, especially as the entire pride usually has to be darted to prevent an attack while removing a snare off a single member.

Zingela was a fast learner and whenever he heard a compressed air dart gun being primed, he knew exactly what was going to happen next. I also found that dipping the back of a dart in Dettol enabled Zingela to quickly single out a darted animal in big herds simply by following the pungent scent. This was to become a very effective technique, honed and perfected over the years, and the next generation of Weimaraners – Landa, Manzi, Impi, Moya, Diezel, Matambu and Roo – were all imprinted on Dettol. We even used that trick during large-scale nyala game captures in Zululand, where teams with dogs easily located any 'Dettol' antelope.

A major concern for wildlife vets are African wild dogs that are often caught in poachers' snares. Unfortunately, these highly endangered animals with large bat-like ears often leave a protected reserve to escape other apex predators such as lions and hyenas. They roam widely and can easily get under fences, which is one of the main reasons why they are snared in community areas. Once caught, they attempt to chew through the wire noose in a frenzy to get free, breaking teeth so severely that they sometimes have to be euthanised as they can no longer feed themselves. On one occasion while doing game capture for the Mpumalanga Tourism and Parks Agency, wildlife game capture manager Ertjies Rohm darted a snared wild dog just as the sun was setting. It was a superb dart-shot from more than eighty yards away, but when the animal bolted with the snare still attached into thick bush down a steep mountainside, we thought we had lost it for good. True to form, Zingela took us straight to the drugged animal in pitch darkness and Ertjies was able to remove the cable noose and treat it.

As I've said, snares are the sickest, most brutal form of savagery for wildlife. I once watched Ertjies dart a snared wild dog where the wire had cut through its penis sheath. We named him *Pieletjies* (*pieletjie* is a 'small penis' in Afrikaans) and fortunately he went on to live a good life after some intricate surgery. On another occasion, Ertjies rescued a wild dog whose trachea had been severed by a noose and was breathing messily through its windpipe. Luckily, we saved the animal, although it no longer had vocal cords, so could not call the rest of the hunting pack. He became a loner, extremely unusual with these extremely social animals that are one of the few species that take care of elderly or disabled pack members. I often wonder what became of him.

We also regularly used our dogs for darting predators at night, which is somewhat nerve-wracking for us mere humans, but routine for them. I use thermal night-vision goggles, but even so, it's the dogs who tell me where to go. In fact, they are so effective that I have on several occasions tracked on foot rhinos horribly injured by poachers with only a sliver of moonlight and my dogs to guide me. That's how much we trust our animals.

But having said that, one night Manzi, my Weimaraner, and I were looking for a darted lion in the long grass and literally stepped on top of it. The drugs had not yet taken full effect and Manzi and I nearly jumped out of our skins as the big cat tried to get up, snarling with great vigour. Suffice to say, we ran like the wind. I usually use Manzi for tracking rhino, so maybe that was the cause of his uncharacteristic lapse of concentration.

Perhaps my most unusual case of dealing with a sick animal was when I received a callout concerning a suspected rabid impala ram that had been spotted by tourists on a game drive. At that time, there was a raging rabies epidemic in much of the Lowveld and any animal thought to be rabid was immediately destroyed. This I could do on my own, but as Zingela was arguably the most rabies-vaccinated dog on planet Earth, I always took him along.

When we reached the tourist vehicle, the field guide told us that the impala seemed to be having some bizarre sort of seizure or fit, which is why he suspected rabies. It had since moved off to the south and Zingela, nose to the ground, took off like a rocket with me trying to keep up.

Barely a minute later, he cornered and bayed the buck. It was indeed acting strangely, standing at an angle and staring at me vacantly, not even attempting to run away. I couldn't take a chance with the rabies outbreak, so swiftly grabbed it and pinned it to the ground, killing it instantly by cutting its throat. I then noticed that the impala's skull was severely fractured, perhaps from a fight with another ram or running into a tree, which indicated its weird behaviour was due to brain damage, not rabies. In any event, euthanising it was the most humane thing to do.

When I returned to the tourist vehicle dragging the impala behind me like a Neanderthal, the international guests were enthralled at how quickly and efficiently everything had been taken care of. They were especially impressed by Zingela, all wanting to stroke him and take photographs while I spent the next half hour answering questions about the work we did. It also gave me an opportunity to explain how effective dogs are in the bush. Nowadays, we regularly give live demonstrations to tourists, which are proving extremely popular.

In fact, the only times I don't take a dog out with me on veterinary work are when dealing with buffalo or when close to crocodile waters. A dog is croc caviar, so to work one on a river bank is downright crazy.

With buffalo, it's equally foolhardy as when they see a dog, the herd immediately closes ranks and attempts to chase it off or gore it. The frightened dog followed by a herd of highly agitated buffs will always run straight back to its handler. For the unfortunate handler, this gives a new significance to the phrase 'scared shitless' – not to mention an appointment with a rectangular pine box if he's unable to get out of the way.

As always, there was an exception, one that probably delayed my own date with a coffin. I was tracking a gunshot-wounded buffalo that unfortunately had to be destroyed and took Zingela with me as backup. It was extremely fortunate that I did. The buffalo, in classic fashion, had circled back on its own trail of blood and was waiting to ambush me in thick bush. I had no idea it was there.

But Zingela, who was off-lead and forty yards ahead, did. He instantly stopped and 'pointed' at the thicket.

At first, I couldn't see anything, but Zingela wouldn't budge, rooted as still as a statue in pointing stance. I continued staring at the bush until gradually a murky figure materialised in my line of vision. But even so, the foliage was so dense that I couldn't make out if I was looking at the front or back of the animal. I shouldered the 45/70 lever-action Marlin rifle, cocked the hammer slowly and took aim, waiting for the slightest movement to provide some point of reference.

Then an almost imperceptible twitch of an ear gave the business end of the buff away. I fired in quick succession for its shoulder area. Six rounds later and I heard the animal give a distinctive death bellow. When a buffalo is mortally wounded, its last breath is often a deep, throat-rattling roar.

I was sure the animal was dead, but even so, Gerard, a fellow ranger, and I approached with painstaking caution as it's well documented that a 'dead' buffalo sometimes gets up like Lazarus. It's one of the most dangerous of the Big Five, so Gerard fired a few more shots for added life insurance.

Taking Zingela with me on that buffalo cull was the correct decision, but one must always prioritise a dog's safety as there are so many lethal bush hazards to consider. Consequently, I nearly always prefer to work off-lead, particularly when tracking black rhino, which come at you like a torpedo if they get your scent. As mentioned before, the most practical way to avoid a rhino in full charge is to climb the nearest tree, which is fine for the handler but not so much for a dog on a lead. Despite its bulk, a black rhino sprints at thirty-five miles per hour, so there is no time to release the lead from the dog's harness or collar while scrambling up a thorny acacia. A dog can usually dodge a full-tilt rhino charge, but its lead can easily get snagged around bushes and pin it down. If that happens, the dog has no chance.

This is particularly relevant to us, as K9 Conservation uses dogs every day to monitor rhino populations on our contracted areas. Our handlers have to know exactly what to do in tight situations, particularly when a two-and-a-half-ton beast comes hurtling out of the bush with little warning. This means we only put dogs on rhino scent when we actually find tracks, then call them off the moment the pachyderms are located. The rangers do a head and ear notch count, and record what condition the animals are in and whether they are in any potential danger, such as being close to areas where we know poachers are infiltrating.

Poachers also sometimes poison rhinos, lacing cabbage leaves with highly toxic pesticides so they can hack the horns off a dead animal without gunfire giving their position away. This has a massive ripple effect on the environment as not only does the rhino die agonisingly, so does all other wildlife feeding off the carcass, such as hyenas, jackals and, of course, vultures. Sometimes a whole flock is destroyed on a single corpse. This is a bonus for the poachers, as dead vultures are considered powerful *muti* and fetch good prices. As these carrion scavengers circling in the thermals are often the first sign that something has died in the bush, there's a widespread belief that they have prophetic powers. The severed head of a vulture is consequently not an unusual sight at horse races to 'assist' punters in predicting winners.

One of the key signs that an animal has been poisoned is if the flies around the carcass are dead. This phenomenon is not restricted to land, as fish poaching syndicates also use poison, dumping toxins into rivers above fixed gill nets and killing all aquatic life for hundreds of yards downstream, including crocodiles. Once gutted, poisoned fish are edible and are sold at bushmeat wet markets. The poachers couldn't care less about what eco-havoc they cause, and part of the problem is that chemical poison is bought in bulk by farmers and easily accessible. It's sprayed on crops and citrus orchards to keep bugs away, and although there are strict control measures, bags of the killing powder are regularly pilfered by the syndicates.

When K9 Conservation was registered in 2011, one of our biggest obstacles was that many fellow game rangers were not convinced that using dogs in the Lowveld would be effective. The main problem, they said, was the heat, as dogs would not be able to operate in scorching temperatures for most of the day. This would seriously hamper patrols, and I was warned of situations where dogs had died from heat exhaustion in the Greater Kruger National Park system. The baking hot ground can also burn a dog's footpads. This, they claimed, was the Achilles' heel of running dog APUs (no pun intended).

To some extent this is true, but learning to manage the welfare of animals is the most important part of the job. It goes without saying that our dogs are exceptionally fit and we monitor them closely in the field. When one gets hot and starts seeking shade, it is immediately rested and another dog handler takes over. By leapfrogging, we are able to operate at all hours and have never lost a dog to overheating. Also, much of our work is done after sunset as dogs track equally well in darkness.

Another cast-iron rule is that we never work our dogs for at least two hours after they've eaten. The reason for this is that a dog running on a full stomach can get gastric torsion, where the stomach twists inside the abdominal cavity, often resulting in a very painful death.

Much of our dog training is imprinting our animals. In other words, getting them to follow specific scents, such as human sweat or spent cartridges in the case of poachers, or blood when tracking wounded or dead animals. All dogs know how to follow a scent, as their noses are superbly designed to do exactly that, but without training, they will follow random, rather than specific odours. Depending on the breed, a dog's sense of smell is up to ten thousand times more powerful than ours. They possess up to three hundred million olfactory receptors in their noses compared to about six million in humans, which is why we rely on sight rather than smell. Proportionally, the part of their brain that processes different scents is forty times greater than ours. Also, of course, all our dogs are gun-trained. The last thing you want is for your dog to run off when a shot is fired.

More challenging is training the handler to have absolute trust in their animals. A dog knows its job far better than a human does, so unless a handler learns how to interpret a dog's body language and understand its incredible inherent skills, he or she will get nowhere. This requires many, many hours of repetitive training, and unfortunately some so-called anti-poaching dog units do not understand that. These guys fail – often spectacularly – because of the handler's incompetence, not the dog's, and to some extent this has given the industry a bad name.

There is absolutely no doubt that the use of well-trained working dogs and skilled handlers has been one of the most significant game changers in conservation. From chasing poachers and helping vets track injured animals to finding blood spoors, sounding danger alarms and sniffing out evidence, these incredible animals are truly our best friends. The inspiration I got from Zingela years ago, where he showed me that dogs are the ultimate incorruptible, loyal and effective partners in the bush, has been proven correct again and again.

Many of us owe our lives to our dogs. The weakest link is humans.

27

Indian Adventure

One day, out of the blue, a call came through from a man with a foreign accent. He introduced himself as Kiran Rahalkar, a representative from the Wildlife Conservation Trust of India. He wanted to know if K9 Conservation could assist with setting up a dog unit for his organisation, but he needed to come and check out our operation first.

Of course we could, I replied, and said he was more than welcome to see first hand what we do with our dogs for conservation.

Kiran proposed visiting us with Aditya Joshi, his work colleague, and if everything went to plan, the two of them would be trained as handlers at our headquarters. He said they wanted four dogs for the Wildlife Conservation Trust (WCT) that would be permanently based in India, working on various wildlife projects. Anke and I were very excited about this and dates were set for the training course to last about three months.

The two Indian conservationists arrived at Eastgate Airport, a short drive from Hoedspruit, and we immediately got on like a house on fire, introducing our soon-to-be very good friends to our way of life and the dogs we worked with.

The best way to learn how to handle a dog and apply its skills to conservation work is to do so in a real-life environment. And that's exactly what happened. For the next three months, Kiran and Aditya shadowed our every move, coming out with us on daily operations, foot patrols and poaching callouts, just as they would be doing when they returned to India.

Apart from training them on how to track and communicate with working canines, a lot of attention was focused on the dogs' welfare in the bushveld. This was one of the reasons why the WCT chose us, as we share a very similar environment to India and almost identical terrain. Heat remains one of the most limiting factors as dogs, of course, don't have sweat glands and regulate their body temperature by passing air rapidly over their tongues and blood-rich capillaries in their mouths. The hotter the temperature, the harder they pant, so the biggest threat is humidity coupled with heat. Very few dog owners ever take the trouble to touch the ground and gauge the temperature on the scalding rocks, or crouch down to feel the intensity of heat radiation. When a dog is seeking shade, it is saying it's too hot.

We also pinpointed the many other hazards and threats of the natural environment – particularly predators and reptiles, including snakes, that we envisaged the dogs would be exposed to in India. However, the biggest killers are vehicles. Driving through villages, the sad number of decaying corpses is stark evidence that dogs cannot judge or dodge a speeding car. I had lost Zingela that way and in India they have far more traffic than we do.

Our friends were exceptional students and soaked up everything we taught them. As they were already accomplished conservationists and used to working outdoors, they soon picked up tracking skills, and Moya, my female Weimaraner, liked Kiran immensely. We also worked with several other breeds to see which dogs would suit the requirements of the WCT the best.

The three-month training course was soon over, and our next mission was to cut through all the bureaucracy to get the four dogs we had selected to their new home in India. This proved to be far more laborious than the course itself. However, just as Kiran and Aditya were leaving, Anke got some bad news. Her father, who had been diagnosed with stage-four bone marrow cancer the year before, was now critically ill. On 29 August, her mother called to say it was time to come and say goodbye. In a whirlwind of emotions and lack of sleep from an APU operation the night before, she hastily packed and left for Pretoria. She got there that afternoon, just in time to bid her final farewell to her father. He passed away early the next morning.

We attended the funeral a week later and, though I regrettably had never met her dad, Paul Kruger, it was evident from the memorial service that he was revered by many. I wanted to be there to support Anke, but unfortunately my clothes closet consisted of only khakis and olive-green uniforms, so we picked up what little formal clothing Hoedspruit shops had on offer, a black long-sleeved, button-up shirt and black pants. After all the years in the bush, I feel naked without a handgun, so a pistol also made the trip up to Pretoria on my hip. It wasn't until several years later that Anke heard from some mourners at the service that it was commonly believed I was Anke's bodyguard, with whom she later fell in love and married. Though we laughed at the rumour, Anke admitted that it sounded rather romantic and had no problem adopting it as truth.

Driving back to Hoedspruit, my diaphragm went into spasm and I felt seriously off-colour with headaches, sweats and chills. The next morning my body temperature fluctuated wildly, and a quick test at the doctor's clinic proved positive for malaria. Two weeks prior to Anke's dad's funeral, we had visited her family at Marloth Park bordering southern Kruger, and that was where that pesky Anopheles mosquito had infected me. Malaria sucks – believe me, you don't want to get it – and for the next two days I didn't care if I kicked the bucket or not. Luckily my recovery was quick, and I suppose that after living for forty years in the bush and being bitten by millions of mozzies, as we call them, I was lucky that this was the first time I had come down with the disease.

We weren't given much time to recover from either the funeral or my malaria as a week later Kiran called from India, saying a tiger had been poached and her two cubs needed to be located and rescued. They needed the four dogs we had selected to be sent over right away. However, we still had a mountain of government red tape to deal with, particularly stamp permits and medical clearances, so the big bosses of the WCT contacted the Indian embassy in Pretoria to speed up the process. It certainly worked, and for the next few days we were given VIP treatment at the embassy, driven all over the place to get everything sorted, and then off to the airport.

I had my day carry-pack with me, containing a pair of stainless-steel handcuffs and my indispensable Leatherman Super Tool. In the mad rush to complete all the paperwork, I forgot to unpack the bag as I was about to clear customs. Handcuffs, not to mention blades, are strictly *verboten* on any plane, and as the official took the cuffs out my pack, his quizzical expression indicated that he thought they were … well, kinky. My explanation that I was a game ranger and had forgotten to take the items out of the pack I always carried was not believed. Anke's face turned redder than her hair as laughter from the gathering crowd erupted behind us. For the record, those handcuffs were only used on criminals. Unfortunately, both the handcuffs and my beloved Leatherman were confiscated, but at least we were allowed onto the plane.

With a couple of security officials trailing us to the boarding gates, we took off, heading via Turkey to India. The layover at

Turkey was anything but pleasant as it involved Anke getting a full body search at customs and a fourteen-hour layover – which happened on the way back as well. We had erroneously relied on a booking agent to arrange our tickets so spent a total of twenty-eight hours at the airport.

Eventually landing in Mumbai, we were met by Kiran and his big smile. At the freight carrier collection point, we picked up our four dogs – Moya, Impi, Hira and Ace – all top trackers that had been trained to the highest standard, and began the five-hour trip to Kiran's parents' house in Nashik, an ancient holy city in western India's Maharashtra state.

The drive through the seething metropolis of Mumbai is an eye-opener for anyone from rural Africa. Millions of people buzzed around like an overheated beehive, while litter was strewn everywhere and the aroma of the downtown area was at times overpowering.

Eventually exiting the city and heading north into the countryside, we wound our way through the Gats Mountain range and stopped for the dogs to touch Indian soil for the first time. After a delicious curry lunch with Kiran's family, we drove for ten more hours to Nagpur, a massive industrial city slap-bang in central India, and also known as the 'tiger capital'. The traffic was insane, with every size, shape and make of vehicle imaginable – including some that I couldn't identify. Kiran explained that the trick of driving on these crazily congested roads was to only look ahead. If you looked back, you would have an accident. I believed him.

The music blaring loudly in our two-ton panel van was very traditional and kept the hired driver and Anke and me awake. In fact, I was hypnotised, and although Anke was looking a tad pale, we both were embracing the adventure of it all. It was unlike anything we had ever experienced. Finally, sometime during the night and after several seemingly near-death traffic experiences, we stopped at a McDonald's and ordered burgers and chips, much to Anke's delight.

But not for long. She took an almighty bite and a second later her blue eyes turned red and nearly popped out as she gave a shriek that would have put Tarzan to shame. It turns out that there is even more chilli in a Big Mac than there is in traditional Indian food. I'm something of a chilli fan and loved it, but from that moment on, Haldiram's desserts, cookies and sweets washed down with lassi buffalo yogurt became Anke's diet of choice for the next twenty days.

The next morning, we met up with the WCT team, all great people and extremely accommodating and friendly. We were given a guided tour through the head office, and it was only then that I realised the sheer scope and size of their project. Essentially, their work revolves around mitigating human–wildlife conflict in the most populous country on the planet. Much of India consists of thousands of small rural villages barely a few miles apart and connected by wildlife corridors where a plethora of game – tigers, blue buck, sambar deer, Asiatic lions, leopard, pangolins, wolves and of course Asian rhino – roam freely. Without massive wilderness areas and only a few small game reserves in the central part of the country, wildlife has to coexist with humans, and there are often clashes with predators such as leopards and tigers coming into the gardens of people's homes. The WCT focuses on protecting the animals in these crucial corridors.

The work of our dogs was going to play a large role in the country's wildlife management, with the Weimaraners Moya and Impi involved in the tracking and detection of wild animals, while Hira and Ace, both Malinois, would be used in poaching and wildlife contraband control in the corridors.

A rented house in Nagpur was our base for the next couple of weeks as we headed into the countryside to train and acclimatise the dogs to this new world. And it was certainly a different experience, continuously bumping into huge crowds of people while every street had its own resident 'gang' of feral animals, including dogs, boars and cattle. Of particular concern was the infestation of an invasive, highly noxious weed growing on the sides of the roads and in crop fields called Parthenium. It has a very dangerous pollen that causes allergic reactions in animals and humans and, if inhaled, it can kill dogs. We paid special attention to avoiding these toxic plants.

Most Indians have never seen a Malinois or Weimaraner, and the dogs got a lot of attention on our evening walks. So did Anke and I, as the rural areas around Nagpur are far off the tourist route and we were obvious foreigners, particularly Anke with her stunning red hair.

We spent many days out in the bush tracking and indicating wild animals, and the dogs did very well on tiger scent, in particular. We even tracked a tiger right on the outskirts of Nagpur a few times, with Moya and Ace indicating that they were very close to it, although we didn't see it ourselves.

One of the animals that Indian conservationists are extremely wary of is the sloth bear. We came upon the tracks of one, and Kiran abruptly turned around and instructed us to head in the opposite direction as fast as we could. As he scanned the bush, he said rangers were more frightened of these bears than they were of tigers.

'If a tiger gets you, you're dead,' he said. 'But a sloth bear scalps and gouges out the eyes of its victim with its big claws, leaving the person blinded and horribly ripped up, but still alive.'

Indian forest rangers are not armed with rifles and instead carry long tomahawk-style axes that they keep razor sharp. Kiran said that these tomahawks were the first line of defence for most rangers and they used them to ward off bears.

Another massive threat to conservation in the countryside is the number of live electrical wires circling fields on the outskirts of villages. These are hooked up to the main power lines at night and conduct millions of volts of electricity. This is to keep deer and other wild animals from destroying crops, and any creature that touches this almost invisible wire is killed instantly, including elephants. These wires are highly illegal but relatively common, and a huge headache for the WCT. We found one around a crop field and kept a very keen eye out for others wherever we went.

There are also many temples and shrines dotted around the countryside and we visited a few while on training exercises with the dogs. I was surprised to find an impressive amount of ancient Stone Age tools such as hand axes and spear points in the eroded gullies and flat plains.

Every day turned out to be a new adventure, including when sampling the local cuisine. Like hobbits, we made frequent stops at various vendors and food stores along the busy roads to eat curry with a myriad different dishes. All were very hot and spicy and my digestive tract soon adapted to the amazing food, but Anke remained firmly focused on the hunt to find non-chilli cuisine.

We also headed up to Pench Tiger Reserve for a Panthera convention and had a chance to go looking for tigers in India's premier reserve. We got to hear tigers mating down a wooded gully but unfortunately didn't get a glimpse of them.

We then visited Kiran's family farm at Nashik where the dogs were going to be based. The countryside is more open and very similar to South Africa, so we carried on training and acclimatising them there. The locals heard of the arrival of 'strange' dogs, and at first there were crowds of people coming to see what all the hype was about. Luckily, after a few days they dispersed.

The time finally came to head back home. It was sad to say goodbye to our friends, but extremely gratifying to see how happy the dogs were with their new handlers.

The trip back home went well apart from another layover in Turkey, and Anke was happy to eat non-spicy food again. We remain in regular contact with Kiran and Aditya and they keep us updated on how well the dogs are doing in India's conservation efforts. Among many other conservation duties, they have already been used to track down man-eating leopards as well as finding the human remains of the big cats' victims.

What pleases me most is that our dogs, born in Africa, are now becoming conservation champions in India.

28

Pangolins – Hope and Despair

Another escalating conflict we and fellow conservationists are increasingly involved with is rescuing pangolins, the world's most trafficked animal.

It happened almost by default. All wildlife poachers are on our radar and pangolin rescue and recovery became an ad hoc extension of the work we were already doing. Our paths crossed with other people saving these severely persecuted creatures, and in so doing, we became part of the Limpopo Pangolin Collective. This collective is highly secretive and so far off the radar that certain things cannot be mentioned.

There are about twenty of us working under the authority of various SAPS teams and we're all volunteers. Members don't charge for their services or claim expenses. However, it's a very tightknit group and volunteers still need to earn their way into a Pangolin Collective as the guys pulling the strings will only work with people they trust. The South African Police Service Provincial Stock Theft and Endangered Species Unit always accompanies us on operations.

These are vastly different to fighting rhino cartels and they're the only anti-poaching operations where we do not use dogs, unless specifically to sniff out animals hidden in residential areas. Instead, it is a true subterfuge 'sting' manoeuvre where our people pose as buyers and we then grab the sellers. Consequently, a successful rescue is totally reliant on our network of sources and there are no shoot-outs in the bush, wild car chases or bullets flying at police roadblocks.

These elusive nocturnal creatures, which harm no one, are usually caught by opportunists – cattle herders or someone stumbling across a pangolin in the bush who knows its worth on the black market. They then try to find buyers. Our sources hear about this, agree to purchase the animal, and meet the sellers somewhere in a nearby town. The deal is seldom, if ever, done in an isolated area, as a lot of money is about to change hands.

At the agreed location, the sellers – there are usually three or four involved – show photographs with the date and time of the capture electronically stamped, and a short mobile phone video to verify the pangolin is alive. Proof of life is crucial, as although dead animals are also 'bought', their value is greatly reduced. The buyer then shows his bag of money.

While all of this is happening, the rest of the Pangolin Collective, dressed in plain clothes and carrying concealed firearms, hang around nearby, either in the street or drinking coffee in a cafe with a clear view of what's happening. All are within striking range of where the sting is going to go down.

Satisfied that there is the correct amount of cash, the sellers then take the buyer to see the pangolin. It is usually stashed in a box or bag in the boot or backseat of a car. The buyer, our guy, makes a pre-arranged signal and we spring into action. Within seconds, we have the suspected poachers face down on the ground and handcuffed. As this happens in busy urban areas, large crowds soon gather that can become belligerent, so we get the suspects to a police station as quickly as we can.

Most pangolin poachers are either small-time crooks or amateurs – unlike the hardcore, well-armed rhino syndicates. It's a completely different setup and many of those involved in the trade are illegal immigrants from Zimbabwe. But perhaps the biggest difference is that, unlike confrontations in the bush, this is seldom a life-or-death situation for the team, although it certainly is for the pangolin. We speak to each other civilly and I often say to them, 'Please guys, we don't want to put you in jail again. Stop doing this.' If I said that to a rhino poacher, he'd laugh in my face.

Obviously, if the pangolin snatchers do make a successful sale, the next stage is far more professional, as the syndicates then get involved to smuggle the poor creature, still alive, through airports to the Asian markets.

The courts take pangolin poaching far more seriously than bushmeat crime, mainly because pangolins are internationally endangered. Consequently, they are aware that the IUCN is watching. If convicted, a pangolin poacher can spend seven or more years in jail, whereas meat poachers are usually released on minimal bail the next day. The slow judicial procedure makes a snail look like Usain Bolt, but the harsher sentences definitely are having an effect.

Just as consequential as the arrest is getting the pangolin to a vet, as rescued animals are almost always in a stressed and critical condition. The lifespan of a captured animal, from the moment it is caught to reaching the Asian market, is at most two weeks. So, every minute is crucial. The vet immediately X-rays and sticks a drip into the animal, as it is without fail severely dehydrated and its digestive tract lethally clogged by being force-fed maize or rice. Pangolins eat live termites and larvae, and their bodies only secrete enzymes to digest food while foraging. We have to get them back into the wild quickly, because if they don't walk and forage, they won't heal. It takes an experienced eye to judge when to release a sick pangolin, as to do so too early would result in the animal dying in the bush. Conversely, if kept inside for too long, it will starve to death through lack of digestive enzymes.

Once the vet has examined the animal, it is taken to a top-secret rehabilitation location to recover. There it is fitted with a GPS or satellite collar and assigned to handlers who will watch over it, initially around the clock, then every few days for several months until it is healthy.

Sadly, even with this intensive care, at least thirty per cent of rescued pangolins die. The trauma and incorrect diet is simply too much for them. The death rate is even higher with pregnant animals that abort their foetuses if stressed.

Those that do survive are eventually set free into carefully selected host reserves that have to meet certain requirements, such as being a minimum of eight thousand hectares and with as little human disruption as possible.

However, even once free they face problems, as many safe reserves still have electric fences with a live strand just off the ground that shocks small animals and reptiles. When this happens, a pangolin's instinctive defence mechanism is to roll into a ball as its armour scales are impervious to even a lion's fangs. However, by curling up, the live electric wire automatically twists into the creature's torso and kills it. There's a lot of controversy over this type of fence as the low-slung live strand does not stop people from coming in or animals from going out. But it kills loads of other wildlife, including snakes, chameleons, tortoises ... and pangolins.

The fact that these harmless, inoffensive, painfully shy creatures are so dreadfully abused is one of the planet's sadder stories. There are eight groups of pangolins, of which the four Asian species are listed by the IUCN as critically endangered, while the African species – ground, giant ground, white-bellied and black-bellied pangolins – are listed as vulnerable.

About a hundred thousand are poached every year, killed for their scales and organs, which are used in traditional medicine and touted as a cure for anything from stomach disorders to cancer and asthma. Like rhino horn, a pangolin's scales consist of medically worthless keratin, the same substance as human hair and fingernails. The meat is also considered a delicacy in China and Vietnam, fetching huge prices at posh restaurants. So, a pangolin has virtually every strike imaginable against it.

For many years, the Asian species were the primary target of poachers and traffickers due to the proximity of the markets. But now that their numbers have plummeted in the Far East to what some consider to be one step away from extinction, traffickers are increasingly turning to African pangolins. This was highlighted in April 2019 when Singapore customs seized twenty-eight tons of pangolin scales smuggled from Nigeria. It's estimated that seventy-two thousand pangolins were slaughtered for that haul. In other words, almost two hundred a day died in one year from one country alone.

Not all pangolins are destined for the Far East market, however. In west and central Africa, pangolin scales are highly prized as *muti* and fetch good prices. One of the more bizarre beliefs is that a scale worn around one's neck will turn bullets into water. The dead animals are also sold by weight, so poachers force-feed them cement to raise the price.

Fortunately, that is not the case in South Africa. Although considered powerful *muti* by *sangomas*, the animal has spiritual significance and is thought to bring good fortune and rain for one's crops. Conversely, if you kill a pangolin, your family will be cursed with bad luck for the next seven years.

So, we have powerful allies among the traditional medicine people who reinforce how important this animal is, a key reason why we retrieve so many poached pangolins alive – unlike the dire situation in Asia and west Africa. That alone gives some hope for these cruelly persecuted creatures. At least in our neck of the woods.

Despite the fact that it's the most trafficked animal in the world, very little is actually known about African pangolins, such as exactly how long they live, their home range, or even how many babies they have. Scientists are only now collating all this data by studying rescued pangolins in rehab centres as these creatures are so secretive and solitary that most people don't even know they have them on their properties. Pangolins only emerge at night, and even then, their eyes do not reflect light so are not picked up by torch beams. Dogs will find them, of course, and that is why two of the dogs we sent to India are specifically pangolin imprinted.

At the moment, we are only doing about three or four raids a year and, although that's not high, thanks to our sources, the success rate in nailing pangolin poachers is impressive. So much so that in 2021 when we were awarded Pangolin Collective badges to acknowledge our work, we learnt that we are the second-most-successful unit in the world after Malaysia.

Not bad for a small group of volunteers operating on a shoestring budget at the bottom end of Africa. And when one considers that more than a million of these timid and strangely beautiful animals have been trafficked in the past decade alone, it makes these efforts all the more worthwhile.

29

The Finale Sting

Finally, three long years after submitting information implicating the bushmeat poaching syndicates in Finale village on the northern banks of the Olifants River, police told me they were now ready for a raid.

As mentioned previously, I had got the incriminating data from a poacher I had caught on a Liverpool property who had sung like the proverbial canary with Anubis growling inches from him.

Initially, police were reluctant to act against the village's poachers as they had not been caught red-handed, so to speak. However, with the wealth of information we had, including names, addresses, GPS co-ordinates and photographs of syndicate leaders, police high command green-lighted the 'sting'. I call it that as the suspects never knew we were coming for them. However, manpower was limited so although the operation was led by police officers, backup was provided by rangers from my company and our trusted *compadres*, the Hoedspruit Farm Watch.

The strike team met on the outskirts of Finale at about midnight on Thursday, 9 April 2020 – just before Good Friday – where Anke and I picked up the source who was going to show us each suspect's house. Although we had precise locations of where the alleged poachers lived, I still wanted the source physically to point out their houses. We needed to be absolutely certain no mistakes were made as I knew it was unlikely we would soon get another opportunity like this.

The procedure for the raid was simple. We would start at the closest suspect's house and from there move on to the other suspects, surrounding each house so no one could escape when police knocked on the door. We would arrest the alleged poachers, search their premises, bag evidence and take photographs and videos. All members of the raiding party were shown photos of the target suspects and warned that there would be other people, including children, in most of the houses so we had to keep disruption to a minimum.

The source sat in the lead vehicle with heavily tinted windows and wore a balaclava so he would not be recognised. Behind us was a police lockup van where the suspects would be detained, followed by a convoy of K9 Conservation rangers and Hoedspruit Farm Watch.

At about 1 a.m. on Good Friday, we drove into the village, timing our entry as we knew from sources that all the suspects would be at home and the weekend holiday revelries would not yet have begun. We had to act fast, needing to be out of the village by sunrise before residents awoke. Every one of us was armed and also carrying handcuffs and pepper spray. By my side was Landa, who would sniff out anything tainted with animal blood. Landa was better than anyone else – human or dog – at finding evidence, but we also brought two Malinois belonging to a friend in case other residents surrounded us or brawls broke out if suspects resisted arrest. This was crucial, as any police operation that gets blockaded by hostile civilians could go south fast, resulting in chaos. We call this a 'Black Hawk Down' scenario, reminiscent of what happened to American forces in Mogadishu in 1993.

The closest house on the list conveniently belonged to the alleged leader of the main poaching gang. The police investigating officer knocked on the door and the suspect himself answered. We quickly moved into the house and started searching the building. Within minutes we had found a large cache of wild game meat in a deepfreeze – so much so that we simply unplugged the freezer and loaded it straight onto one of our trucks. Multiple strips of drying warthog, waterbuck, eland, nyala and kudu biltong were hanging from the ceiling like ghoulish decorations. Landa also sniffed out various animal horns, knives, machetes and bloodstained clothing, as well as a pile of snares in the outside yard. He indicated something suspicious with almost every step he took. The amount of incriminating evidence was overwhelming, and I photographed it all as we stashed it in the police van.

Then it was off to the next house further down the road. We knew this suspect well as he was a repeat offender with several previous poaching convictions. Once again, bushmeat was stashed virtually everywhere we looked, either in deepfreezes or biltong strips hanging from the roof rafters, and the easiest way to move it was simply to load the freezer onto a truck as we had done at the previous house. In the yard, Landa sniffed out a stack of steel-wire snares and some knives and axes.

The third house raid netted two suspects, and in the search we also found a bushpig's head, while various blades or knives were seized as evidence.

On entering the fifth suspect's house, also a previously convicted poacher, we were told he was not at home. However, a quick search found him hiding in one of the rooms. He put up quite a fight, not dissimilar to something you would see on WrestleMania, and we had to subdue him before snapping handcuffs on his wrists. The same evidence as in the other houses was found and seized – meat caches in deepfreezes, biltong, knives and animal horns.

We then surrounded the next suspect's house, and once we identified ourselves and said we had a search warrant, he became extremely aggressive. Fists flew, but we soon overpowered him through sheer weight of numbers, shoving him into the police van as he hurled abuse at us. A hoard of wild meat and butchery equipment was found in his house as well as a zebra hoof.

The eighth suspect hid as soon as the police knocked on his door and we found him lying curled up inside a mattress underneath a little boy lying on top of the bed.

He too was handcuffed and escorted to the police van while more bushmeat was seized.

The final suspect was the girlfriend of one of the poachers. We found bushmeat, snares and an impala skin hidden in a tree just outside the boundary of her yard. Even though it was clear she was involved, confirmed by our sources, we could not legally pin the contraband on her.

By 4 a.m., as planned, the sting was over. We now had Finale's nine most notorious suspected poachers in custody without a shot being fired. The convoy did a rapid U-turn and sped back to the Hoedspruit police station, where the suspects were locked up and the deepfreezes plugged in to stop the meat that was to be used as evidence from rotting. All other evidence, from knives to animal skins, was stashed for further processing.

As Anke and I arrived home in the early morning, desperate for some sleep after a hard night, my phone started ringing. It was a source telling me the village was buzzing with news of the bust. There had never been such a perfectly targeted raid before, nailing the alleged poaching kingpins with clinical precision. Villagers could barely believe that in one fell swoop all the suspected syndicate leaders were behind bars. And it had happened while they were fast asleep.

The suspects' first appearance at Hoedspruit Magistrate's Court was a bail hearing. Unsurprisingly, all were released on a pittance, and then the fun and games with the overworked judicial system began. I was a key witness as I had obtained most of the initial information, so I knew I would be tied up in court appearances for some time. But even so, I thought it would be relatively painless as the raid was a slam dunk. The mountain of poached meat, the huge pile of snares, butchery utensils and filleting knives we had confiscated at each suspect's house was overwhelming.

Unfortunately, the prosecutor did not agree. The second hearing, which I had to drive for almost an hour to attend, was postponed until the following week. Then the next. And the next … until I was travelling into Hoedspruit every Wednesday, only to be told to come back in seven days' time. This continued for close on two years, and the cost in time, petrol and money was staggering. Even worse, there seemed to be no end in sight as no one, including the prosecutor, could set a firm date for the trial to proceed. The only good thing about this, I reasoned, was that the alleged poachers also had to pitch up for each hearing, costing them as well. Even if they eventually got off scot-free, the snail-paced process would be a form of punishment in itself.

And so it continued. Every Wednesday, come rain or shine, the suspects and I would bump into each other outside the courtroom. They would look at me with hostility, which I understood, and I would look back in a sort of staring contest. They knew who I was long before this trial and I knew most of them.

Then I thought, to hell with this. We could either be childish and glower at each other, or I could use this as an opportunity to break some ice. We were all bored out of our minds in any event, so one morning I walked up to them as they lounged outside the courthouse and said, 'Howzit guys.'

They nodded as a reply and I pulled out a packet of cigarettes.

'*Gwayi?*' I asked. Want a smoke?

They all took one – even the non-smokers to give to their buddies later.

We chatted a bit, the conversation somewhat stilted, then we were all called into the courtroom. Once again, the case was postponed until the following week. Their anger and frustration were as palpable as mine.

The next week we spoke again, this time a little more easily. I had heard through my sources that one of the poachers had hurt his leg while fleeing from rangers at a game reserve near us.

I offered him a cigarette and, noticing his limp, asked, 'What happened to your leg?'

'I fell,' he answered.

'Oh. Was that when you were running away from rangers last Friday?'

He looked at me, astonished. The rest of the suspects burst out laughing. They were stunned at how much I knew from my sources and also highly amused at their colleague's discomfort.

That really broke the ice. It carried on in this vein every week. We even started bantering about their activities.

'Hey, I heard you were poaching on that farm and got nailed by a warthog,' I said to one, and we all fell about laughing.

'*Eish* Con. How did you know that?' he asked, eyes wide with astonishment.

'I know everything.'

In a bizarre way, we were in this together. Sure, I was a key state witness and they were the accused, but the continuous stalling and lack of any meaningful progress to bring the trial to a conclusion was freaking us all out. By now, I had the mobile phone number of each suspect and decided to contact them individually to bring matters to a head.

'Look,' I said. 'I'm going to tell the prosecutor to put this case on ice. Nothing is going to happen to you now, but make no mistake – charges have not been dropped. This case will still be pending. So, if you guys keep coming into our areas and I arrest you again, you will be in even more trouble as it will be a repeat offence. Just leave us alone. Okay?'

They all agreed. At the next court appearance, we had a smoke together, not as a peace pipe but as a compromise, and I then went to talk to the prosecutor. He thought I was coming to complain so went on the offensive, saying that the evidence had not been properly bagged and listed. I could tell he was getting further and further bogged down by his workload, so knew he too would welcome some form of resolution.

'Okay, we can get all the evidence listed again, but it will take time,' I said. 'But here's what I suggest. This case has been going on for far too long anyway, so let's put it on hold until we come up with more specific evidence.'

He readily agreed and the case was moved from 'active' to 'pending'. Crucially, charges were not dropped, so I still had leverage with the nine suspects.

As good as their word, poaching in our areas by the Finale syndicates quietened down to a fraction of what it had been. They were, by and large, leaving us alone, although I would be lying if I said they were no longer poaching. For example, there was some confusion when some syndicate members went down the Olifants River and started snaring crocodiles, not knowing that we guarded twenty-eight miles of the river's southern bank. Most of the poaching activity is now on the northern side.

The extraordinary outcome of this bizarre trial is that I now know some of the top poachers in the village personally and we have a tenuous relationship. We're not friends by any stretch of the imagination, but we're not arch-enemies. These particular guys are not evil; they are people who are good hunters in their communities and that's how they make their living, even though it's illegal and destructive. Our relationship is a little like two countries squaring up against each other but keeping lines of communication open. We're simply doing that in a conservation context.

Crucially, I also have their phone numbers. Whenever I hear that one is active, I simply call him. The calls usually go something like this.

'Listen man, I know it was you who snared that impala on (X) reserve. I don't want to come and arrest you again, so *yegela* – stop it now.'

'I need food for my family,' the poacher will say.

'Then get a job.'

'I can't. I've got a criminal record.'

'Well, then get a casual job picking fruit or something like that. They won't ask about your record.'

The poacher will laugh. 'Con, you know what it's like.'

I do know. He had a point; jobs are scarce. But that's something out of my control.

'Look, I don't want to arrest you again,' I repeat. 'Then we all have to go to court again for another two years.'

'Okay.'

I've had more than a few conversations like that, politely warning the syndicates to stay away from our protected areas, and mostly they have taken the advice. Something that does give me a glimmer of hope is that one of the syndicate leaders we arrested now actually has a proper job. He told me so on the phone.

In breaking down barriers, the Finale sting was more successful than I ever imagined. Sure, we did not get a conviction, but to some extent the previously intransigent chasm of mistrust and hatred that existed between us and the lower levels of the syndicates has in a small way been bridged. The poachers certainly don't invite me to any parties, but they accept that we are doing our job and will leave them alone if they don't come into our areas of protection.

I suppose it can be argued that all this does is move the problem elsewhere. But as I have said before, in Africa you take what wins you can.

30

Our Family and Other Animals

I got my first dog as a young boy wandering around the untamed bush and mountains on Mauricedale, our family's game reserve outside Malelane near the Kruger National Park. Trooper, a Rottweiler cross Rhodesian ridgeback, was my constant companion in those carefree times and never left my side during school holidays.

I was an avid hunter as a youngster, stalking mainly skittish impala and warthog, and became completely at home in the wilds. Trooper was my initial dog 'mentor' and we had many adventures together, honing skills that led me to the point where I am now. Say what you like about hunting, it teaches you more about bushcraft than anything else in your formative years. So too does a good dog, and perhaps the most important lesson I learnt from Trooper was that training dogs is a two-way street – you teach them as much as they do you.

My second dog was Bamba at Windy Ridge, an equally faithful companion, and then came Zingela. There is no doubt that Zingela was the greatest teacher and friend I ever had. He was on another level to any dog I've come across and was with me for seven faithful years. From Bongani to Kruger and Sabi

Sand Wildtuin, the two of us with little formal training broke new ground in highlighting the incredible value of dogs in the bush.

Zingela, more than anything else, was the main catalyst in Catherine and me forming K9 Conservation. The key thing I learnt from him was that we could operate day and night with equal ease, and if we were hot on the trail of poachers, they could not hide, no matter what time it was. Their only chance of evading us was to reach a getaway car or escape into areas we could not enter without permission. I will go further and say that to a significant extent, it is due to Zingela's exploits, much publicised after tracking Panjo the tiger, that dogs trained in anti-poaching are now so highly regarded in conservation circles.

Make no mistake; our dogs are not pets. They are hard-working companions and also our family. Most are either German, Belgian or Dutch shepherds, Malinois, or Weimaraners. Malinois were originally bred for herding purposes but have a great temperament for anti-poaching tasks: highly intelligent, obedient, loyal, fast runners and with a powerful bite strength, making them extremely effective in the field. We train them to ignore all animal scents and only pursue human suspects.

The shepherds are also excellent ground trackers for both human and animal quarry, while our Weimaraners are used mostly to locate wounded animals, on darting operations, or for detecting carcasses by air scenting. This is of course generalising, as we also use individual dogs best suited for the specific job on hand, no matter what their breed. Manzi, for example, is a Weimaraner who tracks rhino, while I used Landa also to track lion. The common denominator is that they are all patrol dogs.

These dogs are, in my opinion, true heroes and do more good for this planet than most people can imagine. They are making a real difference and without them, the outcome for the survival – let alone the soul – of our last remaining wildernesses would be in even more jeopardy. Dogs have no concept of this, of course. They do their job because they love it and want to please their handlers. But even so, they do extraordinary work unquestioningly and with a loyalty that takes the meaning of the word to stratospheric levels. They're our brothers and sisters. We work side by side, and every one of them would unhesitatingly sacrifice themselves for us. So far, seven of our canine warriors have sadly fallen in the line of duty.

We get most of our dogs as puppies and they spend their entire lives with us. The puppies are carefully selected for certain tracking qualities and temperaments, and are trained both by us and our more experienced dogs who show them through example how to operate in the bush. When our dogs reach the age of ten or eleven, they are retired and live out the rest of their days at our main base. They go for daily walks and become part of our house pack, where they get pampered as a reward for their loyal service. Their only remaining job is to protect the homestead, as we, like most working in this line of work, have enemies within the bushmeat and rhino horn syndicates.

Our animals all have unique characters. Anyone who thinks a dog is just a dog has no idea. At the time of writing, the dog I work with most is Hashtag, whom I have mentioned before in the chase after poachers through thorn scrub as dense as a wall. I got him when Landa was about to retire and I was offered a puppy with bloodhound and Dobermann bloodlines. This breed is crossed to combine the extraordinary scenting skills of a bloodhound with the bite and aggression of a Dobermann. They're called DBs, and you won't find many civilian owners, as they're mainly used by police dog units.

When I first got Hashtag, he was not only a different breed to what we usually worked with, he was also bundle of trouble unlike any other dog I'd had before. His character was so off the wall and difficult to categorise that I didn't know what to call him, so just settled for Hashtag. He and I are now as close as brothers.

Hashtag was one of Landa's students, and Zingela's son taught him well. It is a great source of pride to me that the dogs I use most on callouts still have direct links to Zingela, as Anubis, another of Hashtag's mentors, was Landa's closest canine companion. Anubis, trained primarily to track humans, is a super-intelligent German shepherd who has also now retired after many hard years in the bush. Self-confident and loyal, he would give his life for me in the blink of an eye if it came to that.

Another interesting dog in our pack is neither shepherd, Weimaraner or Malinois. Jock is about as far removed from those aristocratic bloodlines as you can get. Being part *Canis Africanis*, he genetically has more in common with a poacher's dog than the breeds we use.

Anke rescued him as a mangy five-week-old stray. She was driving to Pretoria from Hoedspruit when a dog crossing the N4 motorway was run over by a taxi right in front of her. As the critically injured animal ran off, she noticed a ball of fur rolling wildly across the road. It was a puppy, surviving because it had been shielded by its mother.

She jumped out of the car to get the puppy, which by then had scampered into a culvert beneath the highway. Anke crawled after it, the narrow, spider-infested pipe really testing her willpower. Stifling her fears, she managed to coax the terrified pup out into the open and her friend grabbed him. She named him Ranger, not knowing that earlier that same day a game ranger had been shot and killed.

At first, Ranger was problematic, unpredictable and difficult to handle around other dogs and people. Perhaps seeing his mother struck and almost certainly killed by a car had irrevocably traumatised him. We didn't know what to do, as although he was an incredible dog, our options seemed limited at this stage.

By chance, Anke heard from an acquaintance about a spiritual healer who had helped the acquaintance relocate a missing pet. With nothing to lose, Anke contacted her. The healer did a session on Ranger and came forward with information that she could not possibly have discovered without forming a close relationship and having knowledge of his past. The first thing the healer told Anke was that there was a 'negative connotation' to the dog's name, perhaps because an actual ranger had been killed the day Anke rescued the traumatised puppy. He was also in pain as his back left leg suffered from an old injury.

'I've worked on it,' she said. 'He will show some swelling and inflammation on that leg over the next couple of days, but that is the body doing the work to heal the trauma.'

Two days later, Ranger started limping. But the limp soon disappeared and the leg never gave him any more trouble. However, a vet mentioned during a check-up sometime afterwards that one of the ligaments below the hock felt strangely stretched and was surprised that Ranger wasn't limping.

Anke also asked about Ranger's 'negative' name, and the healer said that he wanted a name that related to his loyalty and bravery.

'You already have another name for him,' she said. 'Use that.'

Anke wasn't sure what the healer meant, so decided to take her dog for a 'naming walk', as Native Americans do after the birth of a child. Anke and the dog were soaking up the last sunrays on a rocky outcrop when it suddenly came to her.

'Con has always told people that my dog is Jock of the Bushveld incarnate,' she said. 'So, I called out to him: Jock!'

An amazing thing happened. Ranger instantly got up and came over to her. Together they returned to the house, woman and dog, and the connection was tangibly different. Anke came inside crying, 'I don't know how I could have missed it. Of course, his name was Jock all along.'

It was the strangest thing, but it was true. Today Jock's loyalty is absolute. He's Anke's personal working dog and companion who has saved her life several times in the field.

He's her once-in-a-lifetime dog, the way Zingela was mine.

But what is really interesting is that Jock does snake detection – as far as I know, one of the few in the country trained to do so. As a puppy, he had a morbid fascination with snakes and Anke thought it would be interesting to see if she could take this further. She's a qualified snake handler and started using him to sniff out any dangerous species coming into our house. She trained him to indicate where the snake was, but never to attack and risk being bitten. Anke would then catch the reptile, often a mamba or a Mozambique spitting cobra, and relocate it somewhere less hazardous to our health. Sometimes they may or may not have ended up close to areas where poachers like to make themselves at home in the bush. Interestingly, Jock could never sniff out a puff adder, and today many studies have been done confirming that puff adders are 'chemically cryptic', and cannot be detected through scent. The snake responsible for the largest number of snake-related deaths in Africa is actually odour neutral.

Then, one day out of the blue, Anke got a call from an upmarket lodge asking how long it would take to train a 'snake dog'. They were quite surprised when she replied she already had one. Jock is now on continuous standby to sweep the lodge clear of reptiles whenever VIPs arrive, along with his other duties of human tracking and wildlife contraband detection – at which he excels.

Another valued member of our family that Anke brought to Liverpool is her horse called Fire. He's a beautiful bay thoroughbred with kind eyes whose spirit reflects his name. About two years after we started living together, Anke was riding Fire and patrolling the neighbouring game reserve when she spotted poachers' tracks in a drainage line. They were fresh, confirmed by Fire who had also picked up the dead animal scent from their kill and was getting skittish.

They trotted down the drainage line, following the fresh tracks in the sand, when Anke's mobile phone in the saddlebag rang. Fire spooked and bolted up the banks of the drainage line, resulting in Anke hitting her head hard against an overhanging branch of a tree. She saw stars and clung to the horse's neck, then lost consciousness. When she came around, she did not recognise the area they were in. The mountains were out of sight, and she had no idea what direction home was or how far away the poachers were. There was no phone signal, which meant that they were on the eastern side of the reserve and far from home. Despite her groggy state, Anke knew the worst thing that could happen would be if she got separated from her horse and the poachers grabbed her firearm. Feeling weak and nauseous, she managed to wrap a lead rope around her waist and tie herself to the saddle. Some time passed as they wandered aimlessly through grass fields, then everything went black again.

It was nearly dark and I was getting extremely worried. I had no idea where Anke was, and the fact she wasn't answering her phone indicated serious trouble.

Then I heard the sound of hooves on the road coming up to the house. I ran outside, and emerging from the twilight was Anke, slumped over Fire's neck with a rope tying her to the saddle. Her faithful horse had, completely unaided, brought her home.

As with all families, the death of a loved one is a time of bereavement, and it is no different with our dogs. They face scores of daily hazards – lions, leopards, snakes, crocodiles, venomous thick-tailed scorpions. And, worst of all, vehicles. We are always pedantic about the safety of our dogs around these killing machines.

One of our first losses was Vixen, a German shepherd patrol dog in the Sabi Sand Wildtuin. I got a frantic call from a ranger gabbling that he had been talking to a gate guard when a lioness came bounding around the side of his truck and grabbed Vixen right in front of him. The big cat then dragged the dog off into the bush.

I got there five minutes later and headed into the thick scrub on foot with the ranger breathing down my neck. His rifle was pointed more at me than the lioness we were tracking, so I hastily told him to unload his weapon. As we followed the blood trail through the neck-high grass, I suddenly tripped over something and sprawled onto the ground.

It was the bloody corpse of the dead dog. Which was alarming enough – but even worse was that a snarling, emaciated lioness was right next to it. We retreated at speed.

I called Pete, and returning in the back of his Land Cruiser to Vixen's body, we managed to chase the lioness off the now half-eaten carcass by throwing water at it. We didn't want to kill it, but the starving animal was in such a bad way it was later put down due to concerns it could become a threat to humans.

Vixen was buried at our base, and years later I found out the true story. The ranger had lied. He had left her tethered in the back of his truck while he had snuck off to a nearby village to do some shopping. If he hadn't left his post, the lioness would not have got his dog.

Another huge loss to us was Max, a loyal and fearless Malinois who had an amazing relationship with his handler. Max was let off his lead to go to the toilet early one morning and didn't return. His handler went looking for him and to his horror, saw that his beloved Malinois had been killed by a fifteen-foot python, which now was in the process of swallowing the dog whole. The ranger freaked out and shot the python – something expressly forbidden as the snake was only doing what it does naturally. The ranger was inconsolable.

Handlers do become extremely attached to their dogs, none more so than Patric, one of our best rangers. He had just come off an anti-poaching patrol and was relaxing in a boma with his German shepherd when a leopard jumped over the ten-foot-high poles. Quick as a bolt of lightning, the leopard snatched the dog, leapt back over the boma wall and was gone.

Patric was sobbing when he told me the story and said he was now going out to shoot the leopard. I absolutely forbade that as it was hardly the hungry leopard's fault. In any event, we are only authorised to shoot an animal in self-defence.

Crocodiles are also an ever-present threat. Virtually every stretch of water where we live is considered dangerous – in fact, rangers have a saying that you should check your bath before getting in. In all our training sessions, we repeatedly stress to handlers not to take dogs to within five yards of any river, dam or lake. This is strictly adhered to and, so far, the only dog we have lost to a croc was when Katleyla, a black German shepherd, ran down to the river for a swim after a scorching hot day's patrol. A second later there was a yelp, and when the ranger rushed to the bank, all he could see was a swirling eddy.

For me personally, the saddest death after Zingela was that of Landa. Zingela's boy and my close working companion was ten years old and had recently retired when I noticed he could no longer urinate properly. I gently prodded his abdomen and felt a hard lump the size of a grapefruit.

Debbie, our veterinarian, took an X-ray and looked at me sadly. It was a cancerous tumour next to his bladder. She said he only had a day or two before his digestive system and bladder started shutting down and he was in pain. The most humane course of action would be to euthanise him.

I asked her to do it at our base. If we took him to the surgery for the final needle, he would sense what was coming. Instead, we would give him a warrior's farewell at his own home.

The dreaded day came, and when Debbie arrived, Anke and I took our entire pack of dogs out to accompany Landa on his last walk. It was gut-wrenching, and Anke and I struggled not to weep until Landa took his last breath. Dogs are acutely aware of what is going on and if Landa saw us upset, he would know just as surely as if we had taken him to the surgery what was about to happen.

He now tired easily, and after a short walk, he lay down next to us. Debbie inserted the needle into the vein and he painlessly went to sleep.

We cried rivers of tears and let the rest of the dogs, Landa's friends and comrades-in-arms, sniff the body lying peacefully on the ground. We have a dog cemetery at the bottom of our training grounds, a true canine Valhalla, and Landa's grave had been dug the day before. I lifted him and walked to his final resting place.

As I lowered Landa into the ground, Anubis came running up behind, snarling and barking. I laid Landa down and backed off, allowing Anubis to process what was happening to his friend. He circled Landa and spent some time sniffing the body. I did not interfere, waiting until Anubis moved off.

Then, almost choking from the lump in my throat, I buried my faithful companion.

31

The Headshot Gang

All poaching syndicate 'busts' are cause for celebration. But one of our more recent ones, in April 2023, was among the most satisfying. Not least because we were up against some of the most skilled and elusive poachers our joint teams have come across in my long career.

We nicknamed them the Headshot gang as they had two shooters who could kill a rhino from some distance with a single headshot. This was far removed from some of the gangs who sometimes took several ill-placed shots to bring an animal down – or even worse, just used some rusted junk rifle with a homemade stock to riddle the poor creature with lead.

We had been chasing this gang for a year or so. Although they didn't come from our area, they were particularly active in the Harmony Block game reserves, a rhino breeding enclave between Hoedspruit and the small mining town of Gravelotte. Most rhino in Harmony Block are dehorned, but unfortunately that now has resulted in poachers shooting more animals to make up for lost revenue. Dehorning is a bit of a misnomer as the animal still has a baseplate and two-inch stub left intact. And although poachers would rather kill a rhino with a full horn, the extent of the full-scale massacre of these beautiful pachyderms is that poachers can no longer be fussy. They kill what they can. As a result, dehorning is now a much-debated issue as even rhinos with a small stump are worth more dead than alive. This could possibly be reversed, as horns regrow like fingernails and are thus a potentially lucrative renewable resource. In my opinion, the only solution to the problem, without rhino being driven to extinction, is to create a situation where the animal is worth more alive than dead.

I was based for three months in Harmony Block during the height of the Headshot gang's invasions in the area, chasing the thugs while assisting a friend of mine who managed one of the reserves. Much of the time was spent in the bush tracking at night with Hashtag, my Dobermann-bloodhound. The problem was that the property hardest hit in the block was small by South African standards, so poachers were able to kill an animal, hack off the horn stump and hightail it through other reserves not far from tar roads where they would be picked up by a vehicle. Hashtag is unstoppable once on a trail, but tracking poachers is a high-speed pursuit, and on small properties we often simply ran out of space and time.

However, Hashtag more than proved his worth in leading us to rhino carcasses, which sometimes were almost impossible to find in the thick bush, and with his nose he 'mapped' the routes the poachers regularly took. This was invaluable information as humans are creatures of habit, and these wildlife killers were no exception, frequently using the same trails.

We did have one major success when hot-pursuing another gang with Hashtag and two Makalali reserve dogs. They managed to reach their getaway vehicle moments before us, but as they sped off, they ran into a Farm Watch roadblock and were surrounded by heavily armed men. The Farm Watch guys searched the vehicle and found a stump of horn with fresh blood and a large-calibre hunting rifle. The men were all arrested – and that alone made my three months living rough in the bush worthwhile.

But we still hadn't caught the Headshot gang, even though we came nail-bitingly close on several occasions. The most dramatic was when a gunshot was heard and Farm Watch locked down routes as Hashtag and I started tracking in the dark. The gang fled through different reserves where we had hot-pursuit permission, and Hashtag and I were on their tail for several miles. Then, just as we were closing in, they reached their getaway truck on a dirt road and sped off. We were, literally, biting their dust. I stared into the dark night, clenching my fists in fury and despair. I wanted them so badly I could taste it.

Our biggest problem was that the gang ran such a tight network that our sources could not infiltrate the inner circle. There were no loose tongues at the shebeen, no drunkards bragging about how much money they were making, which is a hallmark of many other syndicates. Their internal discipline was strict and, as a result, we never knew where they would strike next, or even who most of their members were. They were professionals, moving stealthily in the shadows.

But we still had a trump card. One of Pete's top sources had the determination of a pit bull. He had been undercover for five and a half years, a phenomenally long time for such a dangerous job, and his nerves weren't just made of steel – they were coated in titanium.

At first, even he could not crack the Headshot gang's code of silence. So, we did the next best thing. Bribery. Lots of money changed hands and we got an address to a house the gang was said to use as a base. Our source rented a room nearby and sat down to wait, watching their every move.

Then came the crucial breakthrough. He saw one of the men hiding a hunting rifle under the bonnet of a Toyota double cab and phoned through the vehicle's registration.

'They're on the move now,' he said.

'Superb work, *mfo*.'

The Hoedspruit Farm Watch and police then activated traffic monitors, and soon we had a sighting. The Toyota was passing Hazyview, about fifty miles away, and one of our joint unit guys started following it to keep us updated. The gang was heading north towards Hoedspruit, but once they reached us, we faced a dilemma. They could either go through the town on the eastern route or take the western bypass. We knew they were armed and we didn't have enough people to cover both routes.

So which one would they take?

It was a tough call. Our joint operations unit, consisting of the police, Hoedspruit Farm Watch and ourselves, decided to gamble on them going west, so we set up an ambush, hiding just off the motorway at a junction called Snake Park.

We were right. Our man following the gang radioed through that the Toyota was approaching Hoedspruit and had veered left to take the western fork. He said he would give the order to mobilise just before they reached Snake Park so we could cut them off with minimal disruption to traffic.

Then someone suddenly shouted, 'Go!' All eight Farm Watch vehicles charged out of our hiding spot – but at that precise moment, a group of women started walking across the road oblivious to our pincer manoeuvre. The driver in the front vehicle slammed on brakes as we yelled at the women to move out of the way. That they did, ducking and diving between the cars and squealing in terror.

Then another shout: 'False alarm! Go back! Go back!'

With some yelling 'move' to the innocent pedestrians in front and others shouting 'false alarm' behind, it was a few seconds of chaos, not sure whether to go forward or back. We hurriedly reversed, almost backing into one another.

I barely had time to catch my breath when thirty seconds later another call came through.

'Mobilise!'

This time it was genuine. The Toyota was almost at the junction, an extremely busy intersection, and we sped out of our hiding spot in clouds of smoke and screaming rubber, surrounding the suspects' vehicle. We were all armed to the teeth and wearing balaclavas, so other motorists in the immediate vicinity started shrieking at full volume, believing they were being hijacked. I shouted to them that we were only after the people in the Toyota double cab and that they must move on. A group of farm workers in a truck were taking no chances and leapt out of the back and fled into the bush.

Seconds later, we had all suspects out of the Toyota and face down on the ground. The whole operation, from the moment we got the call to mobilise to the time we had the Headshot gang suspects handcuffed, took about a minute. It was that fast; that efficient – despite the preceding chaos.

We now had to wait for police from the Provincial Stock Theft and Endangered Species Unit to arrive. They were about three hours away, which was potentially problematic as a lot of people from nearby villages use the Snake Park junction and they are not always keen on helping law enforcement. An angry crowd can gather like a swarm and try to release suspects, especially as some impressionable villagers consider poachers to be antihero celebrities. To counter this, whenever someone asked what was going on, we replied that these men were about to raid their village and we had caught them just in time. Satisfied that we were the good guys, they left us alone.

While waiting, we looked under the bonnet and found the rifle. Our source's information had been bang on target, as usual.

When the police arrived, their forensics team did a thorough search, finding hunting equipment and a huge stash of cash as well as a bag of crystal meth. They also found two valid firearm licences, which was bad news for us. The key factor in this bust – the sole reason for the eighty-mile motorway pursuit – was that we believed the suspects had an unlicensed rifle. If that wasn't the case, we would have no option but to let the gang go free to kill more rhinos.

I shook my head. This did not ring true. 'Why did they hide the rifle if they had a licence?' I asked one of the cops. 'Surely that indicates guilt?'

He nodded. 'I think you're right. We're checking if the licences and the rifle match.'

They didn't. One was for a .375 and the other a .458 – both designed for big, thick-skinned animals such as rhino. The firearm hidden in the bonnet was a .308, also popular for hunting medium to large animals. It had a serial number. But no licence.

The men were arrested on the spot.

We also now knew that the gang had two more big-game hunting rifles, so police subsequently launched follow-up operations to confiscate those. Once found, they will be sent off for ballistic tests to establish if there are any matches with bullets taken from poached rhinos.

Another big plus was that we grabbed the syndicate leader in the raid. It turned out he's high up the ladder in the wider poaching hierarchy, dealing directly with buyers in Johannesburg.

On the downside, we only got one of the gang's suspected two snipers. At the time of writing, the other shooter is still at large. But we will get him.

However, just as we were putting the Headshot gang behind bars, I got terrible news. Our ace informer, who had been directly responsible for the success of the raid, had died. He had been ill for some time with blood pressure issues and advanced diabetes, which had not stopped him from doing his job, but we thought he was getting better. Sadly, that was not the case. He was a true wildlife conservation hero and, thanks to him, we put several syndicates out of action during the years he worked together with us. His phenomenal operational statistics are as follows: seventy-nine crucial information reports on poaching activity; fifty-four prime suspects followed; and twenty-three arrests of rhino poachers. Every one of those reports was gathered at extreme risk to his life.

Pete, Anke and I were shocked by his death. Although we worked closely, so secretive was the nature of our operations that we always had to wear balaclavas and bulky tactical clothing. As a result, he didn't even know Anke was a woman. When she eventually took off her balaclava after one raid and shook loose her luxuriant mane of hair, he exclaimed, '*Umfazi!*'

He then took off his balaclava and Anke responded, 'You're a man!' He thought that was hilarious.

For obvious reasons, we could not attend his funeral. I will always regret that.

Humba gahle, mfowethu. Go well, our brother.

32

Big Joe

The tipoff came as a brief text on one of our WhatsApp groups. It was a simple message: Big Joe was on the move in our territory.

Joseph 'Big Joe' Nyalungu is alleged to be one of the most powerful rhino poaching kingpins in the country – and, whether that is true or not, the media regularly refer to him as such. Not just the local newspapers; even the BBC explicitly mentioned him in a 2018 feature titled 'The strange figures behind a secret trade'.

The fifty-eight-year-old former policeman is, at the time of writing, facing at least five cases involving rhino poaching, racketeering and murder. His first arrest was in 2011, and he has appeared in court so often that newspapers use the phrase 'umpteenth time'.

So, when a joint security unit we were part of tracked a grey Toyota bakkie that had allegedly been used in a recent rhino poaching incident at Lydenburg, we sprang into action. Thanks to intel provided by various agencies – including the Provincial Stock Theft Unit and the Hoedspruit Farm Watch – we knew exactly who the bakkie belonged to. Big Joe Nyalungu himself.

Hoedspruit Farm Watch immediately set up a roadblock on the motorway outside town at the Klaserie One Stop service station and were in position in less than ten minutes, while Anke and I jumped into my V6 Land Cruiser with a racing chip in the engine. We were about sixteen miles away, as was Pete, so we were doing some low-level flying along the main road to get there in time. In fact, Pete almost burnt out his turbo in the process. Other trusted APUs and farm watches also mobilised barely minutes after the alert had gone out. This was the biggest operation we had been in for some time, with even a plane and helicopters patrolling above. From the air, we must have looked like the cartoon Wile E Coyote and the Road Runner hurtling along the motorway. Except we were deadly serious. The speed of everybody's response was remarkable, a well-oiled and cohesive unit of dedicated people.

When Big Joe saw Farm Watch guys dressed in bright orange and yellow jackets ahead, he did a rapid U-turn and hightailed it north towards the small town of Kampersrus. Our joint unit radioed ahead and a roadblock was hastily positioned at Kampersrus as another security vehicle chased the grey Toyota. As the chase vehicle came around a corner, the driver observed Big Joe suddenly stop and a suspected passenger leap out the bakkie clutching something and bolting across the road into sickle thorn bush. However, the fleeing suspect also dropped a bag, which could have been done as a decoy.

Big Joe continued speeding north and was going so fast to avoid police that when flagged down at Kampersrus, he crashed into another vehicle. Miraculously, no one was seriously injured.

Police searched the wrecked bakkie, finding a stack of cash wrapped in a plastic bag hidden under the seat, and Big Joe was handcuffed and taken off to prison.

The search was now on for the other man, and all available police, Farm Watch members and APUs converged at the spot where he had fled into the sickle bush. The wickedly spiked thorns were almost impenetrable so Anke and I ran up a nearby pathway leading to a posh housing estate. We hadn't brought

Hashtag or Jock, as a colleague, Ruan de Flamingh, already had two tracker dogs at the scene and there would have been dogfights with our canines on the same scent. Ruan owns a security company called Green Trax and we have worked closely together before. I knew he and his dogs were more than capable.

It was a massive manhunt, with police and Farm Watch vehicles stretched out along the motorway and quadbikes roaring around the bush, but the thorns were too thick. When Ruan and his dogs emerged, they were absolutely shredded, and the most likely scenario was that the suspect had escaped into the housing estate close to where Anke and I were. We suspected he had an accomplice there. But as we had no search warrants, we couldn't pursue further and he escaped.

However, police recovered the dropped bag, which contained six .375 bullets – specifically used for thick-skinned animals – as well as a rifle silencer and three bloodstained hunting knives. All potentially incriminating evidence. The challenge for the legal team now was to link the DNA from the knives to six rhinos that had been poached in the area over the past few weeks.

In any event, Big Joe was behind bars. He's no stranger to the legal process as he's been on the wildlife investigation radar for more than a decade. In one case, rhino horns were found in his car, and in the follow-up investigation, police confiscated a metal trunk containing more than R5 million (about £200,000) hidden in his luxury house in Hazyview.

The news of his arrest after a dramatic high-speed chase reverberated around the country. This was a massive media story. We didn't kid ourselves that someone as influential as Big Joe would remain behind bars for long, guilty or not, but this round belonged unequivocally to the joint task team.

That night, Anke and I poured ourselves something strong with lots of ice and toasted an extremely successful job. Anubis and Hashtag sat by my feet. Anubis was a retired warrior, but I was sorry that Hashtag had not been with us on this operation, the highest profile one for many years. Especially as the spiritual heirs of Zingela had been with me on almost every major raid since K9 Conservation was formed in 2011.

The results speak for themselves. Since K9 Conservation took over contracts to protect specific areas in the Sabi Sand Wildtuin, we have not had a single rhino poached in eight years on our watch. Compare that to almost thirty rhinos poached in the surrounding areas in just one year after the 2020/1 Covid-19 pandemic. We have unfortunately lost a few rhinos in other reserves, but in most cases, we have eventually caught the culprits. Men such as Ishi, whose gang killed four rhinos in one of our protected areas – and who was also allegedly linked to Big Joe – were finally brought to justice.

To some extent, that's also true with meat poaching in our areas. This is far more widespread and difficult to control, as the judicial system does not take the crisis as seriously as we do. An impala garrotted by a wire noose does not garner the same outcry as a poached rhino or scaly pangolin. Despite that, our success would be a fragment of what it is without our service dogs. The Finale village sting, for example, was mainly due to information I gathered from a meat poacher caught by Anubis.

However, I cannot stress strongly enough that although I started the company, our triumphs are always due to teamwork with the police, various farm watches and highly committed bush veterans such as Rory Guthrie and Pete. There is no place for egos, internal turf wars, or personal glory in this line of work. Those who ignore this simple credo do not last long in the conservation industry. It doesn't matter who brings down a syndicate, as long as the people plundering the planet are stopped in their tracks. That's the bottom line. That's what we care most about.

As far as I'm concerned, the real heroes are the dogs. These incredible animals have been used in the bush for centuries and we are by no means the first to do so. Zingela's forebears, for example, were trained to track in the forests of Germany during the Middle Ages, while one of the best-loved wilderness stories of all time, Jock of the Bushveld, is about a man and his dog.

The simple reality is that we could never have achieved many – if not most – of our successes without dogs. Consequently, I believe that people like me, Richard Sowry, Henry Holsthyzen, Pete and Rory were significantly ahead of the curve in grasping how incredibly effective canines would be in anti-poaching units. We played a large role in pioneering the methods used today and are constantly modifying techniques with ever-increasing success. This has proved to be a genuine game changer, and modern tracker dogs are no longer just service animals. They are, as I have repeatedly said, bushveld warriors. Barely thirty years ago, no one would've guessed that the wildernesses would be dominated by poaching cartels intent on the extinction of wildlife, and there is no better ally to take them on than a well-trained dog and handler. Zingela taught me that, and his spirit lives on in the working dogs we use today.

I have learnt infinitely more from my dogs than they have from me. I have taught them to obey my commands, but in return, they have taught me about the meaning of life. For life is not about greed, killing and profit – which may be obvious to most, but try telling that to the poaching syndicates. It's about loyalty, allegiance, honour and integrity. Dogs are the most loyal, unselfish creatures in the world. The work they do for conservation is incalculable. They find wounded animals; they track humans trying to kill wildlife; they sniff out almost-impossible-to-find incriminating evidence; and they keep rangers as safe as possible in the bush combat zones raging across the African continent.

This brutal conflict is not over. The end is not even in sight. Maybe it never will be.

But we will never surrender. The soul of the planet is at stake.

Epilogue

Nearly six years after the start of our relationship, Anke and I decided to tie the knot, but not in a normal wedding ceremony. It would instead be a handfasting ritual, a centuries-old Celtic tradition in which hands are tied together to symbolise the binding of two souls.

We planned our big day to be in keeping with this ancient rite for over a year, organising a ceremony in the bush among our many other daily chores and duties. The months flew by, rapidly approaching December, when the mighty baobab tree up in the Drakensberg Mountains would be in full bloom. That would be where our ceremony would take place.

I want to end the book with an account of this beautiful event, as Anke and I had accomplished so much in the past years. When the day of the handfasting arrived, we could not have wished for anything better, with friends flying in from around the world. Everything went impeccably to plan. My mother, Elaine Bell, has described the most important day in our lives in the epilogue below.

* * *

I have been given the great privilege to write the prologue to this book, and now the end, with the epilogue – the marriage of my son, Conraad, and his soulmate, Anke.

The ceremony was to be held halfway up a mountain under the spreading branches of a massive baobab. Conraad and Anke had come across this beautiful tree – sacred in African folklore – and had decided it would be a fitting venue for their final vows to one another when the time came.

In preparation for my journey north to attend the ceremony, my car, named Sebastian, was loaded to the hilt, his nose pointing north to take me from KwaZulu-Natal to Limpopo Province, a journey of five hundred miles. With me in the car was the wedding gift from the family – a specially commissioned painting from wildlife artist Vincent Reid, whose work is highly prized. His speciality is baobab trees. Photographs of the tree where Con and Anke would take their vows were sent to him, and he did not disappoint in the final depiction of the tree. It was wrapped up securely along with everything else I could think of that might be needed for this adventure.

Our families were coming from far and wide to be together a week before the wedding. The New Zealand contingent, the Cape branch, the Holland lot and the two oldies from KwaZulu-Natal. Me being one and Leisje (Zoltan's wife – Con's stepmom) the other. A lovely villa organised by my daughter Kendyl and Peter outside Hoedspruit was the rallying point for the days before the celebration. Friends were arriving from Switzerland, America, the UK, other parts of South Africa and, of course, Anke's family from Pretoria. It was as if a fuzzy blanket of love and goodwill had been thrown over all of us. Probably the last time that we would all be together under one roof at the same time. We all mucked in and gave help wherever it was needed. As the handfasting ceremony was a hike up the mountain, the final gathering and reception was in a rustic bush camp at the base.

The day of the celebrations arrived. We gathered at a rustic camp at the base of the baobab mountain at 11 a.m. on 3 December 2022. A line of nine 4x4 vehicles, each with about eight passengers, left in convoy, the way up the mountain dizzyingly steep, the journey slow. The first stop was for a family of giraffe crossing in front of the line of vehicles that stopped to face us and give us their blessing. Giraffes have significant spiritual connotations as their long necks are thought to connect them to the supernatural world.

It took over an hour to get to the baobab tree. We disembarked, in awe at the beauty before us. The baobab tree has a very short flowering time once a year, sometimes lasting only five days. Below the tree lay a carpet of large white flowers, with their crinkled, powder-puff petals and big cluster of stamens, while a few blooms still clung to the branches.

The beauty and stillness affected us all. My expectations for weddings usually include orange blossom, layers of tulle, a long train, flower girls, page boys, and the men in top hats and tails! There's usually a long limousine carrying the bride, with white ribbons fluttering.

Not this one. The bride and her maid of honour, Carli, bounced their way up the mountain in a dusty, trusty Land Rover. The rest of us were dressed in a mixture of bush clothes and casual gear; the only bling was worn by Anke's mother, Cess, and me!

Under the tree, a circle of quartz crystal stones gathered from the mountain enclosed the space where the blessing was to take place. All the guests were seated on tree stumps outside the circle.

Con waited inside the circle with Jen, a spiritualist healer, their confidant and friend, who was to perform the ceremony. She clasped a leather-bound book in her hands.

Out of the bush emerged Anke, looking like Titania, Queen of the Fairies in Shakespeare's *Midsummer Night's Dream*, in a softly flowing tulle dress, carrying a bouquet made up of leaves and raptors' feathers gathered on bush patrols. Braided into her free-flowing red hair were owl feathers.

Both Anke and Con wore patrol bush boots – to the horror of Teresa, my stepdaughter, who had designed and made the wedding dress. The effect was stunning and the guests gave a collective gasp. The traditional 'something old' was a lapis lazuli bracelet, 'newly' designed, the stones 'borrowed' from the earth. And the 'something blue' was, of course, the colour of the stones. The words spoken encompassed all the spiritual blessings of nature. Con and Anke then turned and together faced each cardinal point – north, south, east and west. As they did so, Jen spoke beautiful words accompanying each direction.

Then, appearing from nowhere, a spectacular blue swallowtail butterfly flew directly above them, circling both Con and Anke in a figure of eight. It hovered for a few moments and then slowly melted away into the bush.

It was a simple ceremony filled with a spirituality that touched everyone. I put my hand on the old baobab tree afterwards and felt the pulse of Africa through my hands.

The journey going down the mountain was not as harrowing as the up-slope, and to the delight of the bride and groom they came across the same herd of sable antelope that they had encountered on their first date – in exactly the same area of the bushveld.

The reception party was held on the lawns of the bush camp under the trees with coloured lights and blazing braziers and we danced barefoot on the grass until the early hours. We all made our little speeches but the warmest was when Anke told Con that her wedding gift to him was a beautiful dark silver-grey Weimaraner puppy. Her name, Kalandra, means 'The Lovely One' in Greek.

She who would fill the gap left by Zingela and Landa.

I will end the epilogue as I did the prologue:

I have a son of Africa; he lives on a small farm nestled below the castellated top of Mariepskop Mountain and Moholoholo peak in Limpopo Province. It lies in the valley between the Blyde and Olifants rivers, where the Drakensberg Mountains start to make their way down to KwaZulu-Natal, and there form a great backdrop fortress with the mighty Maloti Mountains of Lesotho. This is the story of the small footprint he has left on the soil of Africa. One day the winds of time may wipe this footprint away, but I dare say his spirit will hover over the bushveld forever.

Maktub. It is written.

ACKNOWLEDGEMENTS

There are too many friends and family to thank individually in the acknowledgements, but I would like to single out a few.

My deepest gratitude to all fellow conservationists, game rangers and all our dogs who dedicate their lives to keeping the balance of the natural environment.

To my amazing, beautiful wife Anke de Rosner – you are truly my soulmate.

To all my closest friends over the years: Rob McQueen, Ruud Aalders, Dirk Meyer, Harem, Brick and others, thank you for everything and all the adventures. The late Aaron Nkuna and Elmond Ndlovu, you will forever be remembered in the pages of this book as true fellow field rangers and also good friends.

A very big thank-you to Hoedspruit Farm Watch. We are privileged to work alongside your well-trained and dedicated members. *Julle is Ysters*!

Thank you, my dear mother Elaine Bell. Without you this story would not have been written. You spent hundreds of hours going through all my diaries and listening to all the stories told over the years.

Graham Spence, thank you for all the hard work you put into this book.

Rory Guthrie and Peter Wearne, you remain vital pillars of K9 Conservation's efforts and successes. Without men like you there would be many fewer rhinos alive today. It is a great privilege to have you on our side. Catherine Corrett, thank you for believing in the dogs and the vision of Canine Conservation Pty Ltd, you contributed in so many ways.

To my wonderful family, thank you all for your support and for being there when needed. To all other special souls, thank you for being a guiding influence in my life.

My Uncle Louis John Havemann, you were a pain in the arse, but they were necessary and hard lessons that have kept me alive, so thank you. My late grandfather Coenraad Havemann, I will never forget you and your wise bush ways. My Late father Zoltan de Rosner, I love you.

To our fallen heroes – Landa, Max, Vixen, Valkyrie, Yule, Shacka, Makulu, Hunter, Wakala, Gypsey, Zulu, Katlyla, Diesel, Moya and Nibiru – the paw prints of your memories will never be erased.

Zingela, one of my closest companions in life … I hope our paths cross again one day. Thank you for showing me the way.